CW00925492

Truth That Never Dies

WIPF *and* STOCK *Publishers*
199 West 8th Avenue, Suite 3 • Eugene, Oregon 97401
Tel. (541) 344-1528 • Fax. (541) 344-1506
Web site: www.wipfandstock.com

CASCADE *Books*
PICKWICK *Publications*
WIPF & STOCK
RESOURCE *Publications*

Dear Nigel,

Greetings from Wipf and Stock Publishers! We trust this note finds you well.

Here are your presentation copies of *Truth That Never Dies: The Dr. G. R. Beasley-Murray Memorial Lectures 2002,Äì2012.*

Your book is ACTIVE and available for order.

Retail price: $27.00

Cost to you with 50% author discount: $13.50
(Note: Books purchased at the author discounted rate are non-returnable.)

To receive your author discount you may place an order directly to our customer service department. Please inform them that you are an author ordering your own book and provide them with your account number, **28396.** Online orders are not set up to calculate author discounts.

How to contact us:
Phone: (541) 344-1528
Fax: (541) 344-1506
Email Orders: orders@wipfandstock.com
Marketing Coordinator: Amanda@wipfandstock.com

When the title is made ACTIVE it will be available via:
Wipf and Stock Publishers Customer Service: Immediately
wipfandstock.com: 10 days
Amazon: in 6–8 weeks
Ingram: in 4 weeks
Kindle: 3-6 months

Thank you for your partnership in publishing this book.

Truth That Never Dies

The Dr. G. R. Beasley-Murray Memorial Lectures 2002–2012

edited by

Nigel G. Wright

PICKWICK *Publications* · Eugene, Oregon

TRUTH THAT NEVER DIES
The Dr. G. R. Beasley-Murray Memorial Lectures 2002–2012

Pickwick Publications
An Imprint of Wipf and Stock Publishers
199 W. 8th Av.e, Suite 3
Eugene, OR 97401

www.wipfandstock.com

ISBN 13: 978-1-62564-476-3

Cataloging-in-Publication data:

Truth that never dies : the Dr. G. R. Beasley-Murray memorial lectures 2002–2012 / edited by Nigel G. Wright.

xiv + 222 p. ; 23 cm. Includes bibliographical references.

ISBN 13: 978-1-62564-476-3

1. Beasley-Murray, George Raymond, 1916–2000. 2. Baptists. I. Wright, Nigel, 1949–. II. Title.

BX6331.3 W754 2014

Manufactured in the U.S.A.

Biblical citations from NIV, TNIV, and NRSV

Dedicated to Ruth Beasley-Murray,
and in memory of George.

Contents

Preface

IN 2002 SPURGEON'S COLLEGE London established a series of lectures in honor and in memory of Dr. George Raymond Beasley-Murray who had served with distinction as its Principal from 1958 to 1973, and died in the year 2000. Himself a graduate of Spurgeon's, George had gone on, while serving in two Baptist pastorates, to qualify himself as a highly competent New Testament scholar of world rank. He was to serve as President of the Baptist Union of Great Britain and to be a prominent figure in national and international Baptist and ecumenical life. The motivation behind the lectures lay in the conviction that there was much in his legacy that demanded to be given further thought and reflection, not least at the beginning of a new millennium into which his various contributions could be extended. The lectures were to be delivered at the annual Assembly of the Baptist Union of Great Britain, wherever in the United Kingdom it might be held. The series yielded eleven lectures in all over the period 2002 to 2012. The present volume now collects those essays and by so doing extends their own contribution indefinitely.

Those giving the lectures were invited to take some aspect of George's theological or denominational work and reflect further on it in ways that would inform the churches' present and future life, practice and mission. As will be seen, some have chosen to do this by giving thought to a theme or concern clearly rooted in George's writing. Others have paid attention to his own life and ministry and have built on that. The lecturers themselves all have had some particular engagement with George as either his students or as fellow scholars, teachers or later students at Spurgeon's College. To be a British Baptist in the second half of the twentieth century was to be indebted in some way to the man. When I began my preparation for ministry at Spurgeon's in 1970, benefiting from the last three years of his tenure there, it was as much George's reputation as that of the College that drew me. I have never had cause for regret on either ground.

I am grateful to Wipf and Stock for the willingness to publish this volume under its Pickwick imprint. Initial editorial work has involved for me the somewhat ironic task of transposing a series of lectures written and delivered uniformly by British scholars in British contexts to British audiences into American spellings and grammatical conventions.

Although a lengthy task this has not been an overly difficult one, but it has required certain decisions. I have, as is usual, retained the original spellings when other British writings than those of the lecturers have been cited directly. I have varied this, however, in the case of verbs and nouns in which the authors have preferred the *–ise* form (as in "realise" or "realisation") and have conformed to the American preferred usage of *–ize*. As this also continues to be an accepted usage in British English it seemed better to have a degree of equalization at this point. Each lecturer has had liberty to present their chosen topic in the way that best suited them. I have sought to reflect this individuality in the lectures gathered here. All in all, the work of adapting to American usage in a publication produced in America seemed a small price to pay for having these lectures in print.

A word of thanks is due to the colleagues who accepted the responsibility of writing and delivering these lectures and who cooperated in the editing of this volume. My warm thanks to all those who contributed and who are introduced in the pages that follow. In addition to their intrinsic value the lectures reflect some of the events, issues, and personalities of the time in which they were written and so have come to have their own historical value.

Finally I am pleased to record that when delivered nearly all of these lectures benefited from the presence both of Dr. Paul-Beasley-Murray and Mrs. Ruth Beasley-Murray at some personal cost in the traveling involved. It is to Ruth that this book is dedicated.

Dr. Nigel G. Wright
Editor, Principal Emeritus, Spurgeon's College

Contributors

Dr. Paul Beasley-Murray is a former Principal of Spurgeon's College (1986–1992) and from 1993 the senior minister of Central Baptist Church, Chelmsford. Like his father a New Testament scholar, Paul is the author of a number of books, including *Radical Believers* (1992) and *The Message of the Resurrection* (2000). His "personal portrait" of his father, *Fearless for Truth* (2002), is frequently referred to in these lectures.

Dr. David R. Coffey OBE is one of the most prominent British Baptists of his generation, having served as President of the Baptist Union (1986–7), General Secretary of the Baptist Union (1991–2006), and President of the Baptist World Alliance (2005–10). He is the author of several books and has been awarded two honorary doctorates.

Dr. John E. Colwell taught theology and ethics at Spurgeon's College from 1994 to 2009. He is the author of *Living the Christian Story* (2001), *Promise and Presence* (2005), *The Rhythm of Doctrine* (2007), and *Why Have You Forsaken Me?* (2010). He is now the pastor of Budleigh Salterton Baptist Church, Devon.

Dr. Anthony R. Cross is a Baptist minister and perhaps the foremost expert on George Beasley-Murray's theology of baptism. He is the author, among other books, of *Baptism and the Baptists: Theology and Practice in Twentieth-Century Britain* (2000), to which George Beasley-Murray contributed a Foreword, and *Recovering the Evangelical Sacrament: Baptisma Semper Reformandum* (2013) and is responsible for editing and publishing a wide range of scholarly works. He is a member of the Faculty of Theology and Religion, University of Oxford.

Dr. Ruth M. B. Gouldbourne is a minister of Bloomsbury Central Baptist Church, London and previously served for eleven years as a tutor in church history at Bristol Baptist College. She is the author of *The Flesh and the Feminine: Gender and Theology in the Writings of Caspar Schwenckfeld* (2007), and co-author with Anthony Cross and Brian Haymes of *On Being the Church: Revisioning Baptist Identity* (2008).

Dr. Stephen R. Holmes is Senior Lecturer in Theology at the University of St. Andrews. He previously taught at Spurgeon's College as a Research Fellow, and at King's College London. He is the author of a number of works, including *God of Grace and God of Glory: An Account of the Theology of Jonathan Edwards* (2000) and *The Holy Trinity: Understanding God's Life* (2012).

Dr. Mark Hopkins is an historian who teaches at the Theological College of Northern Nigeria in Bukuru. His research into Victorian Nonconformity at Oxford, in which C. H. Spurgeon was a major subject, was later published as *Nonconformity's Romantic Generation: Evangelical and Liberal Theologies in Victorian England* (2004).

Dr. Bruce Milne taught systematic and historical theology for ten years at Spurgeon's College before migrating to Canada to become senior minister of First Baptist Church, Vancouver, from 1983 to 2001. His widely used book *Know the Truth: A Handbook of Christian Belief* was published in its third edition in 2009, and other books include *The Message of John: Here Is Your King* (1993), and *Dynamic Diversity: Bridging Class, Age, Race and Gender in the Church* (2007).

Dr. Michael J. Quicke was minister of St. Andrew's Street Baptist Church, Cambridge before becoming Principal of Spurgeon's College from 1993 to 2000. He is now Professor of Preaching and Communication at Northern Seminary, Chicago and is well known for his trilogy *360 Degree Preaching* (2003), *360 Degree Leadership* (2006), and *Preaching as Worship* (2011).

Dr. Brian Stanley is Professor of World Christianity and Director of the Centre for the Study of World Christianity at the University of Edinburgh. He began his academic career as tutor in church history and Academic Dean at Spurgeon's College. His books include *The Bible and the Flag* (1990), *The History of the Baptist Missionary Society, 1792–1992*

(1992), *The World Missionary Conference: Edinburgh 1910* (2009), and *The Global Diffusion of Evangelicalism: The Age of Billy Graham and John Stott* (2013).

Dr. Nigel G. Wright is editor of the present volume and Principal Emeritus of Spurgeon's College where he was Principal from 2000 to 2013. A former President of the Baptist Union, his publications include *The Radical Evangelical: Seeking a Place to Stand* (1996), *Disavowing Constantine: Mission, Church and the Social Order* (2000), *A Theology of the Dark Side* (2003), and *Free Church, Free State: The Positive Baptist Vision* (2005).

1

Fearless for Truth[1]

Paul Beasley-Murray

Earlier this year I made the long journey from Chelmsford to Carlisle and back again all for the sake of ten minutes. In those ten minutes I was given the opportunity of convincing a group of salesmen that my biography of my father was the best thing since sliced bread! I began by acknowledging the difficulty of the task.

First of all, biographies are not normally the most gripping of books. It was the British biographer Philip Guedalla who said, "Biography is a region bounded on the north by history, on the south by fiction, on the east by obituary, and on the west by tedium."

Secondly, biographies written by relatives or friends can often be sickly sweet. For that reason Arthur Balfour, the former Tory Prime Minister, said "Biography should be written by an acute enemy." Thirdly, in Christian circles biographies which sell tend to major on the miraculous and the dramatic. People will buy *The Cross and the Switchblade*, but a biography of a theologian seems to have the kiss of death on it before it has even seen the light of day.

So why on earth was Paternoster publishing the biography of George Beasley-Murray? Indeed, as far as the ordinary punter is concerned, who was George Beasley-Murray? Billy Graham we've heard of, Martin Luther King we've heard of, but who was George Beasley-Murray?

1. This lecture was delivered at the Baptist Assembly in Plymouth on Sunday, 5 May 2002.

I answered that question in various ways. I stated that my father was one of the greatest Baptists of the twentieth Century. Not for nothing did lengthy obituaries of him appear in *The Times* and *The Independent*. I went on to say it was thanks to my father's courageous stand that the Baptist Union of Great Britain retained its cutting evangelical edge and so was saved from the continued decline experienced by all the other mainline churches in Britain. I mentioned his more than twenty books on the New Testament; I drew attention to the fact that long before Bill Hybels had drawn his first breath, my father was into seeker-services with a vengeance. What's more, he conveyed his passion for communicating the gospel to generations of students at Spurgeon's College.

But these facts of themselves do not sell a biography. Indeed, "worthiness" bores most readers stiff. Rather, I suggested, that the secret of this biography lies in its title: *Fearless for Truth*.[2] It was my father's courage and his passion for truth which makes this biography stand out from others. It is this aspect of my father which I wish to highlight in my lecture this afternoon. Needless to say, if you want the full story, then you must buy the book!

The title of the biography was my mother's idea. I believe that she was absolutely right. No title better sums up my father's life than this. For one of his essential characteristics was his passion for truth, wherever that may lead. Not surprisingly, more than one person wrote to me and likened him to Bunyan's "Valiant-for-Truth." Throughout his life my father was concerned for gospel truth, however costly that search might be. Although an unashamed evangelical, he refused to be bound within any one particular evangelical mould, but rather sought to allow the Scriptures to mould his thinking.

To what extent he would have recognized "fearless for truth" as a description of himself, I do not know. For in many ways my father was not a self-conscious person. Indeed, it was precisely this lack of self-consciousness that enabled him to speak and act without worrying how this might affect his standing with others. If he believed something to be right, then he would happily speak and act accordingly, even if those words and actions were to complicate life for him. His approach to life is well-summed up in a short prayer he wrote based on Matt 14:1–12: "Lord, help me to grow into your likeness, *to stand fearlessly for your truth*, to love the unlovely and to forgive those who treat us spitefully."[3]

2. Beasley-Murray, *Fearless for Truth*.

3. To be found in Beasley-Murray, *Matthew*.

So, with that general introduction, let us now look at nine examples of his fearlessness for truth.

His Decision to Follow Jesus

My first example comes from a mission to Leicester by two Spurgeon's students, when my father resolved to follow Jesus Christ. My father described his feelings as a fifteen-year-old boy coming from a nominal Roman Catholic home.

> One evening the preacher took the theme of the meaning of Christ's death. For the first time in my life I, who had seen crucifixes since I was a child, learned that the cross was for my sake; that the love of Christ shown on it embraced me as truly as it did anyone, and that I personally could know forgiveness for ever and eternal life. When that dawned on me it was like the coming of day. I could not hold back from Christ. I went forward to express my desire to receive Him—and went home walking on air.[4]

It took courage to decide to follow Jesus and then stand by that decision, for he received no support from home. Not only was there a lack of understanding on the part of his family, there was a good deal of mockery on their part too. And when it later became clear that this decision to follow Jesus entailed giving up a promising career as a concert pianist in order to respond to a call to ministry, there was consternation and opposition. It took a good number of years before their attitude began to change. For my father following Jesus involved being cut off from his family. Reflecting on that experience he wrote:

> The words of Jesus to his disciples after the refusal of the rich young ruler to become a disciple struck me very forcibly: Mark 10:29–30: "I tell you that anyone who leaves home or brothers or sisters or mother or father or children or fields for me and for the gospel, will receive much more in the present age. He will receive a hundred times more houses, brothers, sisters, mothers, children and fields—and persecutions as well." I learned, in fact, what Jesus meant in teaching us that God was our Father with the corollary that the church was our family.

4. Beasley-Murray, "My Call to the Ministry," 37.

Life between Death and Resurrection

My second example relates to his views about life between death and resurrection, the so-called intermediate state. In an article for *Young Life*, my father wrote,

> Such references as we have to the condition of the departed do not favour the idea that they are in a state of unconsciousness. The latter conception is largely due to taking literally the metaphor of sleep as a figure of death. An example of intense and joyous activity in the world of spirits this side of the Second Coming is the preaching of our Lord to "the spirits in prison," which, I am persuaded, has to be taken as it stands and not made to refer to the preaching of Noah to people once living but now dead. And this preaching was done by our Lord before His spirit was clothed in resurrection![5]

My father repeated these views in an evening lecture course he was giving during the summer of 1947 for the newly formed London Bible College. Unfortunately his view did not find favor with the Council of the China Inland Mission, and so his lecturing career at that stage was brought to an abrupt halt. It would appear that, in this particular lecture my father, on the basis of Peter's reference to the preaching of Jesus to "the spirits in prison" (1 Pet 3:19), speculated on the possibility of a second chance of repentance after death. Present at the lecture were some candidates of the China Inland Mission (CIM), who on their return to the CIM hostel reported my father's comments to some influential laymen who just happened to be there for a meeting of the CIM Council. Although none of them had any theological training, they were alarmed by this "heresy" and immediately got in touch with Dr. Ernest Kevan, the Principal of the London Bible College, to tell him so. Ernest Kevan, conscious of his dependence on these men, for several were on the Council of the new London Bible College, pleaded with my father to withdraw what he had said. My father was astonished and said that these views were ones which he felt were true to Scripture, and were therefore not ones to be discarded lightly. In the end he told Ernest Kevan that he would quietly withdraw from lecturing at the end of the session, so that the members of the CIM could be assured that they would have no need for further disquiet.

5. Beasley-Murray, "After Death—What?" 74.

Whether or not my father was right theologically is a moot point. What is not open to question is the cost which my father was prepared to pay for what he regarded as truth.

Jesus and the Future

From student days my father had on his desk a framed text bearing the words: "His coming is as certain as the dawn." Mark 13, with its eschatological discourse, was therefore a natural choice for his area of research for his London PhD. Described by A. M. Hunter as "the biggest problem in the Gospel," this chapter is quite a challenge to any budding scholar , and not least to a budding scholar from the evangelical wing of the Church. One of the most difficult of verses in that chapter is Mark 13:30: "Truly I tell you, this generation will not pass away until all these things have taken place." Of this verse my father wrote: "In no section of our study is courageous thinking more required than in this."[6] After weighing all the options my father took courage in his hands and argued that Jesus was referring to "a speedy coming of the End." He went on: "Undoubtedly the immediate sense of the saying defines the limits of Jesus' knowledge of the time of the end: it does not say that he knows nothing at all as to its coming; it affirms that it does not lie in his power to define it more closely."[7] "We believe . . . that his conviction of the nearness of the victory was due to the clarity of that vision in his soul."[8]

Not surprisingly such exegesis caused consternation amongst many evangelicals. But my father was not afraid of what others might think. He was concerned for what he deemed to be the truth. F. F. Bruce later commented that it was because "young men like George Beasley-Murray were willing to risk their reputation for conventional orthodoxy by saying what they believed" that there has become increasing openness within the world of evangelical scholarship.

Interestingly, forty years later, in his *magnum opus*, *Jesus and the Last Days*, my father indicated that he had changed his mind, believing that the saying of Jesus in Mark 13:30 relates primarily to the prophecy of the destruction of the temple in Mark 13:2. The factors for this change of mind do not concern us. What is significant is that he was not afraid

6. Beasley-Murray, *Jesus and the Future*, 186.

7. Ibid., 189.

8. Ibid., 190.

to say publicly that he had made a mistake. Here we have yet again more evidence of my father's fearless pursuit of truth.

Baptism in the New Testament

For many Baptists it was not his views on Mark 13 but rather his views on baptism which proved controversial. Indeed, Anthony Cross has called my father's essay on baptism in Paul contained in a collection of essays entitled *Christian Baptism* as "the most controversial work on baptism by any Baptist this century."[9] "Baptism in the Epistles of Paul" proved to be so controversial amongst Baptists because of the overtly sacramentalist position my father adopted. It offended those for whom baptism was primarily an act of witness. The key passage in the essay comes in the conclusion:

> With his predecessors and contemporaries, Paul saw in baptism *a sacrament of the Gospel.* Behind and in baptism stands the Christ of the cross and resurrection, bestowing freedom from sin's guilt and power, and the Spirit who gives the life of the age to come in the present and is the pledge of the resurrection at the last day.[10]

Such a conclusion smacked of baptismal regeneration to some, who wrote letters of protest to the *Baptist Times.* In a subsequent article my father made it clear that in no way did he and his fellow contributors to *Christian Baptism* believe in baptismal regeneration. However, were they to be asked, "Do you believe that baptism is a means of grace?" the answer would be,

> Yes, and more than is generally meant by that expression. In the Church of the Apostles (please note the limitation) the whole height and depth of grace is bound up with the experience of baptism. For to the New Testament writers baptism was nothing less than the climax of God's dealing with the penitent seeker and of the convert's return to God.[11]

The same position was adopted in *Baptism in the New Testament.* Just before it was published my father commented that he would have no friends when it came out, as it was too Baptist for the sacramentalists, and too sacramental for the Baptists!

9. Cross, *Baptism and the Baptists*, 227.
10. Gilmore, *Christian Baptism*, 148.
11. Beasley-Murray, "Baptist Controversy," 8.

As a result of persistent requests to produce a non-technical version of *Baptism in the New Testament* my father wrote *Baptism Today and Tomorrow*. Particularly in the chapter on "Baptism in Baptist Churches Today" my father refused to pull any of his punches:

> For where the cry goes out, "Only a symbol," emphasis is placed on the obedience and witness expressed in baptism. But this obedience is for the carrying out of a rite with virtually no content—and what is that but ritualism? And even the confession is robbed of its significance, for in Baptist Churches baptism is commonly administered *after* confession—and that a confession made in public! The rite then becomes a public ratification of a confession already publicly made. This problem is rendered yet more acute by the methods of mass evangelism that none are so forward in supporting as Baptists; for the essence of the method is conversion by confession, which in the New Testament is expressed in baptism. Carefully handled, this appeal could prepare for baptism. Badly handled, and with a low view of baptism, it could render baptism superfluous.[12]

My father's final contribution to the subject of baptism came in a paper titled "The Problem of Infant Baptism: An Exercise in Possibilities," written for a collection of essays in honor of Günter Wagner,[13] which was perhaps even more controversial than anything that he had ever written. There my father revealed that he had softened his attitude to recognizing in certain circumstances the "possibility" of acknowledging the legitimacy of infant baptism.

> I make the plea that churches which practise believer's baptism should consider acknowledging the legitimacy of infant baptism, and allow members of the Paedobaptist churches the right to interpret it according to their consciences. This would carry with it the practical consequence of believer-baptist churches refraining from baptizing on confession of faith those who have been baptized in infancy . . . It [this position] is at least in harmony with variations in the experience of baptism among the earliest believers recorded in the New Testament (cf. Acts 2:37–38; 8:14–17; 10:44–48; 11:1–18; 18:24–19:6). The great lesson of those variations is the freedom of God in bestowing his gifts.[14]

12. Beasley-Murray, *Baptism Today and Tomorrow*, 85–86, see also 91.
13. Beasley-Murray, "Possibilities," 1–14.
14. Ibid., 13–14.

My father ended the article with a reference to the appeal in the book of Revelation to "hear what the Spirit says to the churches!" (Rev 2:7 etc.): "I leave it to my fellow believer-baptists to ponder whether the 'possibilities' expounded in this article in any sense coincide with what the Spirit is saying to the churches today."[15]

Ecumenism

A convinced evangelical as also a convinced Baptist, my father was also persuaded that neither evangelicals nor Baptists had a monopoly of the truth. Right from the beginning of his ministry he abhorred what he termed the "pharisaism" of the "orthodox." He had a breadth of vision which at the time was unusual amongst evangelicals. In an address given to the College branch of the Theological Students' Fellowship he declared:

> The attitude adopted by many Fundamentalists towards the World Council of Churches is nothing short of scandalous. It is regarded as the first stages of the church of Antichrist. The worst motives are imputed to its enthusiasts; all are tarred with the same brush, and all are tools of the devil, including Karl Barth, the Archbishop of Canterbury and Dr Percy Evans! One is reminded of Hitler's attitude to the Jews; he gained unity by rousing indignation against them; and some Christians evidently find it easier to unite on the basis of hate than love.[16]

All this was well illustrated in what was later known as the "Ipswich affair." On Tuesday 24 January 1967 my father participated in a meeting in Ipswich with the Anglo-Catholic Bishop of St. Edmundsbury and Ipswich and Father Agnellus Andrew, a Roman Catholic priest on the staff of the BBC. The Protestant Truth Society felt impelled to protest that such a meeting should be held and issued a leaflet headed "Ipswich Heroes Betrayed!" The reference was to nine Protestant martyrs who were burned more than 400 years ago by the Roman Catholic Church for their faith. The leaflet continued: "A meeting has been arranged in Ipswich, at the Baths Hall, to seek to unite the Protestant Churches under the Church of Rome." My father was incensed and took issue with

15. Ibid., 14.

16. Beasley-Murray, "Vulnerable Points in the Christian Armoury," 4. (Dr. Percy Evans was the much-loved and irenic Principal of Spurgeon's from 1925 to 1950).

the Protestant Truth Society. His sermon notes for that evening contain the following statements:

> Here is the ground of the unity of the people of God: We are sinners for whom Christ died. We have confessed our sins and have been brought out of our disunity with God in a unity of guilt into unity with Christ our Saviour, who makes us one in Him and with each other by his Holy Spirit. I differ from Mr Spurgeon. Spurgeon was a pessimist with regard to the Churches. And I'm not. I believe in the Holy Ghost! He believed the Church of England and the Roman Catholics as Churches alike to be manifestations of the spirit of Antichrist. Spurgeon was a man of his age, who shared its intolerance as well as its convictions. We keep the convictions and leave the intolerance.

As if preaching such a sermon were in itself not enough, he then published an article in *The Christian and Christianity Today* in which he repeated much of his sermon.[17] In this article my father did not mince his words:

> I'm not ashamed of the Gospel, No. But I confess to being ashamed of some of its defenders. In particular I find myself at a loss to comprehend the tactics of some preachers in their relations with other preachers of the Gospel. There appears to be a competition among Evangelicals to see who can vilify most effectively the people of Christ who believe it is the will of God to end the hostilities within the church.

He attacked the Protestant Truth Society for their "deliberate untruth" in pretending that the purpose of the meeting in Ipswich was "to seek to unite the Protestant Churches under the Church of Rome." "This kind of propaganda," declared my father, "has more in common with the propaganda of Mao Tse Tung than with the Gospel of Jesus Christ."

Needless to say the article provoked a flood of varying responses. The Protestant Newsletter for March/April 1967, issued by the National Union of Protestants, had as its main headline "The Menace of the Beasley-Murrays."

Today ecumenism is no longer an issue in many evangelical circles. But in the 1960s this was not the case. Many evangelical Baptists had deep suspicion of the World Council of Churches. Many an evangelical, and not least an evangelical who was Principal of a theological college,

17. 10 February 1967, 12.

which was dependent on churches for its financial support, would have perhaps kept their head down and avoided the whole issue. But not my father. He was in the business of truth—whatever the cost.

Bultmann's John

To many evangelicals it seemed extraordinary that the Principal of Spurgeon's College should be responsible for the translation of the commentary on John by Rudolf Bultmann, which was published in England in 1971.[18] Bultmann was viewed by them as the "high priest" of demythologization and therefore demonized accordingly. However, my father was unconcerned by their astonishment. In his search for truth he believed it to be important to look at every viewpoint. As he wrote in an article for ministers, "Investigation of the Scriptures which by hook or by crook reaches predetermined conclusions is a denial of the Spirit of truth who is behind them and does no honour to our Lord or His Gospel. The minister who is afraid of truth contradicts alike his calling and his credentials."[19] He was convinced that he could always learn something, even from those with whom he disagreed. Furthermore, he believed that those with whom one disagreed should always be treated courteously.

People would have been less surprised by his decision to head the translation of Bultmann's *John* if they had listened to a Third Programme BBC talk given by my father in 1955. On that occasion he had taken issue with Bultmann's approach to the gospel, and yet at the same time was prepared to acknowledge that Bultmann had made a very positive contribution to Christian thought, and not least in his emphasis on the Cross: "However absurd it may sound, in his desire to make men see their only hope of redemption in the Cross, Bultmann shares the evangelistic aim of a Billy Graham, even though the methods of the two men have no contact."[20]

Christology

Christology—the doctrine of the person of Christ—provided yet another area of contention, where once again my father proved to be "fearless

18. Bultmann, *Gospel of John*.

19. Beasley-Murray, "The Minister and His Bible," 14.

20. Beasley-Murray, "Bultmann and 'Demythologizing,'" 601.

for the truth."[21] The controversy in which my father was involved in a major way was sparked by an address given by the Reverend Michael Taylor, then Principal of the Northern Baptist College, at the Baptist Union Assembly of April 1971. On the Tuesday night of the Assembly Michael Taylor, at the invitation of Dr. G. Henton Davies, the newly installed president of the Baptist Union, gave an address which caused much consternation. In his adddress, titled "The Incarnate Presence: how much of a man was Jesus?" Taylor appeared to question the very basis of the Christian faith. My father, aware of the strong feelings which this address was already beginning to arouse and of the implications which it could have for the ministers and churches of the Baptist Union, at the Thursday afternoon meeting of the Baptist Union Council asked that a notice be put in the *Baptist Times* assuring people that the views of speakers at the Assembly were not necessarily representative of the Baptist Union Council. But Dr. Ernest Payne, the distinguished former General Secretary of the Baptist Union, argued that it was the wrong thing to do because that Council meeting was not a full Council—it was held simply for the purpose of co-opting new Council members. The Council was persuaded by Payne and other denominational leaders to do nothing. For the next few months my father made no public statement about the address, although he was involved in considerable correspondence and discussion with concerned ministers and laypeople.

The matter of the Assembly address came to a meeting of the Baptist Union Council held on 9 November 1971. In spite of my father's pleading to the contrary, the Council by a very large majority recognized the right of Michael Taylor to express himself in the way he did, while at the same time asserting its adherence to the Declaration of Principle contained in the Constitution of the Baptist Union in which Jesus Christ is acknowledged as both "Lord and Saviour" and "God manifest in the flesh." At this point my father felt that he had no option but to resign as Chairman of the Council because he could no longer associate himself with its position. In his formal letter of resignation he went on to comment that his resignation would now free him from "the restraint which I felt laid upon me since the Assembly." At the same time as sending this letter, he wrote a personal letter to Michael Taylor, with whom he had had a three-hour private conversation in his home at Spurgeon's College the previous Sunday. Two of its paragraphs read as follows:

21. See also the final chapter of this collection.—Ed.

> You and I have been placed in positions that are burdensome to endure. You will need great grace to forgive me for my apparent intransigence. It is a question of the Gospel being in my sight of greater account than either you or me. I hope that it may be possible speedily to dissociate discussions from your name and person. That may be difficult at first, but I shall do all in my power to see that it is achieved. You have set in motion forces that will continue to move for a long time. My concern will be to try to direct some of them at any rate in a right direction. If the end of it all is a greater understanding of Christ and the Gospel and a better communication of our message to the world, that will be a wonderful gain. But in the process there will certainly be hurt, for many feel that their faith and the Baptist Denomination in particular is threatened, and people in that situation are not used to quiet speaking. They feel above all that the honour of the Lord is at stake, and they must see that we give him his rightful place in our thought and message.

Over the months controversy continued to mount. In January my father submitted an article for publication in the *Baptist Times* titled "The Controversy Cannot End—Yet," which in essence urged the forthcoming assembly to confess its faith in Christ and to disassociate itself from any Christology which does not recognize his full deity as well as his complete humanity. The editor, the Rev Walter Bottoms, refused to publish the article.

My father thereupon turned his article into a booklet entitled "The Christological Controversy in the Baptist Union" and sent out the booklet together with an accompanying letter on 20 March 1972. In the letter he wrote: "The enclosed article suggests the seriousness of the theological issues involved and these require more prolonged consideration. Surely we shall not shirk to give this? If my interpretation of the issues is false, let it be shown by reasoned statements. I am always very anxious to learn!"

The sending of the letter caused scores of letters of support to be sent to my father. It also provoked strong reaction among the more liberal members of the denomination.

Probably the strongest letters of protest came from Ernest Payne. He accused my father of having misunderstood Michael Taylor, and went on: "You have spent a lot of time and energy translating Bultmann. What if I publicly criticized you for spreading the views of one who is regarded by many as being extremely arbitrary in his treatment of evidence and who reduced the reliable information about Jesus and his teaching to a few verses only?"[22]

In response my father sent Ernest Payne a strong but courteous letter back:

> I wonder whether you have read his exposition of the Gospel of John. I wish with all my heart that Michael had it in him to declare the gospel in the kind of terms that Bultmann makes of John 3:16 and other related sayings within that gospel . . . Naturally I do not accept Bultmann's historical scepticism, but you ought to know Bultmann well enough to realize that he is an exponent of the Lutheran doctrine of justification by faith, despite his absurd limitation of the authentic teaching in the Synoptic Gospels. The extraordinary thing is what he does manage to make of the amount of the teaching of Jesus which he does recognize as authentic."[23]

Dr. Payne was not mollified. Instead he sent a second letter which ended: "You have been stirring up trouble instead of calming it, and have contributed therefore, more than perhaps any other single individual, to the very difficult and dangerous situation we now face."[24]

My father wrote back:

> I did my utmost to prevent a fire raging in the denomination. You will remember that on the occasion of the Council meeting that was at the end of the last assembly I pleaded with the Council members then present to issue a statement with regard to the address of Michael Taylor embodying the perfectly obvious observation that speakers at our assembly bear the responsibility for their utterances themselves, and that the Union is neither responsible nor implicated in them . . . You yourself were above all responsible for the Council declining that advice . . . I believe that you made a grave mistake, and that you thereby made possible the escalation of the discussion to a denominational controversy . . . If the Baptist Union were to be characterized by the theology uttered and implied by Michael Taylor I could have no part with it. That perhaps is of minor consequence, but so long as I am a part of our Baptist Union I feel it my duty to prevent the Union from moving in a direction away from essential Christianity.[25]

22. Letter dated 6 April 1972.
23. Letter dated 12 April 1972.
24. Letter dated 18 April 1972.
25. Letter dated 20 April 1972.

Matters reached a climax on Tuesday 25 April 1972. Delegates from the churches who had come for the debate packed Westminster Chapel from floor to ceiling as they debated and then voted upon the resolution, proposed by Sir Cyril Black, and seconded by my father. Great care had been taken in the drawing up of the resolution that Michael Taylor was not mentioned by name. The issue was about principles, not personalities. Of the several thousand delegates present, only 46 voted against it, and 72 abstentions were recorded. It was indeed a historic vote. There are those who see 1972 as the moment when the tide actually began to turn even though it was some years before the tide began to come in. The ethos of the denomination began to change. Evangelicals began to get more involved in Baptist Union structures. The ginger group, "Mainstream—Baptists for life and growth," was formed, and, whether consequentially or not, the Baptist Union began to experience new life and new growth.

The Battle for the Bible

Unlike many fundamentalists, my father welcomed the advent of Biblical criticism. His approach is well illustrated in a popular talk he gave on the overseas service of the BBC in 1963.[26] "Biblical criticism is as necessary for Fundamentalists as for every one else. For criticism of the Bible is not a process of pronouncing judgment on the Bible, but the investigation of the circumstances of its making—who its authors were, their time and place of writing and why they wrote."

Almost twenty years later my father elaborated on his view of Scripture in a closely-argued paper entitled: "Recovering the Authority of the Bible."[27] For him "the Bible may be referred to as the Word of God, namely in its function as witness to the Gospel." With Luther and Calvin he "affirmed the trustworthiness of the Bible as an infallible authority in matters of salvation and the life of faith"; and with them too he acknowledged that it "contains normal human flaws and failings" which can be sorted out by scholarly study. The final two paragraphs of the paper helpfully illuminate his understanding of the Bible:

26. "The Bible Comes Alive: 4: Through Great Argument." Broadcast on 3 and 5 November 1963.

27. Written in 1982 but not published.

> We should clearly recognize that the concept of inerrancy is concerned with the *form* of the Bible rather than its *message*. Those who formulated it were concerned with the grounding of faith in a rational concept of the Bible. Well meaning as this idea is, especially in connection with a formulation of Christian apologetics, the Bible gives us a different account of its function: it is to present the Word of God to the mind and conscience of the hearer, and by the Holy Spirit's operation to make it the means of salvation, whether entrance into it or continuance in it. The authority of the Bible no more depends on rational proof than the God of salvation does. That authority is self-evidencing to all whose hearts become open to the Holy Spirit. Through the Spirit's operation the revelation of God was given initially (for the Spirit is God at work in the world), through the Spirit the revelation is grasped, and through him its truth and power are known. The Spirit of truth is the life-giving Spirit. The unbeliever who lets the Word of God reach his heart discovers the truth of the Bible by its power to convince and renew and such a one experiences the life.

Unfortunately this approach to Scripture, although common among many evangelical scholars in Britain and elsewhere, does not find favor everywhere. It does not, for instance, find much favor with the present leadership of the Southern Baptist Convention. Happily this was not the case in the 1970s when for seven years my father was teaching at the Southern Baptist Theological Seminary in Louisville and exercising a wide preaching ministry all over the States. Sadly in later years, however, he became *persona non grata* amongst many Southern Baptists—not that this troubled him one whit. To the end, he was fearless for truth.

Significantly, before he left the service of the Seminary, the Board of Trustees in their 1980 annual session passed a formal "resolution" in which they expressed appreciation to my father "for his insight, courage, and commitment in furthering the cause of Christ and the understanding of the New Testament." In the light of the title of my book, *Fearless for Truth*, it is surely noteworthy that the word "courage" features in the resolution.

A Confession of Faith

Even to the end, my father was never satisfied with the "status quo." His watchword was that of Luther's: *ecclesia reformata et reformanda*—the

Church was both reformed and to be reformed. At a Mainstream consultation he gave a paper on "Confessing Baptist Identity"[28] in which he urged his fellow Baptists to "pluck up courage and do for our day what our Baptist forefathers did for theirs, namely produce a contemporary Baptist Confession of Faith."[29]

The word "courage" was significant. Although Baptists in the seventeenth and eighteenth centuries had been happy to produce confessions of faith, in the twentieth century the leadership of the Baptist Union had become very wary of producing a contemporary confession of faith, fearing that it might become divisive rather than unifying. My father begged to differ. Such a confession of faith, he maintained, was "desirable for God's sake, for our sakes, for the sake of other Churches, and for the sake of the world."[30]

It was desirable for God's sake, in so far as it would enable Baptists to "have an understanding of God by which their praise and thanksgiving may rise to genuine adoration." It was desirable for the sake of Baptists, because it "could transform the understanding of their faith which many people hold to be dead. It could also become an excellent basis for instructing new converts." It was desirable for the sake of other Christians, because "there are surprisingly few members of other denominations who have a reasonably accurate knowledge of what Baptists believe." And it was desirable for the sake of the world, in so far as it would help Christians to bear an effective witness to the gospel. "Mission is supposed to be in our blood: it needs to be in our head and in our heart."[31]

He drew his paper to a close with these words:

> A Confession of Faith for today . . . does not need to have negative effects. They could be wholly positive when slanted in the direction of vision for action. We are not wanting a ten point creed corresponding to the Ten Commandments, to which signatures will be demanded from those who camp around the Baptist Mount Sinai! We belong to the city of God. We celebrate with our fellow-citizens beneath an open heaven in the presence of the God of glory and Jesus the Mediator of the New Covenant. We want to catch a fuller glimpse of the reality to which we belong. We need to let it inspire us to action in keeping with this new

28. Beasley-Murray, "Confessing Baptist Identity," 75–85.

29. Ibid., 78.

30. Ibid.

31. Ibid., 78–81.

> world of God's kingdom. Theology is thinking and talking about God. It is dead only when it comes hundredth hand from dusty volumes that got it hundredth hand from even dustier libraries. Theology is done on our knees, our faces turned towards God, our ears attentive to hear from God's Word and what the saints have learned from it. From that mountain top we can see the needy multitudes below. When this is done, visionary theological thinking becomes possible.[32]

Conclusion

After my father's death Spurgeon's College held a celebration of my father's life.

I was given the opportunity to make a brief tribute. I honored my father as a man who loved his family, as a man who loved his Lord, and also as a man who loved truth. Today, I have been glad to honor again the memory of my father as a man who was fearless for truth.

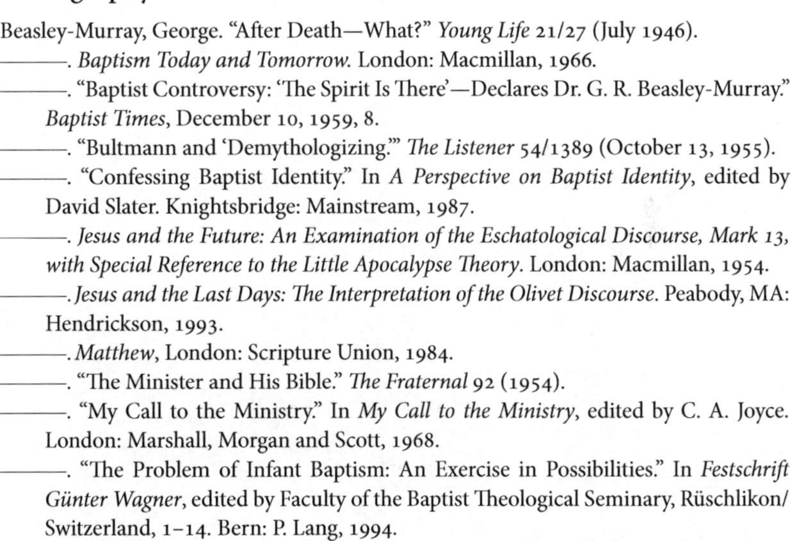

Bibliography

Beasley-Murray, George. "After Death—What?" *Young Life* 21/27 (July 1946).

———. *Baptism Today and Tomorrow.* London: Macmillan, 1966.

———. "Baptist Controversy: 'The Spirit Is There'—Declares Dr. G. R. Beasley-Murray." *Baptist Times*, December 10, 1959, 8.

———. "Bultmann and 'Demythologizing.'" *The Listener* 54/1389 (October 13, 1955).

———. "Confessing Baptist Identity." In *A Perspective on Baptist Identity*, edited by David Slater. Knightsbridge: Mainstream, 1987.

———. *Jesus and the Future: An Examination of the Eschatological Discourse, Mark 13, with Special Reference to the Little Apocalypse Theory*. London: Macmillan, 1954.

———. *Jesus and the Last Days: The Interpretation of the Olivet Discourse*. Peabody, MA: Hendrickson, 1993.

———. *Matthew*, London: Scripture Union, 1984.

———. "The Minister and His Bible." *The Fraternal* 92 (1954).

———. "My Call to the Ministry." In *My Call to the Ministry*, edited by C. A. Joyce. London: Marshall, Morgan and Scott, 1968.

———. "The Problem of Infant Baptism: An Exercise in Possibilities." In *Festschrift Günter Wagner*, edited by Faculty of the Baptist Theological Seminary, Rüschlikon/Switzerland, 1–14. Bern: P. Lang, 1994.

———. "Vulnerable Points in the Christian Armoury." *Spurgeon's College Students Magazine* (Summer 1950).

Beasley-Murray, Paul. *Fearless for Truth: A Personal Portrait of George Raymond Beasley-Murray*. Carlisle, UK: Paternoster, 2002.

32. Ibid., 84.

Bultmann, Rudolf. *The Gospel of John: A Commentary*. Edited and supervised by G. R. Beasley-Murray, with assistance from R. W. N. Hoare and J. K. Riches. Oxford: Blackwell, 1964.

Cross, Anthony R. *Baptism and the Baptists: Theology and Practice in Twentieth Century Britain*. Carlisle, UK: Paternoster, 2000.

Gilmore, Alec, ed. *Christian Baptism: A Fresh Attempt to Understand the Rite in Terms of Scripture, History, and Theology*. London: Lutterworth, 1959.

2

Faith-Baptism

The Key to an Evangelical Baptismal Sacramentalism[1]

Anthony R. Cross

Introduction[2]

George Beasley-Murray was the pre-eminent British Baptist New Testament scholar of the twentieth century and I do not think it would be far wrong to say that most Baptists would consider his contribution to the study of baptism as his most important scholarly work. His Whitley Lectures of 1959–60, published as *Baptism in the New Testament*, are widely and rightly regarded as classic[3] and continue to be

1. This lecture was delivered on 4 May 2003 at the Baptist Assembly in Cardiff. It was later published under the same title in *Journal of European Baptist Studies* 4 (2004) 5–21 and the cooperation of the editors is here acknowledged. The present chapter has undergone slight changes to the text.

2. It should be noted, that as the second Dr. G. R. Beasley-Murray Memorial Lecture, it has been my deliberate policy to try and allow Beasley-Murray to speak for himself. I have striven to expound his baptismal theology as faithfully as possible and to keep critical interaction with him to a minimum. Also, due to constraints of time and space, I have only referred to a limited number of Beasley-Murray's many writings on baptism and related subjects.

3. E.g., Gloer, "Editor's Preface," in Gloer, *Eschatology and the New Testament,* ix; also Culpepper, "George R. Beasley-Murray," 576, who describes it as "the definitive work on the subject for years to come." Fowler, *More Than a Symbol*, 139, calls Beasley-Murray's *Baptism in the New Testament* Baptist sacramentalism's "most articulate de-

in print. However, the irony is that while Baptists have been justifiably proud of Beasley-Murray's major contribution to the study of baptism, one of the historians of Baptist theology at this time has remarked that while he and R. E. O. White "produced what are without doubt the most important, detailed and eloquent examinations of baptism," nevertheless "their impact has been limited." The reason for this, he suggests, is because "much of what they said has either not been read by many Baptists . . . , or have been read but not understood, or have been read but ignored."[4] This is a sad indictment on Baptists who take their name from the rite of Christian initiation. Many times throughout his writings Beasley-Murray refers to Baptist criticisms of other traditions whose baptismal theology does not accord with New Testament teaching, then notes that doing such a thing carries with it the requirement that Baptists themselves also test their beliefs and practices according to the Word of God. For instance,

> (H)ave not we Baptists a duty to set our own house in order? For too long we have regarded it as our vocation to demonstrate *who* are the proper recipients of baptism, but have been unable to supply a coherent account from the Scriptures of *what* that baptism is that must be administered to the right persons. Anyone acquainted with our churches knows that there exist in them traditions as stereotyped as can be found in any other churches, and we are dangerously near to mistaking our own popular traditions for the Word of God as are the rest. We Baptists pride ourselves on being churches of the New Testament. It behooves us to take our own medicine—to cast aside our pride, search afresh the Scriptures, submit ourselves to their teaching, and be prepared for reform according to the Word.[5]

The Issues

The issues at stake are highlighted in two short essays. The first was a brief response to Louis Read's short discussion of "The Ordinances." Here, Read rejects the use of the term "sacraments" understood as "means of

fence"; while Church of Scotland historian and theologian David F. Wright, *What Has Infant Baptism Done to Baptism?*, 5, refers to it as "a landmark in the modern *retractatio* of early Christian baptism."

4. Cross, *Baptism and the Baptists*, 227–28 n. 61.

5. Beasley-Murray, "Baptism in the New Testament," 30, italics original.

grace" on the grounds that it has no meaning pertinent to the Baptist view of baptism and the Lord's Supper. "(A)s things are," he declares, the term "generally conveys a meaning alien to our thought" or "so nebulous to mean nothing." He then objects to the notion that sacraments are means of grace, "imparting benefit to those who participate." Instead, he argues that "ordinance" lacks the ambiguity of "sacrament" and is self-explanatory, implying the institution of both ordinances by Christ and this alone is "sufficient reason for continuing their observance."[6] For Read and the majority of Baptists—both then and now—the purpose and meaning of the ordinances are that in them believers dedicate themselves to the Lord, being responses to God's goodness, portraying the means of redemption and evoking praise and worship.[7]

Beasley-Murray responded in "The Sacraments." His aim is not to defend the use of the term "sacrament," though he remarks that the loose employment of it is inadequate reason for its rejection. But his most severe criticism of Read is that in a discussion of the sacraments "a fellow-Baptist . . . should write with scarcely a reference to the Scriptures." No less than Paedobaptists, Baptists need to "turn again to the documents of our Faith" in order to ensure that they also do not build "on the sands of tradition." He outlines the accepted Baptist position at the time which, to our discredit, has barely changed in over fifty years: "the general emphasis amongst us falls on [baptism's] value as a means of confession and that other significations are subordinated to this main idea. It is normally held to make no difference to the condition of the baptized person; its virtue lies in the expression of spiritual realities already appropriated. Such a view accords with that of [Read] . . . : Baptism is our act for God, our response to His appeal for obedience." Beasley-Murray does *not* deny the confessional nature of baptism, and it is important that this is not forgotten. However, in this article and his other writings, he stresses that "the confessional value of Baptism . . . is a secondary, not primary, meaning of the rite," and that the additional conclusion (namely, "Baptism is our act for God, our response to His appeal for obedience") "is a pure rationalization" which is "impossible to square with the New Testament expositions of the matter." He then summarizes the New Testament teaching as follows: "In every explicit mention of Baptism it is regarded as the supreme moment of our union

6. Read, "Ordinances," 8–9.

7. Ibid., 10.

with Christ in His redemptive acts for us and our consequent reception of the life of the Spirit."[8]

Following his brief review of New Testament teaching, Beasley-Murray asks, "If this be valid exegesis, how can one assert that the important thing in Baptism is what we give to God?" He then comments that objections to a biblical sacramentalism "are usually on other than exegetical grounds." Free Church people, he notes, are disinclined to hold such a view because it appears to contradict the deeply held conviction that people are "renewed in spirit and made heir of salvation on the exercise of faith." It also appears to make baptism "operative instead of symbolic of a crisis already accomplished in the believer," for it "postpones the operation and gift of the Spirit from the submission of faith to the reception of an outward ordinance." And this is precisely Beasley-Murray's point. The key to the problem is "postpone" for "the New Testament knows nothing of postponing a baptism after conversion." This, we will see, is key to Beasley-Murray's argument, that baptism is conversion-baptism.[9] In the primitive Church conversion and baptism were "so indissolubly linked together that they may be regarded as a unity. In such a context," he continues,

> to speak of a Christian dying and rising with Christ and receiving the Spirit of Pentecost in baptism is no magical concept, for the submission of the rite *was* the occasion of surrender to Christ. This is no setting of a sacrament over against repentance and faith, as though baptism made conversion unnecessary, but the intertwining of the two so that baptism is a part of conversion. It is only when the primitive relationship is separated that sacerdotalism creeps in and *opus operatum* becomes the watchword instead of the New Testament principle *nullum sacramentum sine fide*.[10]

8. Beasley-Murray, "Sacraments," 3.

9. E.g., and anticipating our discussion below, see Beasley-Murray, *Worship and the Sacraments*, 5–6, "The descriptions of baptism in the New Testament, and the indications of the apostolic teaching on its meaning, make it plain that the early Church viewed baptism as the completion of conversion to God. The baptism of John the Baptist is described by Mark as a 'repentance baptism' (Mark 1:4), and scholars are agreed that in this context repentance means 'turning to God,' i.e. what we mean by conversion. This way of viewing baptism became normative in the Christian church, whatever else was attached to the significance of the rite" (cf. Acts 2:37–38; 22:16; and 1 Pet 3:21).

10. Beasley-Murray, "The Sacraments," 4, italics added.

However, Baptists have departed from New Testament baptism and in so doing "have overlooked the fact that they have been almost as culpable as others in breaking asunder the unity of conversion and baptism."[11] What he means is that while Paedobaptists have put baptism before conversion, Baptists have put it after it, sometimes by many years, even decades. For Beasley-Murray, Baptists are still not used to the fact that in the New Testament *kerygma* precedes *didache*, preaching precedes teaching,[12] and, though he does not make this explicit at this point, we should note that this is the order in which they appear in Matthew 28:19. He then states that, "If under modern conditions we fear to baptize converts straightway, then let us recognize that in so doing *we have changed the nature of baptism*." So in place of this Baptist tradition of baptism, Beasley-Murray challenged the Baptists of his time, and since little if anything in general has changed, then us too: "let baptism once more be regarded as part of conversion, the moment of supreme surrender rather than the expression of a believer's obedience, and we shall be free once more to teach the New Testament doctrine of Baptism."[13] He concludes his discussion of baptism with a challenge: "If we are to take that opportunity, which Wheeler Robinson foresaw a generation ago would come, of leading the Body of Christ to the true view of Baptism, we shall do it only if we rise to a clearer apprehension of it than we appear to possess today."[14]

The second essay by Beasley-Murray is a brief exegetical study of "Baptism in the Epistles of Paul" which appeared in the 1959 volume, *Christian Baptism*, a collaborative work by some of the leading British Baptist scholars of the next two generations.[15] Edited by Alec Gilmore, *Christian Baptism* proved to be the most controversial work on baptism by any Baptist in the twentieth century[16] coming under a sustained at-

11. Ibid.

12. Ibid., 5.

13. Ibid., italics added.

14. Ibid. On Robinson's baptismal theology, see Cross, "Pneumatological Key," 151–76.

15. Beasley-Murray, "Baptism in the Epistles of Paul," 128–49. On the posts the ten contributors were to hold, see Cross, *Baptism*, 197 n. 55.

16. So Cross, *Baptism*, 228; Beasley-Murray, *Fearless for Truth*, 122–23, and the whole of his discussion of baptism, 120–28.

tack from anti-sacramentalists.[17] Within a very short time the volume was denounced as unbiblical and un-Baptist and it was Beasley-Murray who sought to answer the book's critics. At this juncture, one point needs to be noted. Beasley-Murray stated that the particular exegetical discussions under suspicion[18] related

> to *baptism in the apostolic Church*, not to baptism in the average modern Baptist church. Where baptism is sundered from conversion on the one hand, and from entry into the Church on the other, this language cannot be applied to it; such a baptism is a reduced baptism . . . My concern, along with my colleagues, is to put before Baptists the picture of ideal baptism, as it is portrayed in the apostolic writings, in the hope that we may strive to recover it or get somewhere near it. To insist on keeping our impoverished version of baptism would be a tragedy among a people who pride themselves on being the people of the New Testament.[19]

The Meaning of "Sacrament"

Since the mid-nineteenth-century Baptist understanding of the term "Sacrament" has been clouded by an antipathy towards the type of sacramentalism characterized by the Oxford Movement, whether in terms of the phrases "baptismal regeneration"[20] or the ancient formula *ex opere operato* with its connotation of magical efficacy. But what the overwhelming majority of Baptists were, and still are, unaware of, Beasley-Murray included,[21] is that many early Baptists did understand baptism

17. For details of this controversy, see Fowler, "Is 'Baptist Sacramentalism' an Oxymoron?" 129–50, and his *More Than a Symbol*, 113–33; and Cross, *Baptism*, 196–97, 227–39.

18. R. E. O. White on "The Baptism of Jesus" and "Baptism in the Synoptic Gospels," 84–98 and 98–115; S. I. Buse on "Baptism in the Acts of the Apostles" and "Baptism in Other New Testament Writings," 115–28 and 170–86; and D. R. Griffiths on "Baptism in the Fourth Gospel and the First Epistle of John," 149–70.

19. So Beasley-Murray, "Baptism Controversy'" 8, italics original.

20. See, e.g., Cross, "Baptismal Regeneration," 149–74.

21. Fowler, "Is 'Baptist Sacramentalism' an Oxymoron?" 146–47. Interestingly, however, Read, "The Ordinances," 9, was aware of "a tentative use of sacrament in the early days of Baptist churches." Since Beasley-Murray responded to this article it could be argued that he, too, was aware of this tradition. However, this would not explain why he never mentions it when it would have clearly supported his argument in more than a few places. See, e.g., the discussion of the article by the Presbyterian layman,

and the Lord's Supper sacramentally.[22] It was only during the nineteenth century that this term became widely derided and rejected, used only by a small minority of Baptists.[23] Further, many Baptists were, and continue to be, seemingly unaware that there is no agreed definition of the term "sacrament."[24] "Sacrament" is a term that has to be defined by the writer using it, not read into it by the reader. Here, authorial intention is what is important. That this did not happen can be seen in the controversy surrounding *Christian Baptism* when anti-sacramentalists repeatedly claimed that Beasley-Murray in particular was using the term in a way in which he, in fact, was not.[25]

Beasley-Murray is fully aware that "the term 'sacrament' has . . . varied meanings attributed to it,"[26] and it is significant to note that nowhere does he formally define it. At first this might seem like a singular omission on his part, though, I believe, it was a conscious and wise decision not to do so. Instead he lets the New Testament teaching of baptism—as both a divine and human action—give the term its meaning.[27]

J. M. Ross, "The Theology of Baptism in Baptist History," 100–112, who could only find one reference to the bestowal of the Spirit in baptism prior to 1925, and that in verse 4 of George Rawson's hymn "A Mighty Mystery We Set Forth" (no. 489 in *The Baptist Church Hymnal* [London: Psalms and Hymns Trust, 1900]). The irony is that Rawson was a Congregationalist. For his reference to Ross' work, see Beasley-Murray, *Baptism Today and Tomorrow*, 14–15. Also, Beasley-Murray's discussion on 32–33 shows no awareness of this sacramental tradition in early Baptist thought. For references to the Spirit before 1925, see Cross, *Baptism*, 108–11 and passim, and "Pneumatological Key," 151–76.

22. See Fowler, *More Than a Symbol*, 10–88; Thompson, "New Question in Baptist History," 66–68, 71–72, and "Practicing the Freedom of God," 126–31; and Cross, *Baptism*, 6–17, and "Dispelling the Myth," 128–62.

23. Fowler, *More Than a Symbol*, 86–88; and Cross, *Baptism*, 16–17.

24. E.g., the patristic scholar J. N. D. Kelly, *Early Christian Doctrines*, 423, notes that in the fourth and fifth centuries "the conception of sacrament was still elastic." This is equally the case today.

25. See the discussion in Fowler, "Is 'Baptist Sacramentalism' an Oxymoron?" 141–42 and 147–50, and *More Than a Symbol*, 125–26 and 129–33; and Cross, *Baptism*, 230–39.

26. *Today and Tomorrow*, 13. In *Worship and the Sacraments*, 5, he speaks in terms of the ambiguity of "sacraments," adding, "but my use of the term is intended to convey the simple thought that God has given us sacraments to be employed in the context of worship."

27. That baptism is a divine and human act where the gospel meets faith is repeatedly emphasized by Beasley-Murray. See, e.g., *Today and Tomorrow*, 43, 66; also his "Baptism and the Sacramental View," 9, where, on the basis of baptism in the New

This said, however, Beasley-Murray does mention various definitions of "sacrament," though these tend to be in passing and he neither develops nor endorses them.[28] The only definitions of "sacrament" he favors are a "means of grace" and *sacramentum*, both of which he regards as in accord with New Testament teaching. By "means of grace" he means more than is usually meant, because, "In the Church of the Apostles (please note the limitation) the whole height and depth of grace is bound up with the experience of baptism. For to the New Testament writers baptism was nothing less than *the climax of God's dealing with the penitent seeker and of the convert's return to God*."[29] A sacrament is "the Word of God in action" which "must be responded to in the act of participating." For both Acts and Paul baptism is entrance into the Christian life. This is not at odds with New Testament teaching where "baptism is inseparable from the turning to God in faith, on the basis of which God justifies, gives the Spirit, and unites to Christ." Baptism is, therefore, a medium of grace.[30]

Citing an unpublished Baptist World Alliance report, Beasley-Murray states that baptism and the Lord's Supper are "pre-eminent among the means of grace," though they are not the only means. He tacitly rejects any suggestions of their magical efficacy[31] because "their effectiveness derives from the nature of God, his promises in the Gospel, the work of Christ, the mysterious working of the Holy Spirit, *and the answering of faith of the believer*. Grace is the love of God in action. A means of grace is therefore any channel through which the love of God reaches and enriches the human heart."[32]

He finds the idea of Peter's use of "appeal" or "pledge" in 1 Peter 3:21 as a declaration of faith and loyalty to God as not far removed from the use of the term *sacramentum*, the military oath. For in baptism

---

Testament being inseparable from turning to God in faith, he states that "a sacrament can be a genuine interchange between God and man"; and "Authority and Justification for Believers' Baptism," 66.

28. See *Today and Tomorrow*, 16–17; and his *Baptism in the New Testament*, 7.

29. "Baptist Controversy," 8, italics original.

30. "Baptism and the Sacramental View," 9.

31. Elsewhere, *Today and Tomorrow*, 98, he states unequivocally that "baptism is not a rite that operates automatically."

32. *Worship and the Sacraments*, 9, italics added, quoting a Baptist World Alliance's Commission on the Doctrine of the Church report (1950). For his use of "means of grace," see also, e.g., *Today and Tomorrow*, 41.

"the convert is enrolled in the army of the Lord, and baptism makes his pledge of obedience to God," adding that this is inseparable from baptism as a means of confession before people. He further notes that the early Church's creeds developed from the earliest baptismal confession, "Jesus is Lord" (Rom. 10:9) and were confessions used by converts as they made their surrender to the Redeemer-Lord.[33]

The suggestion that a biblically-based sacramentalism leaves the door open to an automatic, *ex opere operato* understanding of baptism, Beasley-Murray states is ruled out on the basis of Colossians 2:12 and 1 Peter 3:21. In the former is to be found the phrase "in baptism you were also raised to life with him through your faith in the active power of God," while the latter states that "Baptism . . . now saves you, *not* as a removal of dirt from the body, *but* as an appeal to God for a clear conscience, *through* the resurrection of Jesus Christ."[34]

Baptism as a Symbol

It is important to recognize that Beasley-Murray nowhere dismisses or diminishes the importance of the symbolic nature of baptism. What he wants to do is avoid, on the one hand, the merely symbolic interpretation so characteristic of Baptists, especially since the mid-nineteenth century, and, on the other hand, a magical and mechanical understanding of the rite. The strength of the symbolic dimension, he acknowledges, lies in immersion that symbolizes, in a way pouring or sprinkling cannot, the most obvious element of baptismal symbolism, namely the cleansing of sin (Acts 22:16). The stripping off and putting on of clothes symbolizes the discarding of the old life apart from God and putting on the new life in Christ (Gal 3:27; Col 3:9, 12). The act of immersion beneath the water and then the rising out of it is peculiarly appropriate to an action which derives its meaning from identification with Christ who died, was buried and rose again for humanity's salvation. But what he is emphatic about is that it is not enough for the non-sacramentalist to say that what happened to the person so-baptized was that they received the blessing God always gives to the obedience of faith, and the reason for this he states unequivocally is because this is not what the New Testament says

33. *Worship and the Sacraments*, 6. See also *Today and Tomorrow*, 127–28.

34. "Authority and Justification," 64–65. Cf. his "Second Chapter of Colossians," 476–77. In *Today and Tomorrow*, 21–22, he cites 1 Cor 10:1–4 along with 1 Pet 3:21 as warning against a magical-superstitious view of the sacraments.

happens in baptism.[35] Elsewhere he writes, "[Baptism] signifies abandonment of reliance on self for faith in God, the radical turning from sin to God known as repentance, a dying to sin and rising to new life in Christ, a forsaking of life according to this age for life in the fellowship of the Church, the Body of Christ."[36] Quite simply, "to conclude that the understanding of baptism as 'a beautiful and expressive symbol,' *and nothing more*, is irreconcilable with the New Testament."[37] Further, when baptism is viewed as nothing more than a symbol, the emphasis being on the obedience and witness expressed in it, the result is "the carrying out of a rite with virtually no content—and what is that but ritualism?"[38]

The New Testament's Baptismal Sacramentalism: Faith-Baptism

The whole question of the nature of baptism, Beasley-Murray states, "can hardly be answered without reference to the New Testament teaching on baptism," and, as we have seen, his criticisms of the non-sacramentalist position are based on the inadequacy of its exegesis of the New Testament.[39] As we have also already noted, his sacramentalism is "defined" exegetically and exegesis forms the major part of his writings on baptism.

Throughout their history Baptists have understood the authority for believers' baptism to lie in the commission of the risen Lord in Matthew 28:19. Here the making of disciples involves the proclamation of the gospel which includes an appeal for repentance (understood as turning to God[40]) and faith, and that those who receive the word with faith are to be baptized and taught the fuller elements of Christian doctrine and living. But Beasley-Murray notes that this frequent understanding of Jesus' command in terms of making disciples "*by* baptizing them" can be accepted only on the basis of the recognition that it is those who acknowledge Jesus as Lord in the Trinity; that is, on confession of faith in response to the hearing of the gospel, who become "disciples" in baptism. To be baptized in the name of the Trinity is to own the sover-

35. See *Today and Tomorrow*, 23–27.

36. Ibid., 167.

37. Ibid., 32, italics original.

38. Ibid., 85.

39. Ibid., 13.

40. Beasley-Murray, "Faith in the New Testament," 137, "The noun *metanoia* (Hebrew *teshubah*) is the equivalent of conversion."

eignty of God in Christ through the Spirit, and this is in harmony with what he agrees is the earliest baptismal confession, Romans 10:9's "Jesus is Lord." This entails alike the appropriation by the sovereign Lord and the believer's rendering the obedience of faith to him as Lord. [41]

This understanding of the Great Commission is supported by the earliest accounts of the church's mission in the book of Acts. Here the apostolic proclamation of the gospel, the hearing with faith and baptism are constantly linked (Acts 2:37–38; 2:41; 8:31; 8:35–36; 16:14–15; 16:32–33; 18:8; 19:50). But more important than these historical discussions is the nature of baptism itself as expounded throughout the New Testament, particularly the letters. In passages such as Galatians 3:26–27, Romans 6:1–11, and 1 Corinthians 12:13

> the assumption appears to be uniform that baptism marks the passage of a convert confessing Christ in the gospel from a state of alienation without Christ to existence in Christ by the Spirit, under the saving sovereignty of God, and so a member of Christ's people, rejoicing in the forgiveness of sins and the life of the age to come, and anticipating the fullness of that resurrection to the final kingdom.[42]

He remarks that it is significant that passages in the New Testament that provide some of the most important insights into the meaning of baptism "conjoin faith and baptism, as though they were integral to each other." This observation is the hub of the problem for Baptists: "baptism appears to be understood and expounded in such terms as make sense only in the case of baptism received with the response of faith to the Good News."[43]

Galatians 3:26–27 is of foundational importance because it signifies the fundamental element of baptism as relating to union with Christ. "In Christ Jesus you are all sons of God through faith. For as many of you as were baptized to Christ have put on Christ." Baptism here is said to mean "putting on" Christ as one puts on a garment, and in Christ we share sonship to God through faith. "Self-evidently," he comments, "one cannot be in Christ without sharing his sonship; which suggests that it is faith which receives Christ in baptism; accordingly it is the man exercis-

41. "Authority and Justification," 63, italics original.

42. Ibid., 63–64.

43. Ibid., 64.

ing faith who is the object of the divine work in baptism."[44] More simply, "in Paul's view the experience of baptism and that of faith are one."[45]

Therefore, "If faith is to be taken seriously, so is baptism" and he rejects the tendency of many exegetes to "either exalt baptism at the expense of faith or faith at the expense of baptism." This leads to the conclusion that

> Baptism is the baptism of faith and grace, so that in it faith receives what grace gives. Above all grace gives Christ, for Christ is the fullness of grace; faith therefore receives Christ in baptism. If Paul were pressed to define the relationship of the two statements in vv. 26–27, I cannot see how he could preserve the force of both sentences apart from affirming that baptism is the moment of faith in which the adoption is realized—in the dual sense of effected by God and grasped by man—which is the same as saying that in baptism faith receives Christ in whom the adoption is effected. The significance of baptism is the objective facts to which it witnesses, the historic event of redemption and the present gift that it makes possible, embraced through faith in that God who acted and yet acts. Through such an alliance of faith and baptism, Christianity is prevented from evaporating into an ethereal subjectivism on the one hand and from hardening into a fossilized objectivism on the other. The two aspects of Apostolic Christianity are preserved in *faith-baptism*.[46]

It is this final phrase that gives us the title of this lecture and it is worth emphasizing. The crucial 3:27 is especially important, he writes, "as illustrating that the essential significance of faith-baptism is its setting the believer in Christ and that in Christ full salvation is his."[47]

While Romans 6:1–11 "contains the profoundest treatment of baptism in the New Testament"[48] the nature of the relationship between faith and baptism is not Paul's primary concern, which is, rather, the ethical aspect of baptism and how this enables him to counter the antinomian claim, "Let us carry on in sin that grace may abound" (Rom 6:1).[49] Beasley-Murray agrees with those scholars who believe that faith

44. Ibid.

45. "Faith in the New Testament," 141.

46. *Baptism*, 151, italics added.

47. *Today and Tomorrow*, 46–47.

48. "Baptism in the Epistles of Paul," 130.

49. *Baptism*, 143. Cf. "Baptism in the New Testament," 26; "Faith in the New

in God has to be presumed as the background of the whole passage from v. 2 onwards, and, in view of Paul's teaching elsewhere, in Romans and throughout his letters, this cannot be denied. In short, "This chapter has the convert in mind, and all that Paul says of baptism presumes a faith responsive to the grace of God operative in it."[50] Accordingly, "In [Paul's] theology of baptism the divine action and human responsiveness are inseparable and enable baptism to be what it is."[51]

But this said, it is clear in this passage that the divine dimension of baptism predominates and it is recognition of this which shows that baptism is a sacrament: "God is the Actor in baptism," and this is evident in the observation that the characteristic verb tense is the passive: "we *were* baptized," "we *have become planted* with the likeness of Christ's death," "we *were crucified* with Christ," "we *were* and *shall be raised* with him," and these "are acts of God which we can simulate but never produce, as is especially plain when we think in terms of resurrection from the dead." He admits that Baptists have been hesitant to recognize this divine dimension, but what they do recognize, which is often overlooked by other traditions (such as Lutherans and Anglicans), is that "it is *the believer* who is so wonderfully the recipient of the mercy and grace of God!"[52] While Paul's teaching of baptism here stresses our dying and rising with Christ, and the emphasis is "wholly on the divine action," it necessarily implies "the responsiveness of man . . . as indivisibly one with it."[53] There is no place in Beasley-Murray's understanding of baptism for a separation of Spirit- and water-baptism:[54] "A man is not baptized twice, once that God may deal with him and again that he may offer his own response to the divine act; it is one baptism wherein God's *act* is *owned*

Testament," 141; and "Authority and Justification," 64.

50. "Baptism in the Epistles of Paul," 134.

51. *Baptism*, 145.

52. "Baptism in the New Testament," 25, italics original.

53. Ibid., 27.

54. See *Baptism*, 167–71. Cf. *Today and Tomorrow*, 69–70, "As a visible act with a spiritual significance, it is extraordinarily well adapted to serve as the means of entrance into a visible company of the Lord's people and the Body which transcends any one place and time. In the will of God the outward act of baptism, witnessing the entry of a believer into a church of his people, should coincide with the baptism of the Spirit, incorporating him into the Body of Christ." On the central role of the Spirit in baptism, see also *Today and Tomorrow*, 52–60; "Baptism Controversy," 8; and his "Holy Spirit, Baptism, and the Body of Christ," 177–85. For a survey of this question, see Cross, "Spirit- and Water-Baptism," 120–48.

by the believer—a unitary event, wherein glory is given to God by fulfilling the purpose of his grace in the very act of its reception."[55]

What is highlighted by this passage is the problem "of relating the objective work of redemption to the personal appropriation of it," and a great disservice is done to theology if either the former is over-emphasized or the latter is disproportionately magnified. It is necessary, then, to recognize the tension in Paul's thought concerning Christ's redemptive acts and the believer's response to them in baptism. "On the one hand a work of reconciliation has been wrought independently of the will or power of the believer," nevertheless he or she is included potentially in its scope. "It is the work of grace which gives baptism any significance. The believer gratefully recognizes the mercy of God" and is baptized into that death and life. But in all this it needs to be recognized that "The grace of God operative in redemption becomes effective only as it is seized by the judgment of faith."[56] So, while Romans 6:1–11 clearly focuses on the divine action in baptism, this does not diminish the importance of baptism, for "the Christian faith—and therefore baptism—is securely based on the 'Christ-event,' with all that implies; and nothing of man's doing and no theological explanation must ever be allowed to detract from its uniqueness and splendour."[57]

What is set out in Galatians 3:26–27 is even plainer in Colossians 2:12, which Beasley-Murray sees as "an authentic commentary on Romans 6:3–4."[58] We have already noted the objective and subjective dimensions of baptism implicit in Romans 6, but here these are made explicit. This fusion of the objective and subjective elements in baptism is emphasized by the phrase "*in which* you were raised *through faith in the operation of God* who raised him from the dead."[59] Beasley-Murray agrees with the RSV's rendering of v. 12 that the antecedent of "in which" is "baptism" and not "Christ," thus giving the reading, "Buried with Him in baptism, in which you were also raised with Him through faith in the working of God."[60] This also brings the saying close to Galatians 3:26–27,

55. "Baptism in the New Testament," 27, italics original. See also *Baptism*, 145.

56. "Baptism in the Epistles of Paul," 136–37.

57. "Baptism in the New Testament," 25.

58. E.g., *Baptism*, 155; "Authority and Justification," 64.

59. "Baptism in the Epistles of Paul," 140, italics original.

60. *Baptism*, 153–54; "Second Chapter of Colossians," 476; "Baptism in the New Testament," 28.

> for as there, so here, faith is integrated into the baptismal event. *In baptism* the baptized is raised *through faith*. The divine and human aspects of the experience of salvation are accorded full recognition. Not that faith effects its own resurrection; faith rejoices in the grace revealed in Christ and directs itself wholly to the God whose almighty power raised Christ from the dead and raises helpless sinners.[61]

Paul's train of thought is simple: "You were buried with [Christ] in baptism and you were raised with [Christ] in baptism," but it is important to note the significant addition "raised with him in baptism *through faith in the working of God*." The language here "presupposes faith as operative in baptism" in fact, "from the human side, faith is viewed as the operative power of baptism."[62] This interpretation of baptism is wholly in accord with Acts 2:38 where the turning to the Lord is expressed with and in baptism. Beasley-Murray states,

> In such a setting baptism is less a testimony to a faith previously received than a declaration of a faith here and now embraced, an embodiment of conversion to Christ, and a submission to him who is able to save. In such a milieu it is not surprising that the spiritual realities of conversion and baptism are merged together, for in that context they do fall together. Hence Paul puts the meaning of Easter into baptism: by faith the believer is one with the risen Lord, in whom the presence of the new creation burst into this one, and by faith he claims for himself the resurrection life of the new world here and now.[63]

The saying in v. 12, then, means that "baptism is the context in which God makes effective the redemptive action of Christ in the life of the penitent one exercising faith in him."[64] This also makes clear the "vital part in baptism played by faith": "so important a function is ascribed to faith [in Col 2:12], it is difficult to see how the experience described

61. *Baptism*, 154, italics original.

62. "Baptism in the New Testament," 28, italics original.

63. "Second Chapter of Colossians," 476. Cf. *Worship and the Sacraments*, 6. In *Today and Tomorrow*, 48–49, he writes, "Faith is directed to the God who raised Christ from death and so enters into the power of the resurrection. Clearly baptism so interpreted is really conversion-baptism: the believer comes to God through the Christ of the cross and resurrection, and in the momentous beginning of communion in Christ he learns that to be reconciled through the blood of the cross is to be conformed to it and to rise with the Lord (Phil. iii.10)."

64. "Authority and Justification," 65. Cf. "Faith in the New Testament," 141.

can be held to be present without the exercise of faith on the part of the baptized."

A similar understanding of baptism is to be found in 1 Peter 3:21: "Baptism . . . now saves you, not as a removal of dirt from the body, but as an appeal to God for a clear conscience, through the resurrection of Jesus Christ." Here the essential feature of baptism is not the washing of the body but the spiritual transaction in which the baptized makes appeal to God in faith and prayer and experiences the power of the risen Lord to save.[65] Beasley-Murray's conclusion to his study of this verse is worth quoting in full as the climax of his exegetical study.

> The chief lesson of this passage is its emphatic denial that the external elements of baptism constitute either its essence or its power. The cleansing in baptism is gained not through the application of water to the flesh but through the pledge of faith and obedience therein given to God, upon which the resurrection of Jesus Christ becomes a saving power to the individual concerned. Observe carefully: it is not said that the giving to God of an answer saves; the Risen Lord does that, "baptism saves . . . through the resurrection of Jesus Christ." But the response is at the heart of the baptism wherein the Lord makes the resurrection effective. Surely we are not interpreting amiss in believing that once more we have the representation of baptism as the supreme occasion when God, through the Mediator Christ, deals with a man who comes to Him through Christ on the basis of his redemptive acts. It is a meeting of God and man in the Christ of the cross and resurrection; it is faith assenting to God's grace and receiving that grace embodied in Christ. This is more important than Noah and the Flood and the disobedient spirits, but all together combine to magnify the greatness of the grace revealed in the suffering and exalted Lord who meets us in the Christian *baptisma*.[66]

The combined weight of this exegetical study leads Beasley-Murray to conclude that "The inextricable link between Baptism and faith is observable not only in baptismal statements but in a comparison of these with the apostolic teaching about faith." In short, "the New Testament writers associate the full range of salvation on the one hand with baptism and on the other hand with faith."[67] So, if any doubt remains that

65. "Authority and Justification," 65.

66. *Baptism*, 262.

67. "Authority and Justification" 65.

New Testament baptism is rightly understood as faith-baptism then this diagrammatic presentation will dispel it.

The Gifts Promised to Faith and Baptism

Gift of God	Faith	Baptism
Forgiveness	Rom 4:5–8; 1 John 1:9	Acts 2:38; 22:16
Justification	Rom 3–5 (e.g. 3:28); Gal 2–3, e.g. 3:11	1 Cor 6:11
Union with Christ	Eph 3:17	Gal 3:27; Rom 6:3, 5, 8
Being crucified with Christ	Gal 2:19–20	Rom 6:2–11 (esp. 3–4, 6)
Death and Resurrection	Gal 2:19–20	Rom 6:2–11 (esp. 3–4, 5–6 and 8; Col 2:12)
Sonship	John 1:12	Gal 3:26–27
Holy Spirit	Gal 3:2–5, 13–14	Acts 238; 1 Cor 12:13
Entry into the church	Acts 5:14; Gal 3:6–7	Gal 3:27; 1 Cor 12:13
Regeneration and life	John 3:14–16; 20:31	Tit 3:5; John 3:5
The kingdom and eternal life	Mark 10:15; John 3:14–16	1 Cor 6:9–11, Acts 22:16
Salvation	Rom 1:16; John 3:16	1 Pet 3:21

Here we see that according to the New Testament the gifts of grace given to faith are virtually identical with those given in baptism.[68] When the New Testament's baptismal passages are closely examined "an extraordinary duality appears in the means whereby God imparts his saving grace."[69] What we find is that the full range of salvation is promised to faith, but also that it is associated with baptism. Forgiveness is promised to faith in Romans 4:5–8 and 1 John 1:9, but to baptism in Acts 2:38 and 22:16. In Romans 3–5 and Galatians 2–3 justification is by faith alone, e.g., Romans 3:28, but in 1 Corinthians 6:11 it is assigned to baptism. In Ephesians 3:17 union with Christ is through faith, while in Galatians 3:27 it is rooted in baptism. In Galatians 2:19–20 being crucified with Christ is by faith alone, but in Romans 6:2–11 it occurs in

68. This table is based on *Today and Tomorrow*, 27–37; "Baptism in the New Testament," 28; "Authority and Justification," 65–66.

69. "Baptism in the New Testament," 28.

baptism. Sharing in Christ's death and resurrection is by faith in Romans 8:12–13, but in Romans 6:2–11 and Colossians 2:12 it is in baptism. In John 1:12 sonship is promised to faith, but in Galatians 3:26–27 it is related to faith and baptism. In Galatians 3:2–5 and 14 the Spirit is given to faith, but in Acts 2:38 and 1 Corinthians 12:13 to baptism. Entry into the Church, is by faith in Acts 5:14 and Galatians 3:6–7, but in baptism according to Galatians 3:27 and 1 Corinthians 12:13. Regeneration and life are granted to faith in John 3:14–16 and 20:31, but to baptism in Titus 3:5 and John 3:5. The kingdom and eternal life are promised to faith in Mark 10:15 and John 3:14–16, yet in 1 Corinthians 6:9–11 it is given to those who have abandoned the sins that exclude from it, for they have been washed clean in baptism, something also seen in Acts 22:16. Finally, salvation is given to faith in Romans 1:16 and John 3:16, but to baptism in 1 Peter 3:21.

It is clear, therefore, that God's gift to baptism and faith is one, namely, salvation in Christ.

> There is no question of his giving one part in baptism and another to faith, whether in that order or in the reverse. He gives *all* in baptism and *all* to faith . . . God's gracious giving to faith belongs to the context of baptism, even as God's gracious giving in baptism is to faith. Faith has no merit to claim such gifts and baptism has no power to produce them. It is all of God, who brings a man to faith and to baptism and has been pleased so to order his giving.

This New Testament theology of baptism is based on the axiom that baptism is administered to converts. "It is regarded as equally axiomatic that conversion and baptism are inseparable, if not indistinguishable" because "In the primitive apostolic Church baptism was 'conversion-baptism.'"[70] This can all be summarized as follows: "If God gives his gracious gifts to faith *and* baptism, he gives them in association, *i.e.* he gives them to faith *in* baptism, or (which amounts to the same thing) to baptism *in faith*."[71] In the New Testament baptism was never conceived

70. *Today and Tomorrow*, 37, italics original. Cf. 93, 135. See also, e.g., "Holy Spirit, Baptism, and the Body of Christ," 180–81, 185; "Second Chapter of Colossians," 476. In this he anticipates what has become termed "conversion-initiation" by Dunn, *Baptism and the Holy Spirit*, 4–7. For the widespread acceptance of this term for becoming a Christian, see Cross, "'One Baptism' (Ephesians 4:5)," 173–77.

71. "Baptism in the New Testament," 28, italics original. Also, *Today and Tomorrow*, 127, "the New Testament utterances about baptism take it as axiomatic that faith is not

of apart from the faith that turns to God for salvation and any interpretation of baptism that diminishes "the crucial significance of faith is unfaithful to the apostolic gospel."[72]

The concerns of anti-sacramentalists *should* be assuaged when Beasley-Murray writes,

> the really important element in baptism is not the rite but that to which it points—the work of the Spirit in the man who recognizes the claim of the Lord on him by virtue of His accomplished redemption and exaltation. Again and again we have had cause to remind ourselves that Christian baptism is baptism in the name of the Lord Jesus; in it the name of the Lord is called over the baptized, declaring him to be the Lord's, and the name is confessed and invoked by the baptized. It is this confessed relationship with the crucified, Risen Redeemer that is constitutive for Christian baptism and is decisive for its significance.[73]

Elsewhere he puts it this way: "This dual association of the cardinal features of the reconciled life, rooted on the one hand in faith and on the other hand in baptism, appears to proceed from the same consciousness that speaks of faith and baptism in the same breath, as Acts 2:38 and Colossians 2:12."[74] It would seem that baptism and faith turning to the Lord are the exterior and the interior of one reality. Baptists, therefore, "do no service to theology or the Church by playing down the significance of faith in association with baptism, on the ground that faith is in any case the gift of God, and that baptism is primarily the act of God rather than the act of man." He states this plainly, "By grace we are saved—through faith. However much of God is in that faith, [Paul] evidently attaches importance to the human element in it,"[75] and, by implication, Baptists should too.

Baptismal Reform

So how does Beasley-Murray suggest Baptists reform their theology and practice of baptism according to the word of God?

---

merely an accompaniment of baptism but an inherent element of it."

72. "Baptism in the New Testament," 29.

73. *Baptism*, 120.

74. The original mistakenly references this as Col 2:13, "Authority and Justification," 66.

75. Ibid.

First, "there ought to be a greater endeavour to make baptism integral to *the Gospel*." This is seen in Acts 2:38's "Repent and *be baptized*!" Faith was presumed in repentance, but Peter's answer told the crowd how to become Christians: "faith and repentance are to be expressed in baptism, and *so* they are to come to the Lord. Baptism is here a part of the proclamation of Christ . . . An effort ought to be made to restore this note in our preaching."[76] Baptism is also the proper subject for exposition in enquirer's classes. In short, we need to "recover the apostolic concept of conversion-baptism."[77]

Secondly, and following on from the first point, "there should be a serious endeavor to make baptism integral to *conversion*. The preaching of the Gospel is directed to the conversion of men and women" and this involves "not simply the acceptance of an idea but a reception and submission in action. Baptism and conversion are thus inseparables; the one demands the other, for neither is complete without the other."[78]

Many will object that baptism needs to be postponed so that a candidate's fitness for baptism can be ascertained. But we must recall Beasley-Murray's comments that when we do so we in fact alter New Testament baptism. He does not diminish the importance of instruction, which he sees as "always necessary," but notes that it "need not wholly precede baptism" for "much of it can more fittingly come after baptism," adding, "and in any case the instruction ought *never* to cease at baptism." If what he has already said were carried out,

> and the nature and significance of baptism were given their rightful place in the proclamation of the Gospel, hearers would understand what baptism is and that the response of faith should find its fitting embodiment in the sacrament. Above all, whether the time between baptism and conversion be little or much, baptism should be regarded as the ultimate and unreserved ratification of the individual's turning to God and of God's gracious turning to the individual, with all that means of dedication on the one hand and of grace on the other.[79]

76. *Baptism*, 393, italics original.

77. "Holy Spirit, Baptism, and the Body of Christ," 185. Cf. also *Worship and the Sacraments*, 7.

78. *Baptism*, 393–94, italics original.

79. Ibid., 394, italics original.

Thirdly, following on from his belief that the "deeply significant elements in the meaning of baptism should find expression in the baptismal service" and baptismal preparation, the believer should see their baptism as the instrument of their surrender to the Lord and the assurance of their acceptance by God in Christ. "The baptism should therefore be an act of believing prayer," as Jesus prayed at his baptism. This "is naturally bound up with the element of confession in baptism—confession to the Lord and to the congregation." As a minimum, this could be done by means of the opportunity of question and answer, but, where possible, by a brief testimony before the congregation.[80]

Finally, he believes that we should strive to make baptism integral to church membership, observing that "our baptismal practice has tended to obscure the fact that New Testament baptism is at once to Christ and the Body." This is most easily done by means of a service of baptism, concluded with the Lord's Supper, in which the newly baptized is welcomed into the church and partakes of their first communion. To this he adds the desirability of including the laying on of hands as an integral part of the service, underscoring "the aspect of baptismal symbolism as initiation into Christ and the Church by the Spirit."[81]

This said, Beasley-Murray was aware of the present confusion over baptism which has resulted in there being two forms of the rite—believers' and infant baptism.[82] To this end he favors open membership "solely for *members of other Churches* transferring into a Baptist Church,"[83] but "young people confessing their faith and converts from

80. *Worship and the Sacraments*, 7.

81. *Baptism*, 394–95. Cf. also *Worship and the Sacraments*, 7.

82. *Today and Tomorrow*, 158.

83. Ibid., italics original. Cf. 86, "While convinced that the baptism of believers only is scriptural, Baptists know full well that most Christians have not received baptism in this manner; in open membership churches, therefore, a welcome is given to Christians from other denominations, without insisting on their receiving baptism as believers." Elsewhere (*Baptism*, 392), he maintained that Baptists could make "a significant step towards the establishing of closer relations with other Churches," for "in respect for the conscience of our fellow-Christians and the like charity, which we trust will be exercised towards us, could we not refrain from requesting the baptism of those baptized in infancy who wish to join our churches and administer baptism to such only where there is a strong plea for it from the applicant? This would leave room for freedom of conscience for those who believe they should be baptized, despite their having received infant baptism, but it would involve a change of policy with respect to the majority who come to us from other Denominations."

without should never question the need for baptism; they should refrain from both Church membership and participating in the communion service until they have submitted to baptism."[84]

Conclusion

As we have already had cause to note, Baptists have been quick to draw attention to the weakness of purported biblical precedents for infant baptism, but there is the flip side of this which Baptists must not shirk. "The Baptist demand that other denominations face the teaching of the New Testament dispassionately, with a willingness not to be chained to the traditions of earlier generations, and for reform according to the Word of God naturally entails as a corollary a readiness that they take the same medicine and face the teaching of the Scriptures, with a willingness to reform their own ways in accordance with that same Word of God."[85]

This, I believe, we have singularly failed to do. We have not tested our baptismal beliefs and practices against the bar of scripture and neither have we taken much notice of many of our leading scholars who have spent so much of their academic calling studying God's Word, listening to God's people—of whatever tradition—and providing us with rich fare of which with have barely partaken.[86] If this lecture in honor of one of our greatest biblical scholars goes someway to whet our appetite to return again to God's Word then we will be greatly helped to a deeper appreciation of the fullness of the gospel to which we are called to be witnesses. We are all familiar with the fact that we live in a post-Christian culture and as we continue to proclaim the good news of salvation through the life, death and resurrection of the Lord Jesus Christ we must not ignore the fact that the call is still that proclaimed by Peter on the Day of Pentecost, "Repent, and be baptized every one of you in the name of Jesus Christ so that your sins may be forgiven; and you will receive the gift of the Holy Spirit" (Acts 2:38).

The importance of all this for today's Church, I believe, comes out strongly in one of Beasley-Murray's concluding remarks in *Baptism*

84. *Today and Tomorrow*, 88.

85. Ibid., 15–16. See also *Baptism*, 393–95.

86. These are summarized and discussed in Cross, "Evangelical Sacrament," 195–217, and *Should We Take Peter at His Word (Acts 2.38)?*

Today and Tomorrow: “The world is ignorant of the Gospel. The Church therefore is universally on mission, or ought to be. Its proclamation of the Gospel will be far more effective if its baptismal practice is reformed according to the New Testament pattern. In that setting baptism is the conclusion of Gospel proclamation. Any move to rehabilitate that relationship is to be welcomed.”[87]

Bibliography

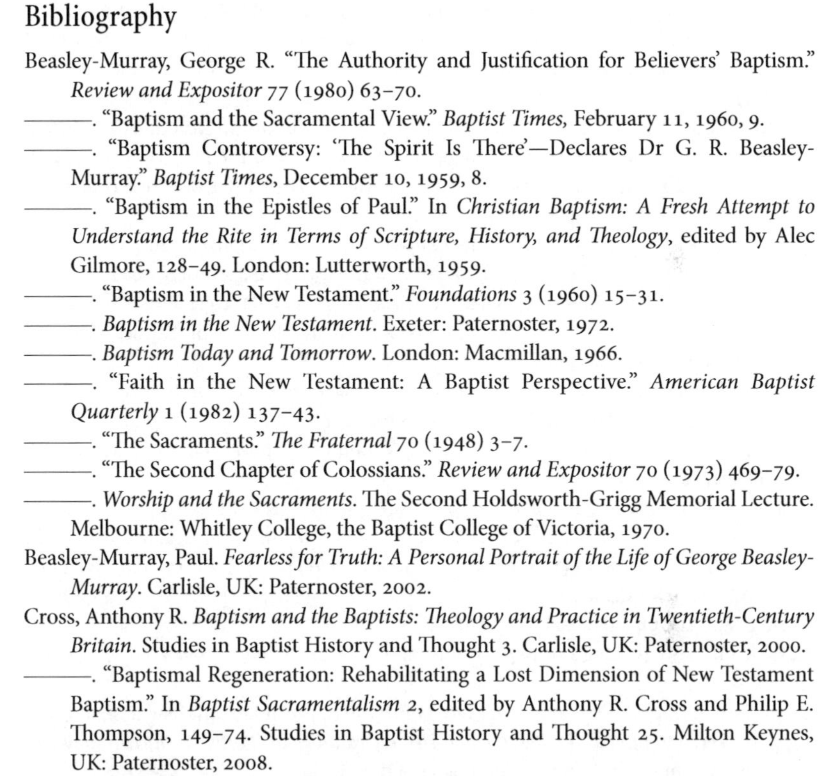

Beasley-Murray, George R. “The Authority and Justification for Believers’ Baptism.” *Review and Expositor* 77 (1980) 63–70.

———. “Baptism and the Sacramental View.” *Baptist Times*, February 11, 1960, 9.

———. “Baptism Controversy: ‘The Spirit Is There’—Declares Dr G. R. Beasley-Murray.” *Baptist Times*, December 10, 1959, 8.

———. “Baptism in the Epistles of Paul.” In *Christian Baptism: A Fresh Attempt to Understand the Rite in Terms of Scripture, History, and Theology*, edited by Alec Gilmore, 128–49. London: Lutterworth, 1959.

———. “Baptism in the New Testament.” *Foundations* 3 (1960) 15–31.

———. *Baptism in the New Testament*. Exeter: Paternoster, 1972.

———. *Baptism Today and Tomorrow*. London: Macmillan, 1966.

———. “Faith in the New Testament: A Baptist Perspective.” *American Baptist Quarterly* 1 (1982) 137–43.

———. “The Sacraments.” *The Fraternal* 70 (1948) 3–7.

———. “The Second Chapter of Colossians.” *Review and Expositor* 70 (1973) 469–79.

———. *Worship and the Sacraments*. The Second Holdsworth-Grigg Memorial Lecture. Melbourne: Whitley College, the Baptist College of Victoria, 1970.

Beasley-Murray, Paul. *Fearless for Truth: A Personal Portrait of the Life of George Beasley-Murray*. Carlisle, UK: Paternoster, 2002.

Cross, Anthony R. *Baptism and the Baptists: Theology and Practice in Twentieth-Century Britain*. Studies in Baptist History and Thought 3. Carlisle, UK: Paternoster, 2000.

———. “Baptismal Regeneration: Rehabilitating a Lost Dimension of New Testament Baptism.” In *Baptist Sacramentalism 2*, edited by Anthony R. Cross and Philip E. Thompson, 149–74. Studies in Baptist History and Thought 25. Milton Keynes, UK: Paternoster, 2008.

———. “The Evangelical Sacrament: *Baptisma semper reformandum*.” *Evangelical Quarterly* 80 (2008) 195–217.

———. “‘One Baptism’ (Ephesians 4:5): A Challenge to the Church.” In *Baptism, the New Testament and the Church: Historical and Contemporary Studies in Honour of R. E. O. White*, edited by Stanley E. Porter and Anthony R. Cross, 173–209. Sheffield, UK: Sheffield Academic, 1999.

———. “The Pneumatological Key to H. Wheeler Robinson’s Baptismal Sacramentalism.” In *Baptist Sacramentalism*, edited by Anthony R. Cross and Philip E. Thompson, 151–176. Studies in Baptist History and Thought 5. Carlisle, UK: Paternoster, 2003.

87. *Today and Tomorrow*, 171. This view, including more detailed proposals for reforming baptismal theology and practice, and strongly indebted to Beasley-Murray’s work, are presented in Cross, *Recovering the Evangelical Sacrament*.

———. *Recovering the Evangelical Sacrament: Baptisma Semper Reformandum*. Eugene, OR: Pickwick, 2013.

———. *Should We Take Peter at His Word (Acts 2:38)? Recovering a Baptist Baptismal Sacramentalism*. Centre for Baptist History and Heritage Studies, Occasional Papers 1. Oxford: Regent's Park College, 2010.

———. "Spirit- and Water-Baptism in 1 Corinthians 12.13." In *Dimensions of Baptism: Biblical and Theological Studies*, edited by Stanley E. Porter and Anthony R. Cross, 120–48. Sheffield, UK: Sheffield Academic, 2002.

Culpepper, R. Alan. "George R. Beasley-Murray." In *Baptist Theologians*, edited by Timothy George and David S. Dockery, 567–87. Nashville: Broadman, 1990.

Dunn, James D. G. *Baptism and the Holy Spirit: A Re-Examination of the New Testament Teaching on the Gift of the Spirit in Relation to Pentecostalism Today*. London: SCM, 1970.

Fowler, Stanley K. "Is 'Baptist Sacramentalism' an Oxymoron? Reactions in Britain to *Christian Baptism* (1959)." In *Baptist Sacramentalism*, edited by Anthony R. Cross and Philip E. Thompson, 129–50. Studies in Baptist History and Thought 5. Carlisle, UK: Paternoster, 2003.

———. *More Than a Symbol: The British Baptist Recovery of Baptismal Sacramentalism*. Studies in Baptist History and Thought 2. Carlisle, UK: Paternoster, 2002.

Gloer, W. Hulitt, ed. "Editor's Preface." In *Eschatology and the New Testament: Essays in Honor of George Raymond Beasley-Murray*, edited by W. Hulitt Gloer. Peabody, MA: Hendrickson, 1988.

———. *Eschatology and the New Testament: Essays in Honor of George Raymond Beasley-Murray*. Peabody, MA: Hendrickson, 1988.

Jones, Brandon C. *Waters of Promise: Finding Meaning in Believer Baptism*. Eugene, OR: Pickwick, 2012.

Kelly, J. N. D. *Early Christian Doctrines*. 5th ed. London: A & C Black, 1977.

Porter, Stanley E., and Anthony R. Cross, eds. *Baptism, the New Testament and the Church: Historical and Contemporary Studies in Honour of R. E. O. White*. Sheffield, UK: Sheffield Academic, 1999.

Read, L. A. "The Ordinances." *The Fraternal* 67 (1948) 8–10.

Ross, J. M. "The Theology of Baptism in Baptist History." *Baptist Quarterly* 15 (1953) 100–112.

Thompson, Philip E. "Dispelling the Myth of English Baptist Baptismal Sacramentalism." In *Recycling the Past or Researching History? Studies in Baptist Historiography and Myths*, edited by Philip E. Thompson and Anthony R. Cross, 128–62. Studies in Baptist History and Thought 11. Milton Keynes, UK: Paternoster, 2005.

———. "A New Question in Baptist History: Seeking a Catholic Spirit among Early Baptists." *Pro Ecclesia* 8 (1999) 51–72.

———. "Practicing the Freedom of God: Formation in Early Baptist Life." In *Theology and Lived Christianity*, edited by David M. Hammond, 119–38. The Annual Publication of the College Theology Society 45. Mystic, CT: Twenty-Third Publications, 2000.

Wright, David F., *What Has Infant Baptism Done to Baptism? An Enquiry at the End of Christendom*. Didsbury Lectures 2003. Milton Keynes, UK: Paternoster, 2005.

3

Preaching the Gospel and Liszt[1]

Michael J. Quicke

I feel truly humbled to be invited back to give this lecture named in honor of George Beasley-Murray, an illustrious predecessor as Principal of Spurgeon's College. In the USA he continues to be remembered with respect and affection. Lunching with a group of academics last week I mentioned that I was coming here and was encouraged by the pool of positive memories that was immediately stirred.

When Paul sent me a copy of his father's biography, *Fearless for Truth*, I devoured it. Some details I knew but much I did not of this good and gifted man. My first visit to Spurgeon's was in early 1965. I went to stay with Paul traveling on my unreliable Honda C90 motorcycle. Later it was to let us down memorably as I was taking Paul to preach somewhere in Suffolk. The bike could hardly carry one person, let alone two people plus sermon notes. On this earlier occasion it broke down strategically on Tower Bridge. Eventually when I arrived, having pushed the machine for miles, Paul greeted me and took me up to the first floor flat, introducing me to his mother. Considerably later that evening his father returned home. I remember thinking it was going to be somewhat intimidating. It *was*, but he was warm and very gracious. And I recall vividly how he went over to his record collection, took out an LP and placed it on the

1. This lecture was delivered at the Baptist Assembly in Cardiff on 1 May 2004. Two short musical excerpts were played during the lecture: The opening bars of Liszt's Piano Concerto No. 1 during the third paragraph, and the beginning of the *Credo* from Beethoven's *Missa Solemnis* during the last paragraph.

record player. Throwing off his shoes he extended himself on the sofa and then music filled the room.

The opening bars of Liszt's Piano Concerto No. 1 thrill the soul. Its passionate unison opening theme, with startling octave leaps, is one of the most dramatic of all openings to a concerto. First, fire and then comes calm. Liszt was a brilliant performer, a large-scale character. His contribution to nineteenth-century music was immense, anticipating what was to come. He began writing his concerto in 1830 and kept rewriting it. In what turned out to be one of the concerts of the century Berlioz conducted it with Liszt at the piano in 1855. I do not think I realized how well George Beasley-Murray could play the piano himself. I was certainly aware of the importance of music to him and the sacrifice involved for him as he turned his back on the piano for the ministry. His biography mentions how compared with Liszt, New Testament Greek "bored him to tears." In forsaking his musical career, he said, "I had an awful fear that I had made a terrible mistake and that I ought to turn back while there was time. Yet in my heart I knew that I could not go back! I was beginning to learn that he who desires to preach the cross must feel its weight."[2]

That memory has forever colored my memory of George Beasley-Murray with its excitement, passion and power to move me. It is not incidental to what I share.

This lecture needs to focus on some aspect of the rich Beasley-Murray heritage. With my interest in preaching it is almost inevitable that I should offer some reflections as a preacher, though this will be on his writing rather than his practice. I only heard him preach a few times but I can still recall some of them–especially a sermon on being ambassadors for Christ. There is a brief debate between Paul and his brother Stephen in *Fearless for Truth* about whether their father was a preacher or a teacher.[3] I contend that four kinds of biblical preacher are legitimate, each with its own dynamics: teacher preacher, herald preacher, pastor or inductive preacher and narrative preacher.[4] Undeniably George was a preacher teacher of the first rank with elements of herald preacher thrown in. (As we shall see, I believe he opened the door for other kinds of preaching too.) His content came out of personal wrestling with the

2. Paul Beasley-Murray, *Fearless for Truth*.

3. Ibid., 62.

4. Quicke, *360 Degree Preaching*, 97–108.

biblical text that involved integrity of intellect and emotion and always with evangelistic fire. He was much less interested in techniques of preaching than in content. As a rigorous textual scholar alert to gospel needs his preaching stirred heads by making us think. His son Stephen comments, "Most of us are not used to hearing such a mind think out loud. Our expectations are low and geared not to the skills of a biblical expert but to showman skills."[5] Sadly there is too much truth in that observation.

I want to focus on his book *Preaching the Gospel from the Gospels.* It's a preacher's book, alive with the sound of preaching. (The number of exclamation marks reveals that alone!). It grew out of lectures given in 1954 to lay preachers in London and was published in 1956. It was a pleasure to take my copy and re-read it and be reminded of first impressions. However, in 1996 it was republished with inclusive language as a complete reworking and expansion. The later book contains most of the gems from the first book but has more than doubled in size. While there were no footnotes in the first book (intentionally), footnotes abound on nearly every page in the 1996 edition with evidence of his voracious reading and writing during the intervening forty years. He also includes an impressive additional bibliography at the conclusion. In preparing this lecture I based my reflections on the 1956 book where the structures of his thought are less overlaid by scholarly references, though I shall obviously refer to his later book.

It is delightful how we grasp something more of the man we honor in these lectures. It is often said that moments of vulnerability ensure authentic communication. Listen to his honest admission as a new Christian (actually omitted from the 1996 version): "I can recall my dismay when first, in an instruction class for candidates for baptism, I heard that the Church is the Body of Christ. "Why" I asked, "does the Christian faith have to be complicated by a doctrine like this? It was many years before I came to see in it the chiefest example of the mercy of God. It is the most precious fruit of the Resurrection."[6]

What a stellar leap from the frank dismay of a new convert to a confident mature theological scholarship that took complicated doctrines and helped us all to understand! Within this writing I believe that

5. Paul Beasley-Murray, *Fearless for Truth*, 62.

6. G. R. Beasley-Murray, *Preaching the Gospel*, 1956, 48.

there are several issues that remain critical for preachers today. I sound out four themes, some general and others perhaps surprising.

Engagement—The Honest Engagement of Biblical Scholarship with Preaching

Thomas Long's important book *Preaching and the Literary Forms of the Bible* reflects on the mutually significant relationship between preacher and biblical scholar.

> I am especially mindful of how deeply those who preach have always depended on the labors of biblical scholars. Serious preaching simply could not occur were it not for their work. I am bold enough to believe, though, that biblical scholarship gains both energy and focus through the urgings and promptings of preachers. . . . The best biblical scholarship is done by those who work while hearing the sound of the preacher concerned about next Sunday's sermon knocking on the study door.[7]

For George Beasley-Murray the two roles were joined at the hip. He writes as preacher; he preaches as scholar. He himself is going to preach next Sunday's sermon bursting out of the study door with accustomed energy. He dares to bring together the best of his contemporary scholarly engagement (and there is some daring as we shall see) to the task of preaching. Sometimes preachers dig so deeply into erudition that burrowing underground they forget their way back to the surface. More frequently, preachers seem only to stay on the surface, nodding to scholarship via remembered fragments of theological college education or devotional commentaries. The old saw observed that you can always tell when a pastor went to theological college by the date of the worthy tomes on the bookshelf and the thickness of the dust on them.

Because of George's depth of mind and academic calling he went far beyond what most of us find possible but he models what every preacher should aspire to. No lazy, popularizing shortcut "people pleasing" communication but solid, rigorous, exacting study for proclamation.

Now that my full-time focus is on training people to preach I often find my students lie at two extremes. One is the seminary student who cannot but help bring an "essay sermon" into the pulpit. For its diligence and footnotes the biblical departments might award an A but no listener

7. Long, *Preaching and the Literary Forms*, 198.

who stays awake could credit it with any more than an E or an F. Bible work is presented in indigestible slabs. ("You'll be *interested* to know that the Greek word here is also found here and here." "No, actually we won't be *interested*!") At the other extreme is the popularizer who knows how to make people smile and work a crowd and whose Bible work is almost missing. (What Greek?). One seems unaware that boredom is a possibility; the other has such fear of boredom so avoids any possibility of depth–the "slick" and the "slack" David Wells calls them. To maintain balance between such extremes is a lifelong discipline and George modeled just such a discipline.

Yet in his scholarship he showed daring and honest engagement with others. Too often evangelicals distrust scholarship unless it is accompanied by a full statement of faith that dots i's and crosses t's in an agreeable manner to the reader. The Old Testament scholar R. E. Clements, a fellow Spurgeon's graduate, observed that George Beasley-Murray combined "evangelical fervour with a love of scholarship" and displayed a "balance and integrity which established a real standard of intellectual honesty."[8] He demonstrated a willingness to go "out of the box." His was no pedestrian, predictable, safe recycling of others' ideas. I remember my surprise that a book for lay preachers had such giant theological ideas lurking on its pages. Without patronizing his readers or trivializing scholarship he brought his best reflections and laid them on the table.

Some names are to be expected. C. H. Dodd was an early seminal influence on George Beasley-Murray with especial impact in thinking through the nature of the gospel and the Kingdom of God. He accepted the fundamental division that Dodd provided between *didache* (instruction for converts by teaching) and *kerygma* (proclaiming the gospel by evangelism). Indeed the whole book concentrates on *kerygma* and especially its emphasis on Jesus attested by teaching and acts of power, crucified, dead, exalted and coming again. But he qualified Dodd's distinction and writes that "it must not be pressed too far."[9] Interestingly, in the light of the preacher/teacher debate he argues that "teaching may be a handmaid of the gospel." Many today would agree that the words *didache* and *kerygma* are far more interchangeable and fluid in practice than Dodd allowed and that they both need each other.

8. *Fearless for Truth*, 68.

9. *Preaching the Gospel*, 1956, 75.

Other significant names are there such as Adolf Schlatter and Newton Flew. George walked and talked with these giants and made his own contributions. However it is the emphasis he gave to the form critic Martin Dibelius that causes amazement. On the first page he explains how he sought to take from form critics a method of approach to the Gospels that enables us "to preach the gospel of the grace of God with more insight and effectiveness."[10] George Beasley-Murray pushed preachers beyond solely grammatical and historical methods of exegesis to consider literary interpretation. While source criticism considers the written sources underlying the biblical text, form criticism seeks to identify the literary forms of the material, "their structures, intentions and settings, in order to understand the oral or pre-literary stage of their development."[11] Between 1919 and 1921 Schmidt, Dibelius and Bultmann each published books applying form criticism to the New Testament. Dibelius listed five categories of Gospel pericopes apart from the passion narrative: Pronouncement story (paradigm), miracle stories (tales), legends, myths and exhortations. George utterly rejected naturalistic assumptions and in his 1956 book takes Bultmann to task for his reductionist stance on miracles. He does not subscribe to tales and legends. He knows as an evangelical scholar he belongs elsewhere. About himself he writes (with a twinkle in the eye), "It is doubtful that Dr. Dibelius would have owned this offspring as in any sense belonging to his family." Yet he dared to bring new thinking into our family as he developed form critical insights into preaching the Gospels in the life of Jesus, miracles, teaching and parables (the four sections of his book). As an evangelical scholar with full bloodied commitment to the authority of Scripture he demonstrates how, from an alien tradition, he can use insights to benefit understanding and preaching without compromise.

So, for example, he recognizes that the Sermon on the Mount has complex form containing "a fairly full outline of two sermons with recollections of anything up to a score of others." He argues that the ultimate form is congruent with the Lord's consciousness of fulfilling his unique understanding of the Messiah lived out harmoniously in private life and teaching. In a rich teaching passage he takes the Beatitudes (Matt 5:3–10)—"the blessed life in the here and now and in the age to come." Each stanza hits home—they begin and end with a promise of the Kingdom of

10. Ibid., 11.

11. Greidanus, *Modern Preacher and the Ancient Text*, 53.

Heaven. "His Kingdom is a Kingdom of Grace. We do not make enough of it!"[12]

Paul Beasley-Murray emphasizes how challenging it was in the 1950s to stress the gospel of Jesus when so many evangelicals focused on the Pauline gospel. In most evangelical churches Paul's letters were the preferred preaching texts. They were *kerygma*—the proclaiming of the gospel—of which the Gospel writers provided the model life and teaching—the *didache*. In a context where Pauline epistles ruled, *Preaching the Gospel from the Gospels* was a "highly significant book which came as an eye-opener for many."[13]

Transition—Awareness of Changing Times

Tides of New Testament scholarship through the twentieth century continue to make impact on preaching in the twenty-first. Form criticism was followed by redaction criticism. While source and form criticism could be said to atomize the Gospels and miss the wood for the trees, redaction criticism sought to be more holistic, viewing the Gospels as entities in which writers had worked over materials, interpreting them theologically. Motives of the different evangelists contrast—John's Gospel has different purposes to Mark's. Redaction criticism with its emphasis on the composition of the whole book and its concern for the theological "intention" of the author has considerable significance for a preacher seeking to discern a text's specific message.

True to form, George's 1996 book pays attention to redaction criticism, identifying its "settings in life" and examining its claims. He rejects radical redaction as perverting the study of the Gospels into recovering the evangelists' theology rather than that of Jesus but believes balanced redaction criticism helps us learn from the evangelists how to do in our day what they did in theirs. Redaction criticism seeded rhetorical criticism that focuses on the relation of form and content and the structural patterns of the received text—"the study of biblical literature as an art-form" with narrative shape. It has renewed much contemporary interest in how biblical authors used structural patterns to signal to readers how their text should be read. This too George acknowledges briefly.

12. *Preaching the Gospel*, 1956, 85.

13. *Fearless for Truth*, 2.

These tides of New Testament scholarship, too briefly described, are part of a complex tradition within culture. What George Beasley-Murray does as he encourages a literary approach focusing on the Gospels may be viewed within a spectrum of preaching possibilities. At the top are the four models of biblical preaching to which I have already alluded—teacher, herald, inductive, narrative. At its base a line represents the churning cultural shift as modernity has given way patchily to post-modernity. This shift is particularly acute for preaching in terms of communication changes as examined by Walter Ong and Pierre Babin.[14] Modernity was characterized by literacy—left-brain thinking that is conceptual, analytical, linear and explanatory. Such preaching uses ideas and is mainly deductive with language that tends to be formal and passive. Its common pattern comprises outlines with points and sub-points neatly ordered. Three heads and nine tails. Post-modernity, however, is marked by secondary orality that combines both left-brain thinking and right-brain thinking with communication that is symbolic, existential, image-orientated and holistic. Its language is self-consciously informal using narrative structures that take hearers on journeys of discovery. In terms of biblical genres the mainly deductive approach is inevitably associated with didactic texts of Scripture, especially the epistles. However the main inductive approach relates to narrative sections, especially preaching the Gospels and their parables.

We should note how this spectrum ties in with recent preaching history. Lucy Rose shows three main kinds of preaching in the twentieth century. Traditional preaching was dominant in the first half with its aim of transmitting ideas and "getting the message across." John Broadus[15] had great impact on most U.S. seminaries. Kerygmatic preaching was strong in the 1960s and 1970s which owed much to C. H. Dodd, Karl Barth and Rudolf Bultmann. Such preaching regarded sermons as events in which God speaks his saving word. Transformational preaching has occurred since the 1980s with an emphasis on preaching that is experienced by worshipers as event and encounter. Its architects are seen as H. Grady Davis *Design for Preaching* (1958) and Fred Craddock *As One without Authority* (1971).

14. Their two seminal works are Ong, *Literacy and Orality*, and Babin, *The New Era in Religious Communication*.

15. John A. Broadus, *On the Preparation and Delivery of Sermons*, was written in the nineteenth century and is regarded as a classic for Baptists in America.

We live in a time of turmoil where an amazing number of preaching possibilities now lie across the map. Such is the contrast between traditional and transformational preaching that many have argued that a "new homiletic" is now challenging the "old homiletic." The old is associated with literary outline form. Indeed it has had the same range of preaching for three hundred years: expository (based on a long Scripture passage), textual (a Scripture verse) and thematic (a topic or theme). However the new seems to offer a bewildering variety. Lowry identifies six models: Inductive sermon, story sermon, narrative sermon, transconscious black sermon, phenomenological sermon and conversational-episodal sermon.[16]

I remain convinced that it is profitless to pitch new against old as though one option has all the virtue. Some summarize their conflict as between exposition and story. Both old and new homiletic have been in grave danger of misusing story. In one it can be reduced to points in an outline and have its narrative power drained out. But in the other there can be such concentration on an art form that gospel can be missed. I argue at greater length in *360 Degree Preaching* that these belong together. Biblical preachers today need to recognize a spectrum of possibilities for biblical preaching and to place an "X" for each preaching event somewhere along this continuum.

George Beasley-Murray worked diligently in this time of transition. There is no evidence that he read Davis or Craddock but much in preaching literature resonates with his convictions. He wished to move the X along the spectrum. This leads to another issue.

Preaching Approach to Scripture

At its best biblical scholarship aids the *approach* to Scripture. Long comments, "The issue raised by preaching is not how to *use*, in a popular way, the gleanings of biblical study but the more central issue of how to approach the Bible in the first place."[17] Biblical scholarship can be used (abused?) to add sermon footnotes which may or may not help a congregation hear the gospel. George Beasley-Murray is not into esoteric details for preachers. His main thesis is that *the Gospel writers were preachers.* Preachers wrote the Gospels and that fact impacts preachers

16. Lowry, *The Sermon: Dancing on the Edge of Mystery.*

17. Long, *Preaching and the Literary Forms*, 7.

ever since. Of course this preaching is post-Resurrection. Everything is viewed through crucifixion and resurrection spectacles. "The event that controlled a true understanding of Him was that which made Him their contemporary, viz the Resurrection . . . Instead of beginning with the birth they began with the Gospel of redeeming love and looked back on the life that brought the new age."[18] Beasley-Murray sums up his argument in this way in the 1996 edition of his book:

> "It pleased God by the foolishness of preaching to save the people," said Paul. Our intention is to consider the further proposition that it pleased God by the foolishness of preaching to give the world the Gospels. (The term "preaching," *kerygma* in 1 Cor 1:18ff. means the message preached but also the act of preaching). The proclamation of the earliest preachers became the material out of which the Gospels were produced . . . the Gospels are the heritage bequeathed to humanity by the labors of preachers.[19]

This approach means that everything in the Gospels can be viewed as preaching. The whole story is preached out. From such oral records the Gospels emerge. Form critical insights abound as he restates how the acts and sayings of Jesus were recounted *as occasion demanded*.[20] Spontaneously in a hundred different settings the apostles tell it as it is, including themselves in the story warts and all. The oral records reveal their oral settings. Today's preachers should understand that approach taken by these first preachers. They should read the Gospels with "expert eyes . . . (they of all people) should best grasp their import, and entering into their spirit should be able to make their message live for others." Because the Gospels are preachers' words, today's preachers share empathy or as he puts it "a more than usual sympathy and understanding."[21] To hear and see the Gospels as preaching documents with voice recording and fingerprints of earliest preachers all over them was the noteworthy contribution in this book. What makes it extra significant is the way he then modeled this in his writing. *Preaching the Gospel* is peppered with expressions like: "Can you hear the voice of the preacher?" This leads us to a fourth observation.

18. *Preaching the Gospel*, 1956, 30.
19. *Preaching the Gospel*, 1996, 8–9.
20. *Preaching the Gospel*, 1956, 17.
21. Ibid., 26.

Imagination—The Role of Imagination in Hearing the Preacher's Voice

As scholar and preacher George Beasley-Murray could not tolerate *eisegesis*. He warns that grasping their import and entering the spirit of the Gospels "does not give the preacher licence to let imagination run riot among the Gospels and produce pictures of fantasy according to whim."[22] Determining the original meaning of a text and understanding its context is essential. However, because the Gospel descriptions were told by the earliest preachers, today's preachers "will try to understand their motives in retelling them; the more they enter into the mind of those men of God, the better they will be able to pass on the stories they first proclaimed . . . the evangelists stamped their viewpoint on the narratives, it was their interests which caused them to select what they heard."[23]

In places he models this "grasping their import and entering into their spirit." In his study of Mark 1 he gives a first person sermon. He moves the X across the spectrum. It is now much more acceptable in evangelical circles where seminary syllabi include first person narrative sermons. You can hear his voice as he steps into Peter's sandals:

> Let me tell you about my wife's mother. On that very afternoon, when we reached home, we found her stricken with fever. My wife was apprehensive. The old lady could not stand many more of these attacks! But the Lord was with us. He had demonstrated what He could do for a person in the grip of an evil power. Why should he not do the like for her in her physical weakness? I hurried out of her room to Him. "Teacher," I said, "she is ill, but God is with you. You can help her, can't you?" He went to her bedside and looked at her. What followed was incredible but for seeing. He simply took my mother-in-law's hand and sat her up. "God is good to you," he said. "You're well now." And so she was. All trace of the fever had gone. "Thank you, Rabbi," she replied. "Yes I am well. God is good. And you are very kind." Then she added, "But I don't see the sense of sitting here. I feel as fit as a fiddle!" She got up, dressed herself and prepared a meal for the whole company of us! That's the Jesus I preach to you! He sets a man or

22. Ibid.

23. Ibid., 27.

> a woman free from the shackles of sin and makes them of use to God and man![24]

Stepping back he asks, "Is this an unwarranted use of imagination? Surely not! We were intended to read the Gospels in this way and to make explicit the motives that prompted their publication."[25] Several times he calls us to listen to the Gospel preachers. Commenting on the hemorrhaging woman in Mark 5:34 he writes, "Cannot we hear the preacher's voice in this narrative—her healing illustrates the power of the crucified Lord to set people free?"[26]

Imagination continues to be a key theme of contemporary homiletics. It is particularly associated with Thomas Troeger. "What are the principles for using our imaginations so that we can receive the *ruach*, the Spirit of the living God to whom our preaching is a witness? The primary principle from which all others are derived is *that we are attentive to what is*."[27] Barbara Brown Taylor writes of "honoring the faithful imagination. Imagination is no pedant presenting systematic theologies for our edification. It has no point to make, no ax to grind. It is more like a child roaming the neighborhood on a free afternoon . . . led by curiosity, by hunger, by hope."[28] Michael Glodo urges a responsible "hermeneutic of imagination" where imagining should be undertaken within the constraints of the grammatical-historical method yet do justice to the place of image and word in Scripture.[29]

This brings me back to music. Many writers on preaching are patently in search of metaphors that do justice to the act of preaching. In the nineteenth century legal analogies of putting a case to achieve a verdict were common. In the twentieth century architectural metaphors of "building" had some popularity. I believe that George Beasley-Murray would have resonated with Mike Grave's recent development of the image of "the sermon as symphony": "Preaching that is sensitive to the orality of Scripture brings the text alive and produces an experience like Mozart's *Requiem Mass* or Handel's *Messiah* for those who hear it. I

24. *Preaching the Gospel*, 1996, 16–17.

25. Ibid., 17.

26. *Preaching the Gospel*, 1956, 64.

27. Troeger, *Imagining the Sermon*, 15.

28. Taylor, *Preaching Life*, 48.

29. See on this Quicke, *360 Degree Preaching*, 83–84.

have come to think of sermon preparation in terms of composition not construction."[30]

In order for a sermon to be an eventful experience that catches hearers up into its passion the preacher must listen first to the *mood* of the text. Graves encourages students to imagine what music might best fit a given text—a crashing Liszt piano concerto, a single plaintiff violin, a massed choir? But second, there is also a textual movement—the progression and structural pattern within the text as the words both say and do things. He calls for form-sensitive sermons where preachers listen to the musicality of the text.

Not everyone will find the music metaphor helpful. One of my students complained, when Graves was a set book in one of my courses, that he was utterly unmusical and the image was no help. I suggested he might use my metaphor of the "preaching swim" to which another student reacted that she hated water and couldn't swim! But for some of us responding to the musicality of the text enriches our understanding of immersion into Scripture. In *Preaching the Gospel* I find much that could be described as "tuning into a text," sensing the evangelist's motives and urgency. One preaching guru in the United States, Eugene Lowry, who is responsible for the sermon structure called "the Lowry Loop," calls preaching an "acoustical event." Lowry has sometimes combined his talent as a jazz pianist with preaching. Just imagine, if he had wished to, how George Beasley-Murray might have developed this gift.[31]

I have merely reflected on four themes in *Preaching the Gospels.* I know that there are others which could be developed. For example, I believe George would have challenged us today by his passion of evangelism that saw preaching's salvation purpose as primary. "It pleased God by the foolishness of preaching to save the people." Preaching is never to be some satisfying exegesis for its own sake but always to save the people. The evangelistic pulse beats through his books and his life. His years in the United States would have brought him into Southern Baptist expectations that every sermon will always issue in an altar call. It would be interesting to know how he responded to that. But I cannot imagine that the alternative too many of us pursue of *never* having an altar call would have been acceptable. God saves by the foolishness of preaching.

30. Graves, *Sermon as Symphony*, 263.

31. Former students have since told me how George did sometimes combine preaching and playing the piano on evangelistic missions.

At one point George spells out his belief about preaching:

> I can think of no more worthy goal for a preacher of the Gospel than to learn how to present the message of Christ to his or her own situation. It demands continuous dedication to the study of the Gospels, with a discriminating use of all the tools that Gospel research has made available, prayer for the love and compassion of the Lord who is their theme, and for the guidance of the Holy Spirit to grasp the message and make it effectively known to our contemporaries.[32]

Behind this his Christian credo stands out. How appropriate it was at the packed thanksgiving service for George that Brian Haymes preached on the resurrection hope and used as his illustration the great *Credo* in Beethoven's *Missa Solemnis*. I could here its triumphant convictions sounding out: "I believe, I believe."

> The heart of the living God pulsates in the Life described in these pages. Anyone who ponders them long enough will enter into the mystery of the passion of God. Like the transfigured Lord, such a one will descend to the plain of humanity's need with a grace not of this world, and in company with the Spirit will bring his or her fellows out of the power of darkness into the kingdom of God's dear Son.[33]

I believe.

Bibliography

Babin, Pierre. *The New Era in Religious Communication*. Minneapolis: Fortress, 1991.

Beasley-Murray, George R. *Preaching the Gospel from the Gospels*. Peabody, MA: Hendrickson, 1996.

Beasley-Murray, Paul. *Fearless for Truth: A Personal Portrait of George Raymond Beasley-Murray*. Carlisle, UK: Paternoster, 2002.

Broadus, John A. *On the Preparation and Delivery of Sermons*. San Francisco: Harper and Row, 1979.

Graves, Mike. *The Sermon as Symphony*. Valley Forge, PA: Judson, 1996.

Greidanus, Sidney. *The Modern Preacher and the Ancient Text: Interpreting and Preaching Biblical Literature*. Grand Rapids: Eerdmans, 1988.

Long, Thomas G. *Preaching and the Literary Forms of the Bible*. Philadelphia: Fortress, 1989.

Lowry, Eugene. *The Sermon: Dancing on the Edge of Mystery*. Nashville: Abingdon, 1997.

32. *Preaching the Gospel*, 24–27.

33. Ibid., 29.

Ong, Walter. *Literacy and Orality: The Technologizing of the Word*. London: Methuen, 1982.

Quicke, Michael J. *360 Degree Preaching: Hearing, Speaking and Living the Word*. Grand Rapids: Baker, 2003.

Taylor, Barbara Brown. *The Preaching Life*. Cambridge, MA: Cowley, 1993.

Troeger, Thomas. *Imagining the Sermon*. Nashville: Abingdon, 1990.

4

New Humanity Church

A Biblical Model for Mission[1]

Bruce Milne

I appreciate immensely the honor of being invited to deliver this Memorial Lecture. I want to say at the very outset, to Ruth and Paul in particular, but to all who have Spurgeon's College in their bloodstream—which includes just about everybody here this evening—that, as far as I am concerned, there is simply no one I have known over my sixty-five years that was quite like George Beasley-Murray. I confess quite unashamedly that he was among the chief mentors of my life, and that he will always hold a unique place in heart. To bring this lecture this evening is, accordingly, a great honor.

In searching for a theme I set myself two parameters: First that it should involve some serious interaction with New Testament Scripture, and second that it contribute in some way to the expanded mission of the Church in our time. And if you really knew George, you will not need my justifying these two parameters.

Now, in essence, this lecture will argue for a particular vision of the local church and its mission, and, in honesty I need to confess that this vision is deeply colored by the experience of my last twenty years

1. This lecture was delivered at the Centennial Congress of the Baptist World Alliance, in Birmingham, England, 29 July 2005. An expanded version of the themes of this lecture was later published as *Dynamic Diversity: Bridging Class, Age, Race and Gender in the Church* (2006).

or so, giving leadership to a special congregation at the heart of a major world city at the far western shores of North America. Without that experience this lecture would never have been composed. However I will also attempt to demonstrate that this particular perspective finds its final justification in certain Biblical perspectives which allow it to transcend the particularity of one pastor's and congregation's story.

This lecture makes no claim to being a contribution to contemporary theological knowledge. My days for attempting such are behind me. However let me balance that qualifying note with the assertion that this presentation is made nonetheless in the sincere conviction that in these next few minutes I have something very important to say to the global witness of Baptist believers at the beginning of the twenty-first century. So, I invite you please, to listen up!

Biblical Grounding

My first parameter was serious interaction with some New Testament Scripture, and the title, "New Humanity Church," is a giveaway as far as the biblical focal point is concerned. I invite your attention accordingly to Ephesians 2:15, translated in the TNIV, "his purpose was to create in himself, one new humanity" (*hena kainon anthropon*).

Ephesians: A "Big-Picture" Letter

Ephesians, as is universally agreed, stands apart within the Pauline corpus. The case for Paul's authorship continues to be persuasively argued, as for example in the recent major commentaries by Peter O'Brien and Harold Hoehner. I cite further a sentence from my 1965 Beasley-Murray lecture notes on Ephesians, "Ephesians bears the marks of genius upon it . . . there is none other in the primitive church apart from Paul who was capable of expressing his own ideas in such a manner." That there is clearly a special timbre to Paul's accent in this letter is certainly to be conceded. But a little imaginative reflection on the circumstances of the letter, goes, in my judgment, a long way to explaining its distinctiveness as well as taking us to the heart of its message. Something of that special provenance came home to me several years ago, when I stood at the site of some of the formative thought which lay behind Ephesians, the Herodian prison at Caesarea, and gazed out into the great, tumbling Mediterranean breakers crashing onto the beach, thrilling at the thought that at the further reaches of that very sea there lay the ruins of ancient Rome, from so many points of view the centre of Paul's inherited world, the "Eternal City" where the apostle was bound, in order to plead his case before Caesar, whenever the Palestinian portion of his imprisonment was concluded.

Granted that evocative, geographical location, the enforced leisure of his incarceration, the nearly thirty years of ministry for Christ which at that point stretched behind him, to say nothing of the sheer fertility of Paul's mind and the reality of the Holy Spirit's inspiration—mix all these ingredients together—and Ephesians turns out as pretty well the kind of writing we might have expected, a "big picture" letter, which ranges far and wide across the vistas of God's mind-blowing, age-long, redemptive plan, to answer our "big-picture" questions, not least concerning the place of the Church in the purpose of God. Not surprising therefore that the theologically sensitized mind of John Calvin should have identified Ephesians as his favourite New Testament letter, or that more recently, John Mackay should have described Ephesians as "the distilled essence of the Christian religion," or that George's research supervisor, Professor C. H. Dodd, should have dubbed it "the crown of Paulinism."

Now, to come to closer quarters, the theme of this thoughtfully crafted writing lies arguably at 1:10 where Paul states the goal of God's entire salvation process, "his good pleasure which he purposed in Christ, to bring all things in heaven and earth together under one head, even Christ." Having arrived at this conclusion concerning 1:10 when expounding through Ephesians in both my pastorates I was not a little encouraged to note that O'Brien arrives at the same conclusion in his recent commentary. In an extended discussion of "The Central Message" of the letter, he asserts, "Ephesians 1:9–10 provides the key for unlocking the glorious riches of the letter."[2] Thus the culmination of all God's purposes, and hence the destiny towards which all that he has made and sustains in the physical and spiritual creation are moving, is here disclosed—"to bring all things together under Christ"—to "crown all things with Christ!" What a magnificent, thrilling perspective, and the preacher in me, as no doubt the preacher in you, is already on his feet, ready to cry to a listening Church and world, "Behold the Lamb upon the throne . . . crown him with many crowns! To Him be the glory for ever and ever!" Well, I will restrain that preacher, not least in the interest

2. O'Brien, *Ephesians*, 58.

of time. But we will stay with the text a few minutes longer as it is critical to all that follows.

The phrase "all things together under one head" translates, you will recall, a single Greek word, *anakephalaiosis*. It is a rare term in the New Testament, but it has several classical usages which throw helpful light on its meaning. I will refer to one: Greek mathematics. When the Greeks wished to add a series of numbers together they habitually listed these, rather as we still do (assuming no calculator is to hand), by writing them one under the other in a column. However whereas we today tend to draw a line at the foot of the list, and write the total beneath the line, the Greeks tended to draw the line above the column and put the total *above* the line, hence they (literally) "summed-up." Paul here sees Jesus as God's "summing-up" of all things.

Hence, whether with ecstatic joy in the case of the redeemed from all the ages and all those heavenly beings who gladly submit to his liberating reign; or in trembling dread, for those beings, both human and super-human who continue in rebellious impenitence—Paul is no universalist, cf. 5:6 "God's wrath is coming on those who are disobedient"—all in earth and heaven will acknowledge this King. The final goal is therefore profoundly Christocentric: "God's purpose in Christ is to unite all things to himself under this one Head."[3] The Lord Jesus Christ, he and no other, will wear the crown on that day. We resonate to Paul Kauffman's great sentence, "Tomorrow's history has already been written . . . at the name of Jesus every knee will bow!"

Finally we should note that since this is the divine purpose it is not merely a possibility to be aimed for, but a destiny to be infallibly realized. Since this is the purpose of the God who "works out everything in conformity with the purpose of his will" (1:11), in a real sense it is already accomplished. "All things together under Christ"—that is the future; quite simply it is your tomorrow, and mine. It is inscribed on every calendar in heaven, and, however unacknowledged, it is also etched into every calendar on earth. To this every life—your life, my life, all life—is moving, whether terrestrial or celestial, and every passing second is a step closer to its realization.

Having stated the glorious divine purpose in the opening sentences, Paul proceeds to explore it in the following paragraphs and a wonderfully encouraging conviction energizes his development of the theme,

3. Hoehner, *Ephesians*, 221.

one that is crucial to the argument of this lecture. This glorious purpose is *not wholly future*. Paul is convinced that it has already erupted into space and time. The historic "first-fruits" of God's triumphant purpose operate at two discernible points, corresponding, not surprisingly, to the two dimensions of the purpose referred to at 1:10. "Under Christ," the headship feature, and "together," the unification feature, Paul proceeds to claim, are *both* already in evidence. As far as the former, the headship, is concerned Paul points to the historic resurrection of Jesus by which God established Jesus "at his right hand in the heavenly realms, far above all rule and authority, power and dominion" (1:20–21). The second dimension of the purpose, the unification, "together," aspect, comes to the centre from 2:11 onwards. Accordingly, in keeping with the thrust, both of the letter, and of this lecture, we pause for a few moments to contemplate the unity of Jew and Gentile in the church.

Prior to Christ's coming the prospects for community between Jew and Gentile were bleak in the extreme. In Hendriksen's succinct paraphrase of 2:12, the Gentiles "B.C." were "Christless, friendless, stateless, hopeless and Godless."[4] Not surprisingly this religious divide was accompanied by a deep attitudinal antipathy. Paul calls it a "hostility" (*echthra*, 14 and 16). Secular and Christian writers combine to emphasize the depth of this mutual hatred. Tacitus for example claims that the Jews "regard the rest of mankind with all the hatred of enemies." Barclay summarizes the relationship: "The Jew had an immense contempt for the Gentile. The Gentiles, said the Jews, were created by God to be fuel for the fires of hell. God, they said, loves only Israel of all the nations that he has made."[5]

This religious distinctiveness and fermenting hostility combined to fix a great gulf between Jew and Gentile. Into that vast gulf, that spiritual and religious no-man's land, had come, in the fullness of time, Jesus the Christ. With his life, ministry, self-sacrifice, and subsequent resurrection from the dead the entire landscape had been altered. Paul signals that with a great adversative, "But now . . ." (13) as he moves on to express the wonder of God's great reconciliation of Jew and Gentile in Jesus. For by him the Gentiles who, as we saw above (12), were profoundly estranged from God's purpose and salvation, have now been "brought near." The intractable enemies have been reconciled and become friends.

4. Hendriksen, *Exposition of Ephesians*, 108.

5. Barclay, *The Letters to the Galatians and the Ephesians*, 195.

The specific means he notes is not just the ministry of Jesus in general but its central act of atonement in particular; the Gentiles are "brought near through the blood of Christ" (13). Following his master he affirms that the new covenant, and hence the new covenant community, is established "in his blood" (cf. 1 Cor 11:25). The apostle will allow no other source for the church than the cross of Jesus. In a real sense the arms of Christ spread-eagled on the cross in his final agony become a fitting symbol of his sacrifice's achievement. For with one outstretched arm he grasps believing Israelites, and with the other he grasps believing Gentiles, and in his person offered up in holy oblation, he unites the two. Accordingly, "he himself is our peace who has made the two one" (14). By his death Christ Jesus (= Messiah Jesus, 13) has "destroyed" the barrier, and hence removed the ground of the hostility. In essence Christ does this by fulfilling in himself the ceremonial law (15), and by bearing, in his propitiatory self-sacrifice, the implications before God of Jewish and Gentile breaches of the moral law (16). Hence he "put to death their hostility" (16b).

The commentators have wrestled with the question of whether the "hostility" here is the same as that referred to earlier, in v. 14, the horizontal enmity which existed between Jew and Gentile; or is it the vertical "hostility" which exists between God and humanity on account of our sinful rebellion against him, which Paul refers to in the earlier part of v. 16? There is much to be said, particularly when other Pauline passages dealing with the achievement of the cross are taken into account, for seeing both dimensions present. So O'Brien, who cites recent study showing that when, in Paul, an aorist participle (here, *apokeinas*, "having slain"), follows the main verb (here *apokatallaxe,* "might reconcile"), "there is a definite tendency towards co-incidental action."[6] In his death Christ does things. In John Murray's insightful phrase, "while our death is our fate, his death is his deed." The cross here has a double effect. It removes the wrath of God and the hostility of humans. That is, it creates a new, reconciled humanity—reconciled with God, and reconciled within itself. Hence we need to understand Paul as claiming that the cross *actually creates community*. By providing the one sufficient means whereby sin can be forgiven Christ's death eliminates all the religious distinctions between Jew and Gentile with their inherent potential for pride and enmity. But it also reaches to the core heart-attitudes which

6. O'Brien, *Ephesians*, 205.

find expression in these specific points of mutual antipathy, by assaulting the fallen attitudes of unlove which inform so much of human relationships. It makes us people with an inherent instinct for love: it creates a "new humanity" (15).

The second-century *Letter to Diogenes* refers to Christians as a "third race" distinct from Israel and the Gentiles. Hoehner spells out the meaning: "It is not that Gentiles become Jews (as Gentile proselytes did in pre-New Testament times), nor that Jews become Gentiles, but both become "one new person . . . a whole new entity . . . a new race which is raceless."[7] The apostle's language here must not be diluted. He is asserting nothing less than a sheer creative action of God indicated by the use of the Greek verb *ktizw* (15: "His purpose was to create in himself one new humanity") translating the Hebrew *bara*, which referred to God's creative acts, particularly the bringing forth of that which did not previously exist (cf. Gen 1:1; 1:21, 27; Num 16:20; Isa 42:5). Just as in his deed of creation he spoke and the universe sprang into being out of non-being, so now he speaks in his deed of redemption, and a new humanity leaps into existence. In 3:6 Paul calls it "this mystery" (Gk. *mysterion*), referring to something previously hidden, which has now been brought to light, implying a real movement from ignorance to knowledge. The creation of the Church is accordingly a prodigy, a wonder, which has been brought about by a supernatural, divine intervention, and hence is, in its way, a divine attestation to the gospel. Lurking in the background, as several commentators suggest, may be Paul's doctrine of Christ as the second Adam in whom the whole race is given a new beginning.[8]

In 3:10, during his inspired, biographical digression, Paul unveils a remarkable, further dimension. "His intent was that now, through the church, the manifold wisdom of God should be made known to the rulers and authorities in the heavenly realms." But what does the church disclose to the heavenly powers? What makes the Church, in Mackay's arresting phrase "a graduate school for angels"?[9] It is the "mystery" whereby "through the gospel the Gentiles are heirs together with Israel, sharers together in the promise in Christ Jesus" (3:6). It is the emergence of the astonishing "diversity in unity," whereby Jews and Gentiles are brought together into a single new humanity as a foretaste of God's

7. Hoehner, *Ephesians*, 378–79.

8. Lincoln, *Ephesians*, 143–46.

9. Mackay, *God's Order*, 84.

universal purpose "to bring all things together . . . under one head, even Christ." F. F. Bruce comments, "The church thus appears as God's pilot scheme for the reconciled universe of the future. The uniting of Jews and Gentiles was . . . God's masterpiece of reconciliation, and gave promise of a time when not Jews and Gentiles only, but all mutually hostile elements in creation would be united in that same Christ."[10]

Thus while the eternal all-embracing purpose of God for the world and all its peoples, as well as the denizens of the heavenly orders, is hidden from the unbelieving world, at two points it breaks through into visibility: the resurrection and headship of Christ and the unifying in a new, supernatural order of existence of those who acknowledge his rule, a "new humanity" in which we see the unveiled face, and touch the outstretched hand of God. Not that all this was immediately perceived or universally practiced. Clearly, and not surprisingly, the older diversities continued to find some degree of expression for a period (cf. Acts 21:20–26). But the principle had been irrevocably established—the "Ephesian Moment,"[11] as Andrew Walls calls it, had arrived for ever, and its greatest day, I believe, is about to dawn!

The implications for our thinking about and planning for the Church are major ones. Specifically we are here afforded a congregational model, which can be succinctly defined as "diversity in unity under Christ." It is a model that achieves two great goals. First, it means building churches that move in the direction of God's purpose for the ages, "all things together under Christ." Second, by virtue of this, it is a plan for congregational life that is profoundly doxological, which is exactly Paul's own response, in the astonishing prayer in 3:14–21. What an utterance it is, ending appropriately in an outburst of praise, which, unsurprisingly, links the glorifying of God to the twin elements of his eternal purpose—"the Church," the body in which all diversities are united together, and "Christ," the exalted reconciler.

> And now to him who is able to do immeasurably more than all we ask or imagine . . . to him be glory in the church and in Christ Jesus, through all generations, forever and ever. Amen!

But we cannot stop there. For the union of Jew and Gentile represents only the paradigm expression of something larger and more compre-

10. Bruce, *Epistles to the Colossians*, 321–22, 262.

11. Walls, "The Ephesian Moment." See further fn. 22.

hensive—the Body of Christ on earth, a unique God-created reality, a "new humanity" in which not only ethnic diversity, but every other major human diversity is overcome. In order to justify that claim we turn, necessarily briefly, to several other New Testament passages.

Galatians 3:26–28

In this passionate letter Paul argues that our acceptance with God lies solely in Christ's atoning self-sacrifice on the cross (3:13) where he bore our "curse," the divine judgment which follows inevitably upon all breaches of the divine law (3:10), with a view to our "by faith receiving the promise of the Spirit" (3:14). This receipt of the Holy Spirit in turn installs us in the family of God: "you are all children of God through faith in Christ Jesus" (3:26), a family where "there is neither Jew nor Greek, slave nor free, male nor female, for you are all one in Christ Jesus" (27–28).

Again we meet the transcending of the ethnic division between Jew and Gentile (cf. 6:15, "neither circumcision nor uncircumcision means anything, what counts is a new creation.") But also, and equally, the social status division between slave and free, and the gender division between male and female are transcended. These extensions, which are clearly implicit in the base passage in Ephesians 2, are critical to the thesis of this lecture. The racial reconciliation is a paradigm of the New Humanity, not its essence. All the major dimensions of human division are embraced and overcome in the new unified life of those who are "all one in Christ Jesus" (3:28).

Colossians 3:10–11

In this companion letter to Ephesians Paul again directs his readers to the exalted Christ who is destined in everything to have the pre-eminence (1:18). In baptismal faith-union with this Christ we are raised to a new life, a new self (3:10) and a new humanity where there is "no Greek or Jew, circumcised or uncircumcised, barbarian, Scythian, slave or free, but Christ is all, and in all" (3:11).

Once more the New Humanity over-reaches natural divisions, Jew and Gentile, and also relativizes social status whether that of slavery or freedom. But here the social divisions are expanded. "Scythians" were viewed as the lowest of the low, "little better than wild beasts," according to Josephus. "The ancient world, just like the modern, was an elaborate network of prejudice, suspicion and arrogance, so ingrained as to be thought natural and normal."[12] The New Humanity in face of these endemic attitudinal evils embraces equally the highly cultured Greek and the anti-cultured Scythian, irreconcilables made one in Christ.

1 Corinthians 12:1–30

The divisions in Corinth are proverbial, and in their way a timely reminder that the New Humanity is always an enterprise in process on this side of the *parousia*. The point of tension here was apparently spiritual gifts, especially the more overtly charismatic ones, and their implications for good and godly order in worship. Again the reign of Christ is paramount—"There are different kinds of service but the same Lord" (12:5). And again the New Humanity transcends diversity and its attendant potential for conflict (in this case around gifts and ministries, and perhaps underlying these, diversities of personality within a local congregation). The secret in all things is the rediscovery of the Holy Spirit's supreme gift of love (12:31—13:13).

1 John 2:12–14

This passage in which John addresses his "new humanity" readers with typical pastoral concern employs a threefold division within congregations of "little, or dear children" (*teknia*, 12, *paidia*, 14), "fathers" *(pateres*, 13, 14), and "young men" (*neaniskoi*, 13, 14). This literary unit in the letter continues to puzzle interpreters. Dr. Terry Griffith observes, "No-one has advanced a satisfactory explanation of the role of 2:12–14 within the body of 1 John." Hence my comments here are necessarily tentative, but I believe that seeing the three categories as a straightforward reference to three generations within the church is certainly worthy of consideration. Whether or not the text upholds it in precisely these terms there is surely confirmation here that the congregations in the first century were no less inclusive in their age-span than ours today, and that the insistent appeal of this letter to mutual love after the pattern of the self-giving love of Christ, cf. 4:19, "We love because he first loved us," had reference to generational distinctions as surely as others. Again the New Humanity expresses itself in a visible fellowship in which diversity is transcended

12. Wright, *Paul for Everyone*, 140.

in a supernatural unity centered in the person of Christ, who is "the true God and eternal life" (5:20).

Hebrews 12:24–26

This remarkable passage identifies a dimension of the unified life of the New Humanity that is rarely focused upon, and yet is hugely significant, not least in affording evidence of the essentially supernatural nature of the new communal life. It is the unity of the present communities of faith with believers of previous ages and with the angelic and other created servants of God who inhabit the celestial order. Such is the plain meaning of this passage, "we have come [in our worship] . . . to the innumerable company of angels in joyful assembly . . . and to the spirits of the just made perfect." We get it wrong when we announce, "Let us begin worship with this song of praise, or hymn, etc. . . ." We do not. We never *begin* worship . . . we only join worship! I recall a College morning prayers, when George remarked, as something of an aside, that the sober reading of Hebrews 12: 24–26 in the setting of the weekly worship service would shake many a Christian congregation to the core. But this too is part of the reality which is the New Humanity, for, as Andrew Walls asserts, "time is valorized by the incarnation" and "since Christ continues to be formed in local communities of his people, whose ways of life are quite different from those within which the incarnation took place, it means that 'sacred time' extends to the entire historical span in which the work of salvation goes on."[13]Accordingly, "Christian faith is necessarily ancestor conscious" asserts Walls, not in the sense of divinizing the dead in Christ, but of recognizing that they actually, if mysteriously, continue to be part of the one Body. And how appropriate to remind ourselves of that dimension of the Body of Christ in a lecture dedicated to one who has moved to the Church triumphant.

Thus our brief consideration of these didactic New Testament passages confirms the claim made above, that the new, communal life of the followers of Jesus which emerged from the Church's evangelistic mission in the New Testament period was a life in which all the principal spheres of diversity were transcended in a new, divinely given unity—the emergence in other words of a radically new kind of human connectedness.

13. Walls, "The Ephesian Moment," 2–3.

Acts 2: The Jerusalem Church

A further line of New Testament evidence is to examine the descriptions within the Book of Acts of the fledgling congregations which emerged in these first decades of the Christian movement. We stop by two of them.

Pentecost was many things, but central to this epochal moment was the communication of the gospel in a supernaturally generated diversity of tongues to the geographically scattered proselyte audience as "Jews from every nation under heaven" (5) confessed in amazement "we hear them declaring the wonders of God in our own tongues" (2:11).

Some commentators have noted a rabbinic tradition that makes similar claims for the giving of the law on Sinai. More likely is the link to Genesis 11:1–9. Thus F. F. Bruce, "The event was surely nothing less than a reversal of the curse of Babel,"[14] an association which of course, if valid, detaches the pentecostal outpouring from merely Jewish, first-century moorings, and positions it squarely within universal history. We compare here words of Jesus, citing Isaiah 56:7, with its eschatological promise, "My house shall be called a house of prayer for all nations" (Mark 11:17). The offspring of Pentecost is nothing less than a global child. The New Humanity in its birthday suit represents massive ethnic diversity embraced in a supernaturally generated unity.

While the ethnic is clearly primary we ought not to overlook two other dimensions alluded to in Acts 2. The first is gender diversity. The account of the praying company upon whom the Spirit descended includes "the women, and Mary the mother of Jesus" (1:14); and the description of the manifestations of the Spirit are notably inclusive: "they were all together . . . tongues of fire . . . separated and came to rest upon each of them . . . all of them were filled with the Holy Spirit and began to speak in other tongues" (2:1–4). Admittedly v. 7 has the bewildered hearers asking, "are not all these men who are speaking Galileans?" But it would be surprising indeed if the women who are already noted as participants in the many-tongued proclamation had no part whatever in this public overflow, not least when Peter's justification of the phenomena cites Joel 2, explicitly including "Your sons and daughters will prophesy . . . even on my servants, both men and women, I will pour out my Spirit in those days, and they will prophesy" (17–18). The same citation has also pointers to another dimension of "New Humanity" di-

14. Bruce, *The Book of Acts*, 64.

versity, the generational—"your young men will see visions, your old men will dream dreams" (17). And all this "diversity in unity" is the fruit of the enthronement of the risen Jesus: "Exalted to God's right hand, he has . . . poured out what you now see and hear" (2:33).

Acts 11:19–26: The Church in Syrian Antioch

The persecution over Stephen scattered the witnessing church. At Antioch the historic breakthrough was achieved as "men from Cyprus and Cyrene" made the critical step, in its way as significant as the legendary "one small step" by Neil Armstrong on to the surface of the moon on 20 July, 1969: "they began to speak to Greeks also, telling them the good news about the Lord Jesus." Padilla claims, "The importance of this step can hardly be overestimated. Antioch was the third largest city in the world."[15] "Almost a microcosm of Roman antiquity in the first century, [Antioch] encompassed most of the advantages, the problems, and the human interests, with which the new faith would have to grapple."[16] The diversity of this Syrian congregation is exposed in 13:1 in the description of the congregation's leadership team, five in number: Simeon the Black, an African; Lucius of Cyrene, a North African; Manaean, possibly a slave of Herod's father, a Palestinian Jew; Saul of Tarsus, a native of Asia Minor, the land bridge to Europe; and Barnabas from Cyprus. As Padilla comments, "A more heterogeneous group could hardly be suggested."[17] Bakke cites the archaeological evidence that the city, not unlike Jerusalem of our own time, was divided into distinct ethnic sectors, separated by walls, in this case five in number: Greek, Syrian, Jewish, Latin and African. [18] Just as the coming of the gospel effectively destroyed the "dividing wall of hostility" between Jew and Gentile, so it effectively destroyed the interior walls of Antioch to enable men, women and children from every sector to come together to hear the gospel and become followers of the "Lord Jesus" (11:20).

This all too brief glance at first generation congregations underpins the exegetical conclusions we reached above. The New Humanity represented a new quality of human community amid the multiple layers and

15. Padilla, *Mission*, 151.

16. Green, *Evangelism in the Early Church*, 114.

17. Padilla, *Mission*, 152.

18. Bakke, *A Theology as Big as the City*, 145–46.

networks of human connectedness which marked the Graeco-Roman world. While never perfected, the quality of this new communal life was nonetheless sufficiently distinctive and noteworthy to be a major ground of attraction to the faith that united them. The social width of these new loyalties is evidenced as Pliny reports to his Emperor concerning "this contagious superstition" of which "many of every age, every class, and of both sexes are accused." Or listen to the later witness Aristides describing Christian lifestyles to the Emperor Hadrian: "They love one another. They never fail to help widows, they save orphans from those who would hurt them. If they have something they give freely to the man who has nothing; if they see a stranger they take him home, and are happy as though he were a real brother. They don't consider themselves brothers in the usual sense, but brothers instead through the Spirit, in God."[19]

The commentators line up in acknowledgment of the significance of this unique lifestyle. "The impact that the early church made on non-Christians because of Christian brotherhood across natural barriers can hardly be overestimated," writes Padilla. "The abolition of the old separation between Jew and Gentile was undoubtedly one of the most amazing accomplishments of the gospel in the first century. Equally amazing however was the breaking down of the class distinction between master and slave."[20] Michael Green comments "When the Christian missionaries not only proclaimed that in Christ the distinctions slave and free man were done away as surely as those between Jew and Greek, but actually lived in accordance with their principles, this had an enormous appeal."[21] The New Humanity which emerged through the New Testament period evinced a new form of human society in which the old polarities—Jew/Gentile, male/female, slave/free, elder/youth—came under increasing pressure, and precisely here lay part of the manifest attractiveness of these new communities.

Now I am hugely torn at this point as the theologian in me longs to explore the congruence of these conclusions with some of the great Christian doctrines. However, I am anxious to move on to the immediate application of all this, and so I have to limit myself to noting that the New Humanity Church, "diversity in unity under Christ," accords with:

19. See Stevenson, *A New Eusebius*, 53.

20. Padilla, *Mission*, 165.

21. Green, *Evangelism*, 117.

a. the nature of the Trinity: and hence is finally to be understood as God imaging himself in his people. Can there be any higher authentication?

b. the mystery of the incarnation: the supreme instance of "the embrace of the different other" in the work of salvation—thus the endorsement of the New Humanity model as the building, in this sense, of "Christ-like" congregations.

c. the visions of eschatology: the "diversity in unity under Christ" as in fact our destined future.

Thus the unity-in-diversity model receives massive endorsement from the Scriptures and the great doctrines that are taught there. However there is a further, necessarily lesser, and yet nonetheless persuasive argument in support of this vision of the Church. It is the flow of history. For the fact is that this model of the Church is massively endorsed by the global realities, that surround us every day. If ever there was "an idea whose time has come" it is precisely this way of doing church.

We can fittingly note the observations of Andrew Walls, in *The Cross-Cultural Process in Christian History.*[22] In a chapter titled "The Ephesian Moment" he explores the nature of the "new humanity" of Ephesians 2:15, recognizing its epochal status. "While the anticipation must have been of two distinct Christian communities, Jew and Gentile, the Ephesian letter has not a dream of such an outcome."[23] This "Ephesian Moment" was "quite brief." The destruction of the Jewish state in AD 70, the scattering of the Jewish church and the sheer success of the Gentile mission meant that the Church very soon became again monocultural, "as overwhelmingly Hellenistic as it had been overwhelmingly Jewish." "But in our own day the Ephesian moment has come again, and come a richer mode than has ever happened since the first century."[24] The evidence for that claim is all around us in this Congress,[25] for the diversity we are celebrating here in Birmingham is disclosive of today's Church as well as prophetic of tomorrow's. Put another way, we need

22. Walls, *The Cross-Cultural Process.*

23. Ibid., 76.

24. Ibid., 78.

25. The reference here is to the huge diversity represented by the Baptist World Alliance Congress.

to let Birmingham challenge and change us, allowing it to set us in our actual and future context.

Let me illustrate this point in a way I personally have found helpful. You are all aware of what I mean by a "Mexican Wave." We attend a sporting event in a large stadium. The game on the pitch is rather boring and so suddenly a section of the spectators jump to their feet and throw their arms in the air. The next section follows on, and so the wave travels right round the stadium and back to the beginning where it may set off again. It's all great fun and often much more memorable than the action on the field of play!

Now, every Sunday a Wave of Worship travels all the way around the world. It begins around the time many of you here in the UK are either heading for bed on Saturday night, or the ministers are coming staggering out of their studies. Right then down in the South Pacific, in West Samoa and Tonga and Fiji, the Christians are heading out to church, and they are being called to worship, and they are on their feet, and they are throwing their hands in the air, as it were, and praising the Lord, and the Wave has begun. At the very same time thousands of miles to the north, at the further eastern edges of the former Soviet Union believers are gathering in smaller numbers, and doing the same. Then the Wave starts moving westwards—it's into New Zealand and Australia, across the time zones, millions now on their feet. Meanwhile the Wave is moving through Asia: Japan, the Philippines, Indonesia, the Lord is being exalted; and now it is into China—how many Christians in China? Only God knows; perhaps up to one hundred million. The wave of worship is sweeping through. And now it is moving across northern Asia and central Asia, and the Southeast, into India and the great ancient churches there. It's into the Middle East, little groups of believers bravely joining, lifting heart and hand in worship; and now it's touching Africa, there on its eastern coast, the historic churches in Egypt and Ethiopia are joining the wave, and then it's the turn of the teeming congregations of Uganda and Kenya and Zambia and across South Africa, millions on their feet, crying, "Jesus Christ is Lord" and worshiping. And so on it goes across central Africa and now into the west. Again these massive communities of Christ in Nigeria, Ghana, Cameroon, others smaller and struggling but the Lord is among them all, and the Wave goes on. Meanwhile it's touching Europe, the Balkans, Scandinavia there to the far north, and the Mediterranean lands and the believers there, and now it's leaping the Channel, and it's your turn here in the UK, and you respond and you are there in your churches and you are on your feet in praise, and the Wave is sweeping through the Iberian Peninsula. And now it is leaping over the sea from Ireland to Iceland, Greenland and finally on to the American landmass; to the Maritimes in the far west of Canada, but even before that it's into Brazil and the exciting new churches there and they are on their feet, millions more, Argentina, and down the eastern coast of Latin America with its lively worship and up the west coast, and the Caribbean Islands get with the beat. And the Wave is coming down through the teeming population areas of the eastern United States and all their churches, and it's moving through Central America where so many love and follow Christ. The Wave is sweeping on and millions more are rising to their feet, across the Canadian prairies, the midwest of the States. And now it is our turn there at the further western coast—California, Oregon, and Washington, and finally our lazy lot in Vancouver. The Lord is being lifted high and we are adoring him our blessed Triune God, and so it goes on, up to Alaska, and across to Hawaii, and finally back to the south Pacific, and the Wave is over for another Sunday! Isn't that exciting? And I am not creating this you understand, I am only describing what actually happens all the way around our world every single Sunday. That is our context, to be a Christian simply means to be a part of that. How could anyone stay in bed? How we need to feel the force, and catch the blessing of all this!

"In our own day the 'Ephesian Moment' has come again, and come in a richer mode than has ever happened since the first century." So claims Andrew Walls. Is it true? In response I invite you to join me in quick overview of the world in which we require to "do church."

Today's Context: The World in Which We Require to "Do Church"

In contemplating our world we can readily identify two significant features, and one significant truth. The first feature: ours is a diversifying world.

In his worldwide bestseller *Future Shock*, written all of thirty-five years ago, Alvin Toffler predicted, "The human race, far from being flattened into monotonous conformity, will become far more diverse socially than it ever was before."[26] By the time he followed that up with *The Third Wave* ten years later, the prediction was already being fulfilled.[27]

Today we are facing social diversity in all of our cultures "as never before" in human history. To quote a chapter heading in Ray Bakke's *The Urban Christian*, "The Lord is Shaking up the World."[28] Ethnic diversity is the most obvious, and visible form of this upheaval. The teeming world cities have become mosaics of national sub-groups. Do you know that supremely important statistic, that by 2050, out of a world population of some nine billion, seven billion will be urban dwellers? Driven by massive international migrations, spawned in many cases by wars and ethnic conflicts, hundreds of millions have abandoned their family roots and set out to find new lands in which to live. Thus for example of the approximately 175 distinct nations identified by the U.N., 135 are significantly represented in my adopted country of Canada. In London children in the school system speak a staggering three hundred different languages. In Miami foreign-born residents number 59 percent of the resident population, followed by Toronto with 44 percent, Los Angeles with 41 percent, and Vancouver, in the global fourth spot, with 39 percent. In Los Angeles the Southern Baptists worship in fifty-two languages every Sunday. In Amsterdam there are forty-four distinct ethnic neighborhoods. Here in Birmingham the ethnic population is 30 percent.

Other criteria of diversification tell the same story. In the sphere of age and generational distinction there is a greater spread of distinct generational identities than at any previous time, impacted largely by the ageing of many populations. Thus in the UK in the period 1901–1981, while the percentage in the under fourteen-year-old bracket fell from 32.4 to 20.5, the percentage over sixty-five more than trebled, from 4.7 to 15. Family structures are also diversifying. To cite U.S. figures, often a social barometer for Western societies, in the period 1960–1990 the percentages of the population in a two-parent family fell from 74 to 54, those in a single-parent family rose from 10 to 17, and those living outside any family structure doubled from 15 percent to 30 percent of the total population. The greater spread of wealth (again I am focusing on Western societies primarily here) has also encouraged greater diversity

26. Toffler, *Future Shock*, 275.

27. Toffler, *The Third Wave*, 360–61.

28. Bakke, *The Urban Christian*, 28.

as more people have access to more diverse opportunities and the significantly enhanced mobility, both social and geographical, which this provides. The greater ease and the speed of travel has also contributed, as has the internationalization of business, as well as a global media and communications network, fuelled by the personal computers and the mobile phone.

Let me illustrate where we are today with this delightful story from the Parsee congregation in Toronto recently. The congregation were happy to welcome a new lady, but were a bit nonplussed by her habit of talking into her cell phone during the sermon on Sunday mornings. The pastor's wife, who always knows of course how much goes into our preparation, decided to take the matter in hand and challenged the lady. "Yes. Of course she was so very welcome, but her husband spent so much time faithfully preparing, could she not show more respect, etc." Then the visitor explained, "Oh, no, no. It's not that I don't respect your husband, but you see during the message I dial up my husband in Baghdad, and he listens to it on the phone and I try and answer his questions as the message goes along, and he is very interested. He's in a secret Bible study of six people and they are all seeking the Lord." Well! So of course the visitor was moved to the front pew. And imagine the joy as few weeks later when, in the middle of the message, the lady cried out, "He wants to become a Christian!" And so the Pastor breaks into his sermon, comes down from the pulpit, and over the phone leads the husband to Christ in Baghdad, goes back into the pulpit and finishes his message, while the congregation are singing hallelujahs in the background.

But as well as the increase in "sheer diversity," i.e., diversity as sociologically identifiable, there is what one might call "experiential diversity." This refers to the diversity I experience in my daily life. In some ways, as far as the implications for forming congregations is concerned, this is more significant. Putting it another way, we inhabit a society today where it is increasingly less possible to escape into ghettos of similarity. ("my kind of people"). The increase of wealth and its wider distribution means that neighborhoods are more stratified; the internationalization of economics, business, and professional life, as well as the greatly increased ethnic diversity, particularly in cities, also increases the diversity of life's daily encounters. I can no longer, or am less and less able, to avoid my "different" neighbor. The implications of all this accelerated diversification, particularly for urban life are far from uniformly benign as you have become only too well aware here in the UK, in the last three weeks.[29]

An Historical Perspective

Paradoxically just as the world becomes more complex and diverse it is experiencing unprecedented trajectories towards unification. This is the reality of globalization. As never before we live in one world. The symbol for life today is the green ball, earth as perceived from space, one world. As Howard Snyder observes, "For the first time children are coming to adulthood with a global consciousness." [30] The usual way to refer to this change is globalization. The academic community and the public sphere continue to debate the precise meaning and significance of globalization. David Held has a more general definition "the widening, deepening and speeding up of worldwide interconnectedness in all aspects of contemporary, social life."[31] No consensus has of course been reached on the positive or negative impact of globalization. Anthony Giddens writes, "We are being propelled into a global order that no one fully understands, but which is making its effect felt upon all of us."[32] But this newborn sense of global identity is hugely important as far as our mental world is concerned. It inevitably stirs the imagination, not least that of the emerging generations, challenging our merely personal and national ambitions, disturbing our narrow preoccupations, and awakening at a certain level, our dreams of belonging to a family which transcends the divisive negativism of so much modern life, and connects us to a community of truth, acceptance and beauty, a community of love, kindness and purity, where we can unite with all our human family, and make a difference in our desperately needy world.

One of the paradoxes of the appearance and growth of this global "skin" is the way in which it has also produced fragmentations and even a certain type of localization. This is explored by Roland Robertson in a book that coins the somewhat unattractive term "glocalization."[33] He notes that globalization always takes place and has an impact in a spe-

29. The reference here is to the bombings on the London transport system that took place in July 2005.

30. Snyder, *Earth Currents*, 24–25.

31. Held et al., *Global Transformations*, 2.

32. Giddens, *Runaway World*, 7.

33. Robertson, *Global Modernities*, 25–44.

cific local setting, and that one of the effects of the global forces is to cause local markets and communities to morph their identity to suit the global forces and in the process become more self-consciously themselves. This glocalizing effect reminds us that in reviewing our world we need to find a place to recognize both these developments which we have surveyed—diversity in terms of social and communal pluralisms at every level, and unity in terms of overarching forces which transcend national and tribal identities.

Today's reality is perceptively caught by a quotation from *The Atlantic* magazine: "the world is coming dangerously apart and rushing precipitously together at the same time." Evangelical sociologist Peter Dray notes the same ambiguity: "on the one hand increasing complexity as we enter the 'network society' where the increasingly extended networks produce increasing complexity." Yet at the same time, "globalization is also concerned with the increasing homogenization of cultures and tastes with the standardized products produced by global corporations with no allegiance to place or community." Hence "globalization is a tension of two processes in making networks more complex: localization within locales, and an overall framework of increasing homogenization of content."[34] We complete this glance at the contemporary world by noting, alongside these two significant features, a significant truth.

Back to the Present

As we saw in our consideration of Ephesians 1:10, God's final purpose to bring all things under Christ has historic precedent. So Ephesians 1:22–23, "He raised Christ from the dead, and seated him at his right hand in the heavenly realms." For Paul, as for his Master, resurrection means reign (cf. Matt 28:18)! And hence his present rule at this moment over all the earth, and here and now in Birmingham.

One thinks of Luther, as the German princes, fearful for his safety, try to dissuade him from his perilous journey to Augsburg, "At Augsburg are the powers of hell!" But the reformer will have nothing of their craven capitulation. "And at Augsburg," he shouted, "Jesus reigns!" We shout it still, in face of all the threats, from bombs and bullets, nuclear holocaust, environmental disaster, and Islamist terrorist mayhem. Jesus reigns! "Jesus Christ is Lord." That is the faith. These three realities, diversity,

34. Dray, *Globalization and the Christian Mission*, 2.

unity, and the Lordship of Christ, are of course the three factors which combine in the Ephesians 1:10 revelation of God's purpose, "all things together under Christ." But this polarized, diversity-in-unity world we inhabit is actually not a "first." In fact at least once before in history that very pattern expressed itself—the world into which the gospel came at the first. So I invite you in a further moment to consider an historical precedent.

The Graeco-Roman world of the first century may not unfairly be described as "skin over cracks." The skin was the empire. Roman empire-building took on a quite specific form. As the legions pushed outwards in all directions, Rome expanded its dominance, and new territories with their native populations were constantly added to its territories. However there was little attempt in most cases to absorb these tribal peoples into a full Roman identity. "The solidarity of the empire was a product of the sheer preponderance of Roman might rather than of direct centralized administration."[35] Not that Rome was less than utterly ruthless in imposing her will if called upon. But she learned how to blend the sheer will to power with a certain sensitivity to local aspirations. Indeed, as Metzger claims, "the secret of Rome's success where others had failed lay in her wise provision for differing kinds of local supervision and control."[36] Patently there were the overarching features, the "skin," to use the earlier image, represented by military dominance, law and (some) institutions, a formal language (Latin), a common language (*koine* Greek), a network of roads, and a religious veneer over an almost endless pluralism (the emperor cult). But the empire in general consisted in a mosaic rather than a melting pot: under this skin lay massive diversity of ethnicity, language, race and culture. The skin was critical, however, for the effective spread of the Christian faith as it provided the highways of communication by which the gospel could rapidly spread as well the means for travel and interpersonal contacts.

But the skin did something else. It created a mind-set, it stirred a longing, it awakened a dream at the horizons of imagination, which projected the individual beyond purely personal and tribal boundaries. It vivified a longing deeply set in every human heart for a larger world of harmony and peace, where ancient hatreds and rivalries would be buried forever, and swords become ploughshares, and spears pruning

35. E. A. Judge in Douglas, *Illustrated Bible Dictionary*, 1344.

36. Metzger, *The New Testament*, 30.

hooks, and wars be no more, and neighbor love will extend across the human borders and reach as wide as the human family.

Not surprisingly, in this environment of intense and often conflicted diversity, and yet alongside it the trappings of wider horizons, one of the major attractions of Christianity, as writers universally conclude, was its offer of community. "Perhaps this was the way," F. F. Bruce suggests, "in which the gospel made its deepest impression on the pagan world."[37] In John Poulton's memorable words, referring to the specific case of the slave-master relationship, but memorably conveying the universal significance of New Humanity Christian community, "When masters could call slaves brothers, and when the enormities of depersonalizing them became conscious in enough people's minds, something had to go. It took time, but slavery went. And in the interim, the people of God were an embodied question mark, because here were some people who could live another set of relationships within the given social system."[38] An embodied question mark, living another set of relationships within the given social system in which the different other was embraced instead of rejected, was loved instead of hated, was a brother or sister instead of an enemy, within a new kind of human existence which was destined to inherit the world.

After the breakdown of the empire (fifth-ninth centuries), first in the West and then in the East, the skin was shredded and peoples retreated behind the walls of nation-states where they remained until the modern period. Accordingly it is arguable that in some senses it is not until the twenty-first century that the skin has re-grown in terms of present-day globalization. Thus for the first time since the first century we have a recovery of certain primary contextual features of the environment in which Christianity made such impressive headway in the beginning.

The point I am making here, as hopefully you will have gathered, is that there is a striking parallel between the world of the first century with its massive local diversities, and its imperial "global" skin, and the twenty-first century, third millennium world, in which we meet this afternoon with its unprecedented "on your face" diversities, and its globalization skin. Now, admittedly the brush strokes here are very broad, and unless my initial biblical section was invalid, the case for the New

37. Simpson and Bruce, *The Epistles to the Ephesians and Colossians*, 277.

38. Houlton, *People Under Pressure*, 112.

Humanity congregation does not hang on the validity of the parallel. However the parallels are interesting, to say the least, and surely worth being thoughtfully pondered. Here again is huge social diversity with a unifying skin that can provide a highway for communication across the various gulfs and contradictions. And "under the skin" the expanding diversity is producing not dissimilar problems: need I say more in July 2005, in central-southern England?

Alvin Toffler warns, "The sudden shift of social ground-rules today, the smudging of roles, status distinctions, and lines of authority, the immersion in blip culture, and above all the break-up of the great thought system "indust-reality" have shattered the world-image most of us carry around in our skulls. In consequence most people surveying the world around them today see only chaos. They suffer a sense of personal powerlessness and pointlessness."[39]

> A society fast fragmenting at the level of values and life styles challenges all the old integrative mechanisms and cries out for a totally new basis for reconstitution. We have by no means yet found this basis. Yet if we shall face disturbing, agonizing problems of social integration, we shall confront even more agonizing problems of individual integration. For the multiplication of life styles challenges our ability to hold the very self together.[40]

"We have by no means yet found this 'totally new' basis for reconstruction." These are Toffler's words, but they resonate surely for every Baptist with a missionary heart, and how can you be an authentic Baptist without such? George Beasley-Murray was such a Baptist, with such a heart, and that is one reason why he lives on in the memory and imagination of so many of us. The world in other words has no real answer to the crisis of our time, the means to hold together in living community the diversities of our burgeoning multi-faceted cultures. And yet an answer must be found, for the global forces forcing these diversities into an ever closer confrontational unity are irreversible.

"We have by no means yet found this 'totally new' basis for reconstruction." But the witness of history as reflected in Christianity's foundational documents, is that in the parallel world of the first century there emerged a group of people who had discovered a totally new basis for social reconstruction, and lived it out, as an embodied question mark,

39. Toffler, *The Third Wave*, 374.

40. Toffler, *Future Shock*, 293.

before the watching world in their local Christian congregations scattered throughout the empire, to such effect that multitudes were drawn as by a magnet to share in their discovery. But we have that answer still available to us today, lying on the surface of the New Testament—the gospel, the great good news of Jesus Christ.

My mind often goes back to a conversation I have reported before, with the mayor of Vancouver. I asked him this question: "Philip, can you tell me one other group that meets anywhere in this city, on a weekly basis, for any purpose, which has a greater diversity than the diversity of our congregations at First Baptist every Sunday morning?" He thought for a while. He was an outstanding mayor who knew his city very well. Finally he replied, "No, I don't think I can." Then I was able to say to him—with appropriate courtesy, I hope—"Philip, doesn't that say something very important about Jesus Christ." You see, by the grace of God, we had become an embodied question mark. and that was a relevant witness, because as a civic servant and leader he was only too well aware of the forces threatening to tear our community apart, and longing accordingly for some solution to the problem. That surely is our gospel, the supremely relevant good news to this explosive society. In face of this threatening culture of potential conflict there is another way, a New Humanity which transcends the diversities and can slay the latent conflictual enmities of the human heart, and create in the Holy Spirit a new kind of person-in-community. As Rene Padilla declares, "Unmistakably the unity [belongs to] the gospel—not simply a result that should take place as the church is 'perfected,' but an essential aspect of the *kerygma* that the apostles proclaimed."[41]

To think of a single current application—what would it mean for the integrity and impact of Christian witness on my continent of North America, if 11.00 a.m. on Sunday morning ceased to be the weekly hour of the greatest segregation, and became instead the hour of greatest integration? The religious and social impact would be, I believe, incalculable.

Listen. I have a dream, a dream of a congregation where people of all colors, from every ethnic identity, find welcome, warmth, dignity, and a sense of belonging. I have a dream of a church where men and women worship and serve together as equally valuable in the sight of God, and equal in their capacity to honor him. I have a dream of a Christian community where children, youth, middle-aged and seniors,

41. Padilla, *Mission*, 144.

boomers, busters, Generation Xers and Millennials, learn to respect and love, and discover their profound need of each other; where people from all wealth and power indexes can live, and relate, and laugh together. I have a dream of a family where singles, and marrieds, and marrieds with families, and single parents, and divorcees, are all affirmed in their worth before God and his people, where differences of personality, and huge diversities of spiritual stories and spiritual journeys, or the lack of them, are no barrier to acceptance—all of that multi-textured humanity, uniting under the conscious, blessed rule of the exalted Lord Jesus Christ through his living Word, in wondering communion in worship with saints and angels. I have a dream.

And I have a dream, of that same exuberant, technicolor family, swept by the Holy Spirit, streaming forth from their worship buildings into the community around them, to throw their arms around it, and hug it to their hearts, sharing with it the joyous good news of Jesus and his salvation, and the practical ministries of love, with the poor, and the lonely, the street kids and the HIV/AIDS victims, the physically and mentally challenged, the unemployed and the addicted, the johns and the prostitutes, the cynics and the broken-hearted, the powerbrokers and the affluent, and the forgotten souls on the park benches. I have a dream!

Let me be clear. What I have just focused on is not First Baptist, Vancouver. But it describes a vision that motivated us and defines the goal of a journey we were privileged to at least set out upon. Let me illustrate what can become possible. I think of a thankfully not untypical baptismal service. We had thirteen candidates that morning. Listen to this diversity:

- a ladies' hairdresser;
- a First Nations Crow Indian chief;
- his wife;
- a physical education teacher from North Vancouver;
- a hospital psychiatrist;
- a former call girl from our Kitsilano district;
- a mom and homemaker from Holland;
- an investment banker from Hong Kong;

- a converted biker from Aberdeen;
- a doctor from a hospital emergency department;
- an eleven-year-old school student from Hawaii;
- a science major from the University;
- and a Hungarian tightrope walker and trapeze artist!

God uses all kinds of things, and I am certainly not claiming that one size fits all as far as congregational life is concerned. God has patently blest homogeneous churches, and continues to do so today. And of course in some locations no other kind of church would be meaningful since the community within which the church functions is essentially homogeneous. I suspect however that such churches are much rarer in actual terms than is claimed, partly because, whether they like it or not, vastly increasing numbers of people in all our societies will in fact be unable to stay around only "people like us," and be forced, whether they like it or not, to be with people different from themselves; and also because, from our examination of the New Testament evidence, ethnic diversity is only one form of diversity that God is calling us to overcome in the New Humanity.

But even granted that some will be led towards a relatively homogeneous path, many will not, if we are open to hear the voice of the Spirit in our time. And as one who has walked on to, and a fair distance along, that particular road I want to come back to you with the good news: it is a great road to travel, which gets better the further you go with it, which emphatically does not inhibit the congregation's mission, but to the contrary actually expands it; which has all kinds of potential to bring healing, hope, renewal, energy, vision, maturity, and salvation in its fullest terms.

We coined a slogan at First Baptist: "Diversity is not a threat to be feared, but a gift to be celebrated." It is a gift, with wonderful potential for enrichment. Sure, there is a price. It is only possible within an environment where there is a willingness to sacrifice as well as to receive. In my later years at Vancouver I learned to say to every potential new member, thankfully the vast majority of whom came to us by baptism: "If you are looking for a church which will give you all you want, then don't join us here. But if you are looking for a church which will give you most of what you want, but also a real opportunity to grow with others who are different, and have something very important to share with you, then First Baptist is the place for you; and incidentally, you will be in great shape for heaven!" I never had a single refusal, but that process was helpful in staking out the ground on which they came to us. But is this really so special or difficult? Is this not simply the living out of believers' baptism, in which I am crucified with Christ and hence die to what pleases me, and suits me, and meets my needs first of all? And is that not where the Christian life, in New Testament times at any rate, actually started, not some high, idealistic pinnacle, to be aimed for in the distant future?

But there is something else, and surely the greatest consideration of all—the New Humanity Church is the fulfillment of a dream in the heart of God. It corresponds to, and embodies, the very purpose of God to which all things are moving, in time and into eternity, the bringing of all things, now divided, into unity under the blessed reign of Jesus Christ our Lord. Hence the New Humanity Church, as a humanly impossible but divinely generated reality, becomes a tangible witness to a Living God at work in the world. And above and beyond that, a model of the local church and its mission which has the potential to enhance directly the everlasting glory of our ever-blessed, adorable, triune God, to whom be all the worship, and the praise, and the honor, for ever and ever.

And so, sisters and brothers, I give you the New Humanity Church: a Church of the New Testament, a Church of yesterday, a Church of the *parousia,* a Church of tomorrow; and, through the gracious ministry of the Holy Spirit, a Church for today.

Bibliography

Bakke, Ray. *A Theology as Big as the City*. Leicester, UK: InterVarsity, 1997.

———. *The Urban Christian*. Leicester, UK: InterVarsity, 1987.

Barclay, William. *The Letters to the Galatians and the Ephesians*. Edinburgh: Saint Andrew's Press, 1958.

Bruce, F. F. *The Book of Acts*. New London Commentary on the New Testament. London: Marshall, Morgan and Scott, 1954.

———. *The Epistles to the Colossians, to Philemon, and to the Ephesians*. New International Commentary on the New Testament. Grand Rapids: Eerdmans, 1984.

Dray, Peter. *Globalization and the Christian Mission*. Global Connections Occasional Paper 15, Autumn 2003.

Giddens, Anthony. *Runaway World: How Globalization Is Reshaping Our Lives*. London: Profile, 1999.

Green, Michael. *Evangelism in the Early Church*. London: Hodder & Stoughton, 1970.

Held, David, et al. *Global Transformations: Politics, Economics and Culture*. Oxford: Blackwell, 1999.

Hendriksen, William. *Exposition of Ephesians*. Grand Rapids: Baker, 1967.

Hoehner, Harold W. *Ephesians: An Exegetical Commentary*. Grand Rapids: Baker, 2002.

Houlton, John. *People Under Pressure*. London: Lutterworth, 1973.

Lincoln, Andrew T. *Ephesians*. Word Biblical Commentary 42. Dallas: Word, 1990.

Mackay, John. *God's Order: The Ephesian Letter and This Present Time*. London: Nisbet, 1953.

Metzger, Bruce. *The New Testament: Its Background, Growth and Content*. Nashville: Abingdon, 1965.

Milne, Bruce. *Dynamic Diversity: Bridging Class, Age, Race and Gender in the Church*. Leicester, UK: InterVarsity, 2006.

O'Brien, Peter. *The Letter to the Ephesians*. Leicester, UK: Apollos, 1999.

Padilla, René. *Mission Between the Times*. Grand Rapids: Eerdmans, 1985.

Robertson, Roland. *Global Modernities*. London: Sage, 1995.

Simpson, E. K., and F. F. Bruce. *Commentary on the Epistles to the Ephesians and Colossians*. New International Commentary on the New Testament. London: Marshall, Morgan and Scott, 1957.

Snyder, Howard. *Earth Currents: The Struggle for the World's Soul*. Nashville: Abingdon, 1995.

Stevenson, J. *A New Eusebius: Documents Illustrating the History of the Church to AD 337*. London: SPCK, 1987.

Toffler, Alvin. *Future Shock*. London: Pan, 1970.

———. *The Third Wave*. London: Pan, 1980.

Walls, Andrew F. *The Cross-Cultural Process in Christian History: Studies in the Transmission and Appropriation of Faith*. Edinburgh: T. & T. Clark, 2004.

———. "The Ephesian Moment: At a Crossroads in Human History." Unpublished paper, http://www.anglicancommunion.org/listening/book_resources/docs/ephesian_moment.pdf.

Wright, N. T. *Paul for Everyone: Galatians and Thessalonians*. London: SPCK, 2002.

5

A Missionary Union

Past, Present, and Future Perspectives[1]

David R. Coffey

Introduction

The text of the preacher was John chapter 13 verse 27. His sermon was titled "Satanic Salesmanship." His theme was the betrayal of Judas. The content of the sermon was rich with Scripture. The aim of the preacher was to communicate the good news of the gospel. The sermon concluded with evangelistic fervor: "Jesus himself will hold out his wounded hands, and plead for their return, but they will harden their hearts and go out into the night. Blackness, when it might be glorious light; gloom when it ought to be wonderful joy. My brother, my sister when you leave this hall—will it be night or will it be light?"[2]

This was George Beasley-Murray applying to enter Spurgeon's College in 1937 and enclosing one of his sermons for the consideration of the College Council. The unfailing enthusiasm for the gospel and the passion for evangelism, which shine out from the pages of this early sermon, would characterize the life and ministry of this richly gifted servant of God until the Lord called him home on 23 February 2000.

1. This lecture was delivered at the Baptist Assembly on 29 April 2006.

2. Beasley-Murray, *Fearless for Truth*, 17–18.

I consider it an honor to be invited to give this memorial lecture for 2006 and take the opportunity at the outset to express my profound appreciation for the abiding influence that George Beasley-Murray had on my life and ministry. I first heard him preach at my home church, Union Street Kingston upon Thames, in the late 1950s, soon after he became Principal of Spurgeon's College in 1958. He was my College Principal when I was a student at Spurgeon's 1963–67 and my mentor in preaching, pastoring and opening the Scriptures for the people of God. Throughout my ministry he was an unfailing encourager, not least during my service as General Secretary of the Union which he himself had served with such distinction.

A missionary union—past present and future perspectives is the theme I would like to unfold and at the outset express the limitations of the treatment of my subject. I am well aware of the privileged position I have held during the past fifteen years and the mission insights I have gained from this service, as well as the preceding years as a member of the Baptist Union Council since 1979; President of the Baptist Union (1986–87); and Secretary for Evangelism (1988–91). I confess to being too near to the events which I have shared in and request that you receive what I now offer as a snapshot taken at this moment of time—not as a permanent record. In other words I would like to revisit the past with the benefit of hindsight and careful reflection.

Kierkegaard is right, "Life is lived forwards but understood backwards" and I need a longer time to view through the rear mirror. So these are current reflections on an exhilarating journey. But remember, it is a journey.

I remember Donald English once sharing with me that trifocal vision is exhilarating if you can manage it! Look back, he said, because if we jettison history, the present becomes distorted; look around, because if we neglect the present, life becomes illusory; look ahead, because if we ignore the future, hope loses its meaning. So wearing the trifocals, let's begin with a backward look.

This Union was birthed in a climate of dynamic mission enterprise. My look back is through the scholarship lens of the late Dr. Leonard Champion, and the studies he contributed to the *Baptist Quarterly*[3] in the early 1980s. In one article he suggested that the most instructive period in Baptist history, which offers the most potential for a living

3. Champion, "Evangelical Calvinism," 196–208.

relationship with the present, is the half-century between 1775 and 1825. It was during this period that the Baptist Missionary Society was founded, as well as the Bible Society, the Baptist Union and a number of Baptist colleges.

In his articles, Dr. Champion cites the work of Clyde Binfield on English nonconformity, *So down to Prayer,* which suggests that the influence of the evangelical movements of the eighteenth century led to a revaluation of mission, a reassessment of organization and a review of doctrine. Dr. Champion indicated that these three elements are essential features of our own era, but suggested a different order: He said that "a renewed theology leads to a rediscovery of mission and the creation of organizations for the fulfillment of mission." Champion then makes two further points. This renewal of theology in the late 18th and early 19th centuries was marked not only by clarity and coherence but also by an intimate association with a living experience of Christ. There was the conviction that the personal experience of God's grace was a lively thing to be shared. The second factor was that those who formulated a renewed theology rediscovered a mission impulse and created organizations for the fulfillment of this mission. They were not only deeply devoted to the cause of Christ, but were renowned for their warm and unfailing trust in one another. Modern-day relating and resourcing has deep roots in our Baptist history.

The central character in this period was, without doubt, Andrew Fuller. As Peter Morden reminds us, Fuller's career and the revival of eighteenth-century Particular Baptist life are inextricably intertwined. "The revitalization of the churches which took place was highly significant and it is no exaggeration to say that the Particular Baptists were transformed from an inward-looking denomination in decline, to one that was confident, outward-looking and missionary minded."[4] But we need the sober reminder that revitalization of missionary endeavor does not last for ever. William J. Abraham's assessment of renewal in general suggests that in the long and ragged history of the Church, (missiological) renewal has never been comprehensive. "It has been patchy, partial, scattered, disorganized and volatile and it has rarely lasted more than a couple of generations. . . . There is no 'big bang' that will solve all our problems; there is no spiritual hurricane that will sweep in off the coast and blow evil away; there is no spiritual vaccine that will prevent the

4. Morden, *Offering Christ to the World*, 184–86.

arrival of new viruses; there is no new messianic figure waiting in the wings to lead us to earthly glory. . . . We must embrace a persistent repentance and a sober optimism in the face of God's final judgment and ultimate transformation of creation."[5]

The life of the Union in the twentieth century bears out this gloomy observation. Whenever I consult Ian Randall's brilliantly concise twentieth century history of the English Baptists,[6] I discover there are recurring themes in his chapter headings. The most striking features of these themes is the long missionary journey of the Union as it faced the perpetual challenge of relevant mission and evangelism in each decade of the last century. There was a constant need for the life of the Union to be refreshed and renewed in the *missio Dei* and, in almost each decade, fresh initiatives needed to be birthed.

In the decades I have served as a minister, let me briefly mention a few of the major mission initiatives which I suggest influenced parts of the Union. As I began my ministry in the late 1960s, *One Step Forward* and *Evangelism Explosion* training programs were beginning to have a major impact on some Baptist churches; some pastors were studying the principles of the Church Growth movement through the writings of Peter Wagner and Donald McGavran; at national level, concern was being expressed about the numerical and spiritual decline in the Union, culminating in the report *Signs of Hope* which was produced in 1979 and recorded a decline in membership from 1952 to 1977. While the Commission which produced the report was concerned about churches "closed in outlook," they concluded that "there does seem to be . . . an unwillingness to be bound by precedent, and a new concern to proclaim the eternal gospel in terms relevant to the contemporary scene and a greater willingness to serve the need of the community in the name of Christ."[7]

At the end of the 1970s, *The Nationwide Initiative in Evangelism (NIE)* was born under the inspiring leadership of Donald English. At the Nottingham *NIE* Assembly in September 1980 over 900 participants were present (5 percent Anglicans, 12 percent Methodist, 11 percent Baptists, 4 percent Catholics, etc). But in spite of some significant achievements (including united prayer, shared evangelism, special inter-

5. Abraham, *The Logic of Renewal*, 154–55.

6. Randall, *The English Baptists of the Twentieth Century.*

7. Baptist Union of Great Britain, *Signs of Hope*, 44.

est groups looking at the urban poor, unemployment and other faiths) the *NIE* floundered as a movement and officially closed in 1983. The *Action in Mission* program sponsored by the Baptist Union was brought into being during the middle of the decade as a response to *Signs of Hope*. By the beginning of the 1990s AIM had the support of about one third of churches in BUGB.[8]

The 1990s brought the *Decade of Evangelism* and within this there was a renewed emphasis on church planting spearheaded by the *Challenge 2000* initiative which advocated tracked and co-ordinated church planting.[9] As a Union, we shared in the national conferences on church planting and endorsed the general emphasis, but during this period we resisted the call to set targets for the Union to be achieved by the year 2000. As Stuart Murray Williams notes, it was evident by 1996 that enthusiasm was flagging and planting was slowing down.

Church planting was harder than had been anticipated, took longer than envisaged and "inadequate attention had been given to how newly planted churches would mature. . . . and there were simply not enough leaders with the skills, experience and training needed for church planting."[10]

During the same decade we saw the emergence of *Alpha*, *Willow Creek*, *Emmaus* and *Cell Church* as programmatic contributions to shaping the missionary congregation and it was obvious by the attendance at conferences that the former two in particular were making a major impact on local Baptist churches. The new millennium opened with greater numbers of local churches committed to either *Alpha* or *Emmaus* and there was a fresh interest in the new program from the ministry of Rick Warren and the Saddleback Community Church, *Purpose Driven Church*. In recent years it is most encouraging that many of our Baptist young people have been caught up into the *Soul Survivor* conferences and *Soul in the City* initiatives, both of which have a strong mission emphasis.

Other Baptists caught a vision for the long term regeneration of communities in partnership with voluntary organizations, with funding from local and national government. They rediscovered the gospel principle that you cannot change lives without transforming communities

8. Baptist Union of Great Britain.

9. Williams, *Changing Mission*, 19.

10. Ibid., 21.

and Baptists have provided some leading practitioners in this field of the regeneration of urban church. The contribution of Terry Jones as the BUGB Urban Mission Adviser has been immensely valuable, drawing on his experience in Toxteth, Liverpool. There has also been an increasing interest in a renewed understanding of community and a recovery of the rich Celtic traditions that refresh worship and community, mission and discipleship.

It has been said that you can tell where a local minister lays their emphasis by where they spend their sabbaticals! Is it Saddleback California; Toronto Canada; Willowcreek Chicago; Fuller Seminary Los Angeles; Northumbria Community; Iona or Taizé; Toxteth Liverpool; St. Thomas Crookes Sheffield? I suggest that our unique emphasis as a Union during this decade of the nineties was to embark on a program of structural reforms that would position us to be shaped by God for his missionary purposes. As we shared and listened to one another in honest consultations it became obvious that many local churches had lost touch with whole cultures within their community and, more seriously, many Christians had lost their nerve to share the good news of the gospel with these "alien" people groups and cultures which have emerged in the last twenty years. It was also apparent in these consultations that many churches wanted to belong to a mission-shaped Union and they were prepared to make a new journey of partnership with their regional association.

As the reform program emerged from the Denominational Consultation of 1996 we saw the signs of a Union willing to be re-imagined for God's missionary purposes:

- *Five Core Values* was our commitment to the gospel and our desire for a renewed passion for God's story
- *Covenant 21* was our commitment to the Church and our desire for meaningful covenant relationships that last the distance
- The creation of our *Mentoring and appraisal program* for ministers was a commitment to life-long learning and constant formation of the missionary pastor
- The reconfiguration of the *Mission Department* to include a network of research training and development was our commitment to thoughtful mission in a complex world. The

Mission Leaders' Network has proved to be a valuable source for the sharing of good practice and I believe the best years are yet to come for this network

- The inclusion of *Evangelists* on the BUGB register of covenanted persons accredited for ministry, was a long overdue recognition of God's gift of equipping the whole church to engage in the task of winning the lost for Christ
- The reconfiguring of *Association teams* was our commitment to bringing mission consultation nearer to the local church.
- The appointment of a *BUGB Racial Justice Co-ordinator* to the Mission department staff is a sign that we are committed as a Union to the multicultural imperative of the gospel
- The recent report of the BUGB *Financial Review Group* reveals a rich financial resource within the Union, admittedly unevenly distributed across the associations, but posing clearly the question "how are we going to deploy our resources for mission?"

In all these significant developments, the commitments we made at the *Wembley Leaders' Day* of 1999 are a reminder of the spiritual dynamic which must inspire all our structural reforms.

There are many more signs of imaginative changes of emphasis which have flowed from this commitment to a long term re-imagining of mission within the life of BUGB. The emphasis on Regional Ministers being trained and equipped for trans-local leadership is a further positive sign. We have assumed a competency for missional leadership when transferring from the local to the regional or the national and I am encouraged that within the next eighteen months we should have a Master's course available for those who are called among us to trans-local leadership. The Union has twice at the annual Assembly (1989 and 1995) committed itself to ecumenical membership with the new national instruments and the potential of creative mission partnerships with member denominations. For all the good work of the CTE Group for Evangelization and the CTBI *Building Bridges of Hope* program (where a succession of Baptists have served with distinction), I share with others a sense of frustration at the lack of progress of all the British churches becoming "united in mission." Those who represent BUGB in the ecumenical structures have worked to move the debate from traditional questions like "who is a true minister?" and "who presides at the Eucharist?" to more mission-focused questions like "how do we proclaim the Kingdom of God in a secular society?" and "how do we engage in God's mission in an alien culture?"

This brief review brings us to the present day and an assessment of what has been accomplished through all this enterprise.

I believe mission is more a heartbeat than a headache for the majority of our churches. I discern that there are many things to encourage, and good mission practice is in place. I observe healthy relationships in renewed associations with local churches. But I also recognize there are danger signs and warnings we need to heed with great seriousness if we are to see some long-lasting fruitful outcomes to our journey of missiological reform as a Union. I discern that the English Church overall is in deep trouble with persistent decline, serious denominational disintegration and social marginalization, and statistically there are warning signs that BUGB needs to note.

When Keith Jones and I began our service with the Union in 1991, you may recall we decided to commence with some Listening Days. We met over three thousand representative Baptists over a period of six months and heard the views of the grassroots. These were invaluable occasions and I was reminded of the importance of "keeping your ear to the ground" when I read recently the speech that Winston Churchill made to the House of Commons in September 1941: "I have heard it said that leaders should keep their ears to the ground. All I can say is that the British nation will find it very hard to look up to the leaders who are detected in that somewhat ungainly posture. Nothing is more dangerous than to live in the temperamental atmosphere of a Gallup Poll—always feeling one's pulse and taking one's temperature."

Whatever Churchill had in mind, we do need occasionally to take the pulse and temperature, and that includes reviewing statistics. I suspect that the published results of the 2005 English Church Census will reveal a further decline in membership for the Baptist Union. For the English churches as a whole, in 1979 12 percent of the population went to church; this declined to 10 percent in 1989 and 7.5 percent in 1998; this is likely to decrease to 6.3 percent in 2005 which is 3.7 million people, and the projected figure for 2015 will likely bring that number down to 2.4 million of the population as regular church goers.[11] In the year 2000 it was estimated that Baptists had seen an 11 percent decline in membership over the decade. Last year we saw an increase in membership from 140,918 in 2003 to 141,584 in 2004 following a 9 percent increase in 2002. Baptisms have also been rising year on year: in 1998 there were 3853, in 2003 there were 4844 and in 2004 there were 4995. I recognize that much of this growth is in the Black Majority churches in London, but it is still an encouraging trend in the face of general decline. Strangely, our 2003 attendance figure was a 20 percent increase over 1998 and we saw a 26 percent increase in baptisms over the same period of 1998–2003. It would seem it is our inability to attract a committed membership to the local church that is the most challenging statistic.

Where have all the children gone? is the report prepared for the Baptist Union Council last November. This revealed there had been a dramatic decline in the number of children attending Baptist Sunday Schools. The apparent loss of thirty thousand children in only two years prompted the BUGB Council to call for a day of prayer in June, and the Mission Department was invited to initiate a program of research into the reasons and remedies for the decline.

I have just concluded my final tour of the regional associations as General Secretary and in every part of the country there are stories of encouragement and mission enterprise. There are new mission initiatives and exciting partnerships, but more than one association reported that roughly one-third of their churches were growing; one-third were declining; and one-third were static. How does a Union of autonomous churches encourage life and growth in those situations of decline? How do we encourage a greater partnership with churches that become stuck in a mission mind-set that is no longer relevant of the needs of their community?

The statistics also tell us that the 25 percent of Baptist churches that grew in the 1990s would style themselves as evangelical. It would be worth examining whether the program of *Willow Creek, Purpose Driven Church* and *Alpha* have been sufficient to offset sharp decline in some churches, or whether all our churches, including those which have followed these programs, are facing fundamental questions about mission practice. I suspect that the benefits of spiritual renewal, which manifestly have emerged from these valued programs, have not always

11. Brierley, *English Church Census.*

spawned the necessary break-through into creative mission and evangelism which brings the local church in touch with a growing number of unreached people groups.

Having noted the encouragements, I suggest there are warning signs for BUGB, and a missionary Union will do well to pause and ask: Is it business as usual for day to day mission? Do we continue consolidating the reforms we have put in place? Is it the time for further radical revisions? Or is it both?

William Abraham has suggested that "not every age or every time is a time for renewal. There are also seasons of consolidation (when) spiritual and theological gains have to be exploited and explored. New experiences need to be examined and evaluated."[12] There are those who suggest that we need no more changes or reforms to the life of the Union for the time being; this is a time for patient consolidation of the reforms in which we have invested, and our gains need to be "exploited and explored."

The consolidation argument is confirmed by the observation of David Bosch that "new paradigms do not establish themselves overnight. They take decades, even centuries, to develop distinctive contours." This underlines the constant emphasis we have made on this journey of denominational reform: that a missionary Union needs to focus on generational change. But Bosch also comments on the value of "thinking and working in terms of two paradigms."[13] You simultaneously conserve the gains you have made and re-imagine a new future. Rowan Williams uses the phrase "mixed economy" which is also helpful. By this he means that the whole Church, old and new, inherited and emerging, should be shaped for mission. My own conviction is we are still living through one of the most intriguing and challenging periods of Church history and I agree with those who describe this era for the British church as a *kairos* moment—what Rowan Williams calls a "thickening of the plot," when a number of things are coming together that will pave the way for the *kairos* moment, God's special moment.[14]

If we care for the future of our missionary Union then we will look down the road and make hard choices, so with my long distance glasses I suggest the following markers for the future of a missionary Union.

12. Abraham, *The Logic of Renewal*, 6.

13. Bosch, *Transforming Mission*, 349.

14. Bayes, *Mission-Shaped Church*, 5.

These features are not totally new but may be seen as a reconfiguration of existing emphases:

The First Mark of a Missionary Union Is That It Knows the Vital Place of Prayer

It is intuitively aware that the hope of the Church is rekindled by turning to God and the *missio Dei*. It is from this basic action that we gain a clear perspective on the world and God's commitment to the world. William Shenk reminds us that "this perspective gains in power only when it is attuned to the appointed time, of God's *kairos*. It means that through prayer we read our times through God's eyes and then respond out of passion for the world. Otherwise we will be engulfed in the prevailing despair."[15]

Recently I was invited to do some studies in the Acts of the Apostles and I was reminded again of the dynamic link between Pentecost and Mission. The early church had a strong sense of the leadership of the Holy Spirit in the mission of the church, and Acts declares the finger of God as the force behind the expansion of their missionary movement. I value those recurring phrases in Acts: "the Lord added to the church" and "the hand of the Lord was with them." David Edwards captures it when he says: "In the Acts of the Apostles the Holy Spirit destroys shyness."

When I was preparing for the Wembley Leaders' Day in 1999, I was drawn to Isaiah 35 and the vision of salvation depicted by the prophet. He describes salvation as rescue for those who are helpless. The people are described as blind, deaf, lame and dumb, which is a reminder of the absolute helplessness of the human condition. You will recall that in the late 1700s it was the custom of the pastors in the Northamptonshire Baptist Association to meet periodically for prayer and fasting. These were ministers clustering together, relating and resourcing each other, concerned for the renewal of the church and its mission to the whole world. John Ryland wrote in his diary in January 1788, four years before the founding of the BMS: "Brothers Fuller, Sutcliffe, Carey and I kept this day as a private fast. Our chief design was to implore a revival in the power of godliness in our souls in our churches and in the land at

15. Shenk, *Write the Vision*, 80.

large." People only pray like this when they see the helplessness of their condition.

I remember reading a challenging letter from Carl Jung to a Christian woman. In his letter to her he said: "I admire you Christians because when you see somebody hungry and thirsty you see Jesus. When you see someone in prison or hospital you see Jesus. When you see a stranger you see Jesus. What I don't understand is that you do not see Jesus in your own brokenness. Why are the poor always outside of you? Can't you see within your own poverty?"

Prayer enables us to see this "poverty within" and prompts the need for a personal transformation before we are sent out by the King as his ambassadors for reconciliation. Many, many times I have said over these denominational reforms what I have said over the local church of which I was pastor: "Lord, this situation needs your touch of power." I believe that in this "*kairos*" time we should be praying to the Lord to come and save us. Ask that, in his mercy, he would come to us as a Baptist Union, as a local church, as a college, as an association, and plead for his gracious power to transform us as a missionary people.

The Second Mark of a Missionary Union Is It Will Be Open to Be Renewed in Its Mission Imagination

When it comes to the renewal of the mission imagination, we need to observe the new child on the block that is Emerging Church, and we need to listen with great care to this new phenomenon. I see this as an Acts 11 moment for the Baptist Union. We are like the Jerusalem Church of the first century faced with the rumors emerging out of "new church" Antioch. Emerging Church in its multifarious forms is brand new and we have not seen anything like it in the preceding decades. We are uncertain what to call it; we find it difficult as a centrally organized denomination to get a handle on something that is so fluid and seemingly spontaneous; and we are reserved about criticizing something we have not truly encountered from the inside—it is a classic Acts 11 situation!

Gibbs and Bolger suggest "in many ways Emerging Church is a fragile movement that can be marginalized by denominational leaders and killed with criticism by theological power brokers. Whatever reservations people may have, these new voices need to be heard. Many of these innovative leaders are looking for mentors rather than critics."[16]

16. Gibbs and Bolger, *Emerging Churches*, 29.

What I find refreshing about Emerging Church is their attempt to read and understand contemporary culture and their desire to take church culturally closer to people. My nephew and his wife are members of the pub church *Bar None* that is based in Cardiff. They say "The aim is to plant ourselves back into the heart of the community, to bar none that are looking for answers or a place to ask questions. Pubs by definition are public space, they feel inhabitable and unpretentious, a quality not always shared by churches."[17] I agree when they suggest we have an overemphasized focus on a "come structure" for church activities. As Andrew Jones of Boaz UK says: "The church should happen in *their* house rather than *our* house."[18] I appreciate the high emphasis on true community and the desire to transform the secular realm. I also think Emerging Church is right to challenge inherited church as to whether we have been living the wrong story. Have we been more concerned with what form the church takes, rather than asking what life Jesus is asking us to live?

From a critically affirming position I am not suggesting that Emerging Church holds all the answers but I think they are posing some highly relevant questions for inherited church. Equally, Emerging Church must be open to the kind of questions Stuart Murray poses:

- Have they the capacity to sustain faith and discipleship beyond one generation, and be reproducible beyond particular examples?
- Have they the capacity to reach the pre-churched and anti-churched as well as the de-churched, semi-churched and post-churched?
- Are they angst-ridden communities of like-minded dissidents united by discontent rather than transforming vision?
- Or are they forerunners of a great movement of missional creativity that will negotiate the journey of the church to a promised land of mission fruitfulness?[19]

Stuart Murray Williams is probably right to suggest that the way forward lies neither with inherited or emerging forms of church, but

17. Williams, *Changing Mission*, 64.

18. Gibbs and Bolger, *Emerging Churches*, 51.

19. Williams, *Changing Mission*, 122.

a symbiotic relationship between these.[20] "Emerging churches need the accumulated wisdom of inherited churches: inherited churches need the stimulus of emerging churches."[21] Emerging Church is tentative and experimental but we should be grateful for their pioneering work, and I hope we can continue to support such pioneering mission through Home Mission projects like "Church from Scratch," and I also suggest that the Union is well-placed to facilitate the kind of mutually helpful conversations that are suggested by Stuart Murray Williams.

The Third Mark of a Missionary Union Is It Will Build Capacity to Create Conversations in a Civil Square

If one of our theological tasks is always to penetrate as deeply as possible into the great existential questions that hang over culture, then I agree with Wilbert Shenk that to be credible "evangelization must engage a culture intellectually, socially, politically and personally (experientially)." Shenk is right to suggest that, "The church is most at risk where it has been present in a culture for a long period of time so that it no longer conceives its relation to culture in terms of a missionary encounter. The church remains socially and salvifically relevant only so long as it is in redemptive tension with culture."[22]

The same question was posed to three men of God: when does life begin? The Roman Catholic priest said "at the moment of conception"; the Anglican said "when the child is born"; the rabbi said "life begins when the children leave home, are married, the dog has died and the mortgage paid." Would that the life questions were as easily answered!

This cultural engagement is a part of our missionary Union that has become increasingly important to our witness and has taken on some urgency in the light of rapid social and cultural changes. It seems that almost monthly at our Didcot offices we are faced with a new set of issues and we are invited as a Union to give a Baptist perspective on issues such as abortion and euthanasia reform; Church and Nation and the future of the monarchy; welfare reform and the plight of single parents; child poverty; relations with other faith traditions; faith schools and government funding; the Equality Act and its implications for the staffing of

20. Ibid., 3.

21. Ibid., 136.

22. Shenk, *Write the Vision*, 48.

Christian organizations; civil partnerships and the local church; Asylum and Immigration polices; the future of the Trident missile program; human trafficking; environmental issues and the care of creation. The list is impressively endless and all credit to my staff colleagues who manage this flow of information on our behalf, with some excellent partnership with our ecumenical colleagues.

We can ignore these challenges and say this is not a priority either for the Union or the local church. That is not an option in mission values, because you do not evangelize a culture by turning your back on the culture. We need to face the challenge and hear the voices and cultivate a response in which all can participate, and not just in the sharing of knowledge. Local pastors need to be equipped and resourced to bring a greater prophetic edge to their preaching—equipping church members for their mission encounters in the world of work.

I am convinced that we need to respond more creatively to these unspoken invitations to a public conversation. Nigel Wright offers a clue to this conversational approach when he suggests that "we should deal with people on the ground of a common humanity. If other people are estimated on the basis of whether or not they are Christians, we are likely to end up dividing humanity into tribal camps. All people are made of one; they are made in the divine image and exist as persons. . . . We should deal with people on the basis of our common questions rather than our differing answers."[23]

So what are some of these common questions?

It is a common question for *faith and science*, when *The New Statesman* warns in an editorial on faith schools against the dangers of subsidizing bigotry. Children deserve the broadest possible access to ideas. Further, faith schools may have a tendency to "ghettoize" communities, and they may teach as fact notions with no foundations in science or history, without supplying the equipment to evaluate those notions critically." Polly Toynbee adds spice to this common question in an article in *The Guardian* suggesting that "the teaching of creationism is a clash of civilizations, not between Islam and Christianity, but between reason and superstition."[24]

It is a common question for *relations with other faith traditions* when, following the publication of the cartoons of Muhammad in a

23. Wright, *The Radical Evangelical*, 130.

24. *The Guardian*, 14 April, 2006.

Danish newspaper subsequently reprinted in a French newspaper, 86% of British people felt the Muslim reaction, or part of the Muslim reaction, was a "gross over-reaction." Muslims in the West still feel they are at a disadvantage. We can, if we choose, think of Islam as strong, menacing, and terrifying. Interestingly, many Muslims in the United Kingdom largely think of themselves as marginalized and ridiculed for their faith. This present time constitutes a critical context for Christian Muslim relations. It is fraught with the danger of distrust, division and destruction. This is a major common question for all of us. A recent Church of England report suggests that the question facing us is not simply: "How can we live and work together as different communities in our society?" rather, "How do we understand and relate to one another in the purposes of God?"[25]

It is a common question for the *veracity of the Gospel records* when Dan Brown's *The Da Vinci Code* is a runaway bestseller and the writer claims as fact that Jesus Christ was married to Mary Magdalene.

It is a common question for *spirituality* when Noel Edmonds says he has become a follower of a book called Cosmic Ordering Service that claims to help you realize all your dreams. He claims that four of his life wishes have already come true.

It is a common question for *human sexuality*, when the culture assumes you cannot be a whole and healthy person unless you are having sex. There is a great line in the film *Vanilla Sky* when Cameron Diaz says to Tom Cruise: "don't you know that when you sleep with someone, your body makes a promise whether you do or not?"

It is a common question for *racial justice*, when the National Front launches a website termed the "Christian Council of Great Britain" stating that the Council is a non-denominational, non-proselytizing body of Christian men and women who have come together to ensure a healthy future for Christians in Britain.

It is a common question for our *religious divisions*, when there is still a Belfast cemetery with a dividing wall separating Protestants and Catholics. The dividing wall goes nine feet underground. These deep "underground walls" which are present in Israel and Palestine and Iraq and many places of the world provide the most urgent of common questions: How do faith communities live with their deepest differences? So how do we respond to these common questions? What part does evan-

25. Archbishop's Council, *Archbishop of Canterbury's Listening Initiative*.

gelization play in encouraging all citizens to ask questions about their culture? I like the way Os Guinness distinguishes between a sacred public square, a naked public square and a civil public square. Sacred square is limited to one dominant religion—Catholic, Orthodox, Protestant, Jewish or Muslim. This is clearly unjust and unworkable because only the established faith has freedom to enter the square. The naked square is where all faiths are rigorously excluded so the public square is totally secular and faith is privatized. The civil square is where people of all faiths share the opportunity, based on religious liberty, to enter an engaged public life on the basis of their faith. This means that a right for a Christian is a right for a Muslim, is a right for a Jew, and is a right for an atheist and a believer of any faith under the sun. "This is not a civil religion: it's what is called a public philosophy . . . we work at building the important things that allow us a robust but civil public debate that doesn't blow us out of the water. So that diversity becomes a matter of richness and strength and not a source of division and conflict."[26]

The Fourth Mark of the Missionary Union Is Its Ability to Foster and Sustain Thoughtful Evangelism

When I was researching for material on the Emerging Church I was surprised and concerned at the genuine antagonism there was to the concept of evangelism. In the interviews conducted by Gibbs and Bolger for their work on Emerging Churches they were given some candid interviews. One leader confessed "that our evangelism is pretty poor. The word barely gets mentioned. Everyone who has become a Christian here has done so through friendships. The people are very cynical about any evangelistic techniques. My own vision is to simply put people, the people of God, out there in the market place and hope that we live a life that attracts people to God. That is the hardest option of all because it is 24–7 evangelism."[27]

Another leader said "evangelism or mission for me is no longer about persuading people to believe what I believe . . . it is more about shared experiences and encounters."[28] Gibbs and Bolger comment that "Emerging churches have a strong desire to distance themselves from

26. Guinness, "Living With Our Deepest Differences," 18–19.

27. Gibbs and Bolger, *Emerging Churches*, 130.

28. Ibid., 31.

the prevailing models of evangelism which they regard as intrusive and manipulative. They seek to work alongside from a position of respect and concern for the whole person. Evangelization is not a hit and run activity but one that entails a long-term commitment."[29]

Michael Paul Gallagher says a great deal of energy can be expended on external trends such as a decline in church going, but it misses the crucial question behind the statistics of religious decline—what is happening to people's spiritual imagination? "If there has been a rapid loss of cultural roots in religion, especially in the younger generation, this constitutes not only a faith crisis of concern for the Church, but an anthropological crisis of concern to anyone who realizes how the loss of such anchors can leave people adrift."[30] He names three wounds that affect the humanity of people: a wounded imagination, a wounded memory and a wounded sense of belonging. In spiritual terms the avenues to faith have become blocked. "In this light, our preaching may need a more aggressive discernment of the assumptions of contemporary culture. This does not mean moaning or denouncing, but offering an intelligent Christian critique of the market-driven images that are around and of the human damage they can do."

I have recent argued for "The big ears church," a church which is attuned to a listening evangelism because the facts speak for themselves.[31] Greater numbers of the population are becoming interested in spirituality. In Alan Billings' phrase, "People may lead more secular lives but they retain sacred hearts."[32] The research of David Hay and Kate Hunt[33] compared a poll of 1987 with the BBC's *Soul of Britain* survey of 2000. This revealed a dramatic increase in people admitting to an awareness of religious or spiritual experience, including an awareness of the presence of God (41 percent increase), awareness of prayer being answered (48 percent increase), and awareness of an evil presence (108 percent increase). David Hay has been researching religious or spiritual experience for more than twenty-five years and he maintains that spiritual awareness is "hard-wired" into every human being. In the language of

29. Ibid., 153.

30. *The Tablet,* September 10, 2005.

31. *Transform,* Winter 2005 (BUGB).

32. Billings, *Secular Lives, Sacred Hearts,* 37.

33. Hay and Hunt, *Understanding the Spirituality.*

Ecclesiastes, "God has set eternity in the hearts of people, but they cannot fathom what God has done from beginning to end" (3:11).

In an attempt to understand the spirituality of people outside the churches, the *Beyond the Fringe* research project of 2003 asked the question of a range of people: "If there is one big question you would like answered, what would it be?" Those who responded had six particular areas of interest, "big questions" to which they wanted answers: Destiny—what happens after we die? Purpose—what is the point of life? The universe—how did it start? God—does he exist?; Spiritual realm—does it have any relevance to my life? Suffering—why is there so much in the world? We may feel confident to offer answers to the questions, but the sobering punch line from the research project says: "There was little sense that answers to these big questions were to be found in the Church or the Christian message (at least as respondents understood it) and there was a general feeling that Christianity was irrelevant to the questions people were asking."[34]

We have been on a missionary journey as a Union for many years and it is deeply encouraging to see how many churches are re-imagining their church program and their buildings in order to be a mission-shaped congregation. But there is a growing awareness that for all the engagement we have as churches with sometimes thousands of people in our local community, through pre-school groups and luncheon clubs and day centers, we need to face up to how we can be more overtly evangelistic in a spiritual age. We may be serving with integrity without strings attached—but where does evangelism come in? One way is to strengthen our listening skills in order to improve our speaking skills. This is one of the insights proposed by Stephen Croft. [35] He suggests that evangelism is normally equated with something to say. Instead he suggests, "before we speak, we first need to listen." We need to attend carefully to the spiritual experiences people are having and see the world through their eyes. Croft reminds us of the three levels of listening in evangelism: I listen in order to gain the right to speak; I listen in order to tailor my message to what you say; I listen in order to learn from your wisdom and insight.

I accept the admonition of Nigel Wright that we have failed as a Union to capitalize on an evangelistic imperative at the heart of a na-

34. Spencer et al., *Evangelism in a Spiritual Age*, 18.

35. Ibid., 132ff.

tional strategy for mission and he is right to draw attention to the Baptist Union Declaration of Principle, where the final statement reads: "that it is the duty of every disciple to bear personal witness to the gospel of Jesus Christ and to take part in the evangelization of the world." We *are* most truly ourselves when we are an evangelistic people bearing witness to the truth and the salvation that are in Jesus Christ. Of all the mission imperatives that are laid upon us, evangelism is at the top. I agree with Nigel when he says "it will be a tragic waste of time and effort if, after all the reforming processes, we were no further forward in delivering a concentrated way of focused evangelism.'[36]

The Fifth Mark of a Missionary Union Is a Commitment to Intentional Discipleship

Last year Channel 4 broadcast a documentary *Hallowed be thy Game.* The presenter, Mark Dowd, suggested that the national game of soccer has become a modern day religion. There is the repetitive chanting and the well-known "hymns" which are sung on the terraces; the frequent signs of the cross made by a number of players when they come on to the pitch; the regular sight of spectators with their hands clasped in what looks like a prayer to the Almighty. More profoundly, advocates of the "football as religion" way of thinking point out that many individuals in a secular society now shape the whole of their lives around their club. There was a chilling scene in the documentary when Dowd approached a group of youngsters outside the Reebok Stadium before Bolton's home match with Manchester United. Presenting them with an empty circle that denoted the whole of their lives' values, he asked them to shade in how much of it is governed by football. One after the other they colored in the empty circle: none of them less than fifty percent, and the majority filling in most, if not all, of the circle.[37]

If we have been asking how you evangelize in a culture that is inherently hedonistic and idolatrous, it is as urgent a question to ask how you practice a deep-life shaping discipleship. David Bosch suggests that people want to enjoy their football matches, rock festivals, television programs, holidays and parties, all of which they "deserve" after a hard day's work. "Sacrifice, asceticism, modesty, self-discipline and the

36. Wright, *New Baptists, New Agenda*, 94–95.

37. See Dowd, "For the Love of the Game."

like are not popular virtues. Much of this has entered our churches, tangible in the prosperity gospel, more effectively camouflaged in mainline churches but present there as well. We all crave for an acceptance in our culture and for a well-defined role within. . . . We have to communicate an alternative culture to our contemporaries."[38] I think the new monasticism has much to teach us at this point. It has been inspiring to see the impact Roy Searle has had during his presidency and how he has introduced even more people to the rich life ministry of the Northumbria Community. I honor the work of the St. Thomas Philadelphia congregation in Sheffield and in particular their life shapes program within The Order of Mission that has emerged out of the fellowship at St. Thomas Crookes Sheffield. They practice the recalibrating of disciples for a missionary environment. They recognize that if we are to develop Christ-like characters we need intentional discipleship in a community context of values based on simplicity, purity and accountability.

William Abraham says the ministry of making disciples is not just a moral imperative, it is a *missionary* imperative. Hosts of people struggle with the life of discipleship because of the incompetence of the church in the art of making disciples. He talks about the intrinsic grammar of initiation and the richness and many-sidedness of initiating disciples into the faith, and illustrates this in the following way:

> If we focus merely on the gospel at the expense of the rest, we will have Christians who never get beyond the first steps of Christian existence. If we focus on the moral and ignore the intellectual, we shall have activists who can make little or no sense of the content of Christian doctrine. If we focus on the intellectual and ignore the moral we shall have legions of dead orthodox on our hands. If we attend only to the importance of church membership and the spiritual disciplines, we shall have nominal Christianity in abundance. If we concentrate only on the richness of Christian experience but ignore the intellectual challenges represented by queries about the rationality of the faith, we shall end with superficial and irrelevant enthusiasts unable to give a reason for the hope that is within them. If we focus only on queries about reflective rationality we shall have networks of eggheads cut off from the treasures of the tradition and deprived of the epistemic practices of the church.[39]

38. Bosch, *Believing in the Future*, 57.

39. Abraham, "On Making Disciples," 65–66.

This is the demanding task of making disciples.

The Sixth Mark of the Missionary Union Is the Recognition and Encouragement of Apostolic Leadership

This sixth mark of a missionary union is the one I feel most passion about because in one sense all that has preceded hinges on this. Alan Roxburgh captures it for me when he says: "Discipling and equipping require a leadership that demonstrates encounter with the culture in action. In days ahead, the gown of the scholar must be replaced with the shoes of the apostle. This is not to diminish the importance of intellectual engagement, but it is a call for a shift of paradigm towards contextual engagement with the culture. Pastor as apostle, is foundational to all other functions."[40]

We need to continue working as a Union until we are truly *reconstituted as an apostolic people.* For this to happen, we need to heighten the profile of the apostolic calling and yearn for an increasing number of expressions of the apostolic church. Most Baptists have an understanding of the apostolic calling. In their best moments they know their calling is not to take the mission out, but to go and meet the mission of God already there. Our problem is we see so many changes in the world around that we become overwhelmed by the strangeness of the cultures growing up around us, and lack the faith to believe that God is present in these alien cultures. History teaches us that when the world around us is changing this constitutes a new calling from the Missionary God because God's loving heart for our needy world never changes. But we need help if we are going to reconstitute ourselves as an apostolic people, and for this God raises up apostolic leadership. The distinguishing mark of apostolic leadership is that it refuses to domesticate the gospel. It should challenge the churches of our Union with the clarion call: "Don't domesticate the ministry!" We need pastors who are prepared to don the shoes of the apostle and walk the streets.

For a long time, I have been suggesting a modest change in our BUGB practice which could be pioneered by pastors and regional ministry teams. This would mean that when a minister receives the call to a new church and a starting date is agreed, the minister moves into the new manse and begins to receive a salary from the church; but the

40. Roxburgh, *The Missionary Congregation.*

start of their public ministry of preaching, leading and pastoring in the church is delayed by up to three months. During the three months, they are encouraged to immerse themselves in the community where their church is located. They walk the streets and meet people. They visit the statutory and voluntary agencies who are present or potential partners of the church. They attend the meeting places where people gather in that community. They read—they listen—they observe. They note the languages and learn the traditions of this community. They soak themselves in the cultures of the community which is to be their home for the years ahead. During this period they share with a translocal apostolic leadership which visits them on site and prayer-walks the streets of the community.

At the end of this period of contextualization they are ready for the induction service. Invitations to the induction are sent to all the community leaders who have been visited in the preceding weeks, as well as to the usual ecumenical guests. For the first few weeks the pastor's sermons are based on sharing with the congregation the sights and sounds and experiences they have had in the community. It is making the point to the membership that this minister is not for domestication.

I share this idea to provide an example of where the BUGB must break some of the current moulds of ministerial practice which might do everything to negate the formation of the missionary pastor. An apostolic church has a commitment to practice the apostolic mission and it is the kiss of death for any community when the church domesticates the ministry and minimizes the apostolic calling. I also think that by creating an induction and orientation program we might see more ministers offering for some of the tough places of ministry which are bypassed because pastors say to themselves "I would not know where to begin in a place like that." Apostolic pastors need the support of a translocal team of apostolic leaders and these translocal teams have their own distinguishing marks. If the prime mark of the church is its apostolicity—then the prime purpose of translocal apostolic leadership is to re-establish the vitality of missionary congregations. I support the essential gift of *episcope,* oversight for pastoral care, but am concerned that in our attention to oversight for pastoral care we may have neglected the equally essential apostolic gifting. In other words, I am as concerned for the domestication of the translocal leader as I am for the local pastor. We need a vision for the release of apostolic gifting that creates regional and national leaders with a passion to see the church re-established as a missional people.

The appointment of the new General Secretary and the renewed debate around the future of the presidency must be seen in this context of missional leadership. This debate needs to be married to the postponed discussion of collegial Baptist leadership that draws in the associations and the colleges and other Baptists who have a translocal leadership. I say postponed because these ideas were in the "Relating and Resourcing" debate but never emerged in the structural reforms.[41] All the building blocks are in place with the excellent dynamics between the regional team leaders, the college principals and the Didcot team—we simply need to build the house.

Let me suggest that these are some of the marks of the collegial apostolic leadership we need to encourage into being in the years ahead.

1. Apostolic leaders convince the church they are a sent people

Central to everything is the apostolic nature of the church that is expressed by its witness to the gospel. Apostolic leadership convinces the Church it is a sent people accompanied by Jesus in its mission in the world. Wilbert Shenk again: "The first essential of leadership, the one above all others in regard to mission, is to see the vision of the reign of God being established in these frontier situations and then to hold that before the church. All else is secondary."

2. Apostolic leadership refuses to domesticate the gospel

They know their task is to challenge churches to engage prophetically with the community where they are placed. They know that worship can become disengaged from mission and discipleship training can become disengaged from mission. They appeal to the churches, "Don't domesticate the ministry!"

3. Apostolic leaders encourage churches to train members for a worldly

41. "Relating and Resourcing" was a report commissioned by the Baptist Union Council with the task of proposing radical revisions to Baptist association structures and other patterns of relating together. The report was discussed in 1998 and led to significant denominational change. See further Randall, *English Baptists of the Twentieth Century*, 517–20.

discipleship

They discourage church members from being held captive to the culture and needs of the organization. They teach pastors to train disciples to be subversive for Jesus in the world of work. We wrongly make the emphasis on baptism and membership rather than baptism and mission. William Willimon is right to suggest that the politics of baptism is a politics of renunciation, and our initiation rites must be strong enough to signify the cost of discipleship for service in the world.

4. Apostolic leaders encourage the Church to know the power of a Sabbath rest

They constantly direct the local church to the well-springs of spiritual refreshment and renewal. They are always asking: Is this community listening to God? Are the people of God discovering what the Spirit is saying to the Church? They promote the principles of healthy church. They discern the health-damaging effects of a toxic community.

5. Apostolic leaders warn the churches they must be prepared to pay the price of mission

They know that apostolic ministry is costly and heroic and apostolic churches must be prepared to pay the price of mission.

6. Apostolic leaders engage in a preaching ministry that is characterized by its prophetic edge

We need daring preachers who use language that "breaks open old worlds with surprise abrasion and pace."[42] Apostolic preachers who follow in the steps of Jesus and his Nazareth sermon; they open the familiar Book and interpret it with fresh meaning for today.

In summary, this is my future perspective. We offer ourselves in prayer to our missionary God and his loving purposes in the world; we say we are open to more experimentation as God leads us; we commit ourselves to care more creatively for the disciples God gives us; to engage in thoughtful evangelism in these strange and alien cultures; to be open for engagement with the common questions of our cultures; to develop intentionally those apostolic leadership teams which will prepare the whole of God's people for their works of service.

42. Brueggemann, *Finally Comes the Poet*, 3.

A French Catholic once said "If you want to build a ship, don't drum up people to gather wood, divide the work and give orders. Instead, teach them to yearn for the vast and endless sea." If we teach people to indwell this unique gospel story that shapes our lives, then this missionary Union will be well prepared for the adventure of sailing in uncharted waters and the building of the ships of future Church will emerge naturally out of a quest to journey on God's vast and endless sea.

Bibliography

Abraham, William J. *The Logic of Renewal*. Grand Rapids: Eerdmans, 2003.

———. "On Making Disciples of the Lord Jesus Christ." In *Marks of the Body of Christ*, edited by Carl Braaten and Robert Jenson. Grand Rapids: Eerdmans, 1999.

Archbishop's Council. *Archbishop of Canterbury's Listening Initiative in Christian Muslim Relations, 2001–2004*. London: Archbishops' Council, 2004.

Baptist Union of Great Britain. *Signs of Hope: An Examination of the Numerical and Spiritual State of Churches in Membership with the Baptist Union of Great Britain and Ireland*. London: BUGB, 1979.

Bayes, Paul. *Mission-Shaped Church*. Nottingham: Grove, 2004.

Beasley-Murray, Paul. *Fearless for Truth: A Personal Portrait of George Beasley-Murray*. Carlisle, UK: Paternoster, 2002.

Billings, Alan. *Secular Lives, Sacred Hearts*. London: SPCK, 2004.

Bosch, David J. *Believing in the Future*. Harrisburg, PA: Trinity, 2005.

———. *Transforming Mission: Paradigm Shifts in the Theology of Mission*. Maryknoll, NY: Orbis, 1991.

Brierley, Peter. *English Church Census, 2005*. London: Christian Research, 2006.

Brueggemann, Walter. *Finally Comes the Poet: Daring Speech for Proclamation*. Minneapolis: Fortress, 1987.

Champion, Leonard. "Evangelical Calvinism and the Structures of Baptist Church Life." *Baptist Quarterly* 28 (1980) 198–208.

Dowd, Mark. "For the Love of the Game." *The Tablet*, January 29, 2005.

Gibbs, Eddie, and Ryan K. Bolger. *Emerging Churches*. London: SPCK, 2006.

Guinness, Os. "Living with Our Deepest Differences." *Lion and Lamb* (Winter 2003).

Hay, David, and Kate Hunt. *Understanding the Spirituality of People Who Don't Go to Church*. Nottingham: Nottingham University Press, 2000.

Morden, Peter. *Offering Christ to the World: Andrew Fuller (1754–1815) and the Revival of Eighteenth-Century Particular Baptist Life*. Studies in Baptist History and Thought 8. Carlisle, UK: Paternoster, 2003.

Randall, Ian M. *The English Baptists of the Twentieth Century*. Didcot: Baptist Historical Society, 2005.

Roxburgh, Alan. *The Missionary Congregation, Leadership, and Liminality*. Harrisburg, PA: Trinity, 1997.

Shenk, Wilbert. *Write the Vision—the Church Renewed*. Harrisburg, PA: Trinity, 2005.

Spencer, Nick, et al. *Evangelism in a Spiritual Age*. London: Church House, 2005.

Williams, Stuart Murray. *Changing Mission: Learning from the Newer Churches*. London: Churches Together in the British Isles, 2006.

Wright, Nigel G. *New Baptists, New Agenda*. Carlisle, UK: Paternoster, 2002.
———. *The Radical Evangelical: Seeking a Place to Stand*. London: SPCK 1996.

6

The Downgrade Controversy

Reflections on a Baptist Earthquake[1]

MARK HOPKINS

THE DOWNGRADE CONTROVERSY OF 1887–88 was at once the most dramatic and most painful episode in the history of the Baptist Union. The wounds it left behind took a very long time to heal, and people were reluctant to do anything that might reopen them. Thus when I started studying it almost a century afterward, I was carefully vetted before gaining access to E. A. Payne's main account, written thirty years earlier and still a closely guarded typescript in Baptist House.

In introducing her own account of Downgrade in her husband's "Autobiography," Charles Haddon Spurgeon's widow Susannah said she had "been led to allow the shadow of the past to rest upon it in a measure, and to conceal, under a generous silence, most of the . . . evidence which could . . . prove the perfect uprightness, veracity, and fidelity of [her] dear husband."[2] A century had passed before some of the evidence held by both sides finally emerged; in the meantime, people who knew just enough to be plausible had produced speculations that were adopted as truths by historians. The basic *mise en scène*, especially

1. This lecture was delivered at the Baptist Assembly in Brighton on 6 May 2007. The lecture has been slightly revised for publication. The historical material draws substantially on earlier research, written up at greater length in my *Nonconformity's Romantic Generation*, ch. 7 "The Downgrade Controversy."

2. Spurgeon and Harrald, *C. H. Spurgeon Autobiography*, 469.

as it relates to Spurgeon's outlook, was never elucidated, bringing about an environment conducive to the proliferation of myths—myths which should now be laid to rest. That is one of the aims of this lecture: to make the story of Downgrade clear. The other aim is to reflect on the issues the controversy embodied, issues of what we may term "religious communion" that are always relevant to believers in Christ who share some things in common and differ on others as they seek to meet and work together.

Beginnings of the Controversy

Study of the Downgrade Controversy should begin in 1883. Up until that year Spurgeon had dismissed the issue of suspect theology among Baptists by saying such things as "there are not above a dozen loose men among us to my knowledge, but an attack upon one might make a martyr of a party, and cause a world of trouble to the many faithful ones among us."[3] But in that year this argument was shot down in flames by his trusted associate Archibald Brown, who unlike Spurgeon was present at the Baptist Union's autumn meetings: "I wish I could believe that the spirit of the age has only tainted about a dozen men amongst us. If so they are able to make a wonderful noise in the way of applause at every 'broad' statement."[4] This precipitated Spurgeon into a two part program: protesting and withdrawing—or fight *and* flight. The protest part mostly came in salvos fired in his monthly magazine, *The Sword and the Trowel*—that in the November 1883 edition was followed by a number of others, with the 1887 Downgrade articles coming as a more sustained barrage following an established pattern. The withdrawal part had two elements: an immediate boycott of Baptist Union meetings (to which he never returned after 1882), and the threat of withdrawing his membership. In 1883 the Union leadership, centered on the secretary Samuel Harris Booth, succeeded in talking him out of that, and avoiding it was a major concern of theirs over the next few years—it influenced both meeting programs and selection of presidents.

It is vital to get inside Spurgeon's mind. We can start to do so with his analysis of the theological situation: he was realistic, seeing that liberalism would become dominant and not lose momentum for decades

3. Murray, *The Forgotten Spurgeon*, 85.

4. Brown to Spurgeon, 16 October 1883, MS letter at Spurgeon's College.

to come. It seemed to him that all the defensive weapons that might be deployed—creeds, witch-hunts and schism—carried more drawbacks than merits. Hence his two part program of protest and withdrawal. But these two were unequal. Right from 1883 he saw protest as a duty, and the path toward withdrawal which was the goal, as he told his brother-in-law: "I have fired the first shot, and the battle is beginning . . . I think I must personally withdraw from the Baptist Union. I do not care to fight, but can be rid of the responsibility by retiring."[5] The flight from responsibility was a recurring theme of these years—his explanation of the Downgrade articles to his friend James Douglas was that members of other denominations kept writing to him as if he were the custodian of truth among Baptists: "I am not that," he said; "it is too bad to hold me *responsible* for all that may occur."[6]

Even close supporters of Spurgeon did not understand this, and were shocked and caught off balance by his resignation from the Baptist Union early in the Downgrade. *Their* program was to keep the Union an environment in which they could be comfortable—and to which he could return. The way the controversy unravelled for them is closely linked to the fact that their captain had abandoned the field of play early in the first half. The unforeseen pressure put on Spurgeon after his resignation obliged him to be seen to be trying to do something, but his heart was never in it, he was not in a position to act effectively, and his failure to achieve his makeshift goals cannot be considered surprising. This will all become apparent as we summarize the main events of the controversy.

Spurgeon wrote the four "Downgrade" articles that gave the controversy its name for the August-November 1887 issues of *The Sword and the Trowel*. He pitched his tone in the shrill register, perhaps because he felt the need to armor pierce the shells that had been harmlessly bouncing off the bunker of silence in which the Union leadership habitually took refuge. His very first paragraph included the three doctrines that would be most in focus through the controversy, but couched in terms that no-one could identify with: the atonement was "scouted," inspiration of Scripture "derided," and future punishment "turned into fiction."[7] Many

5. Spurgeon to W. Jackson, 8 November 1883, quoted in Payne, "Down Grade Controversy," 148–49.

6. Douglas, *The Prince of Preachers*, 163, emphasis mine.

7. *The Sword and the Trowel*, vol. 23, August 1887, 397.

have failed to realize that his main target was the Congregationalists, more of whom had departed further than Baptists from doctrinal positions he considered acceptable—it was his resignation from the Baptist Union, which accompanied the last of the articles, that put the focus squarely on his own denomination.

Another overlooked point is the identity of the item in Spurgeon's ordnance that broke through the silence. It was a paragraph in the first article in which he compared the current state of Dissent unfavorably with the Church of England that elicited nearly all the press debate.[8] Anglicans made unsubtle and uncomfortable use of this, turning against Spurgeon even such a man as William Lockhart, a conservative on the Council of the Union who had up to that point been a friend. (His initial reaction to that first article had been to write Spurgeon a congratulatory letter, and he incorrectly believed that the problem was that Spurgeon's language had later gone over the top.)

This meant that the "Downgrade" was the dominant conversational topic at the Union's autumn meetings in Sheffield. It made Samuel Harris Booth's refusal to give the matter space within the program seem questionable, and when to that were added a couple of derogatory passing references to him, Spurgeon considered that his views had been deemed unworthy of debate and his resignation was therefore justified. On 7 November he left for his customary two month winter break in Menton on the Franco-Italian border thinking the pain was largely behind and a welcome quiet in store. He could not have been more wrong.

Meeting with Spurgeon

Six positions can be identified in the England he left behind—or at least its Baptist portion. Those closest and furthest from him were negligible in number: on the one hand, close supporters who also resigned; on the other hand, unabashed liberals who openly agreed with Spurgeon's presentation of the theological situation while differing profoundly with his interpretation of it. Early in the controversy Spurgeon found their pronouncements helpful, but later they became much quieter, apparently cooperating with Union leaders anxious to press the line that any problem was small and could be addressed if Spurgeon submitted names and evidence. The third position was occupied by the vast majority of

8. *The Sword and the Trowel*, vol. 23, August 1887, 398–99.

Spurgeon's supporters: they wanted to see him return to the Union and saw its adoption of a satisfactorily evangelical doctrinal basis as the appropriate way. (Spurgeon considered this enterprise doomed to fail, but thought it a good prelude to their joining him in resignation.) This leaves three major positions occupied by nearly all Baptists who did not see themselves as serving under Spurgeon's colors. The most sympathetic agreed with Spurgeon that there was a problem—though not with his estimate of its scale nor with his way of addressing it—and thought that the Union should make a statement to vindicate its evangelical nature. The most antipathetic considered that Spurgeon's protest and resignation constituted an unwarranted attack on the Union: he should be pressed to try to justify them, and when that failed he should be reprimanded. Union leadership was divided between these two groups, with the then President and Vice-President, James Culross and John Clifford, in the latter but most of the living former Presidents taking the milder line. In between lay an amorphous mass who thought the entire thing overblown: to them dignified silence seemed the best response, and, when others made that impossible, simple brotherly discussion with Spurgeon.

With the leadership split, it was that last view that prevailed at the December 1887 meeting of the Baptist Union Council: four representatives, known as the "four doctors," were deputed simply to confer with Spurgeon on the maintenance of the unity of the denomination. Booth and Spurgeon corresponded about the terms for this meeting, the former consulting with Culross, Clifford and Alexander McLaren, the other members of the Union delegation. Finally available a century later, this correspondence reveals that Spurgeon insisted that his resignation should not be on the agenda, making that a condition of the meeting taking place, only to find that Clifford had put it right at the top of the agenda statement presented to him by the delegation, which was reduced to three by McLaren's ill-health. It is surely significant that it was during these negotiations that Booth, who had been both hyperactive and hypersensitive since the resignation, accused a bemused correspondent of charging him with being "Jesuitical."[9]

The meeting on 13 January 1888 was polite but frosty: there was no convergence between Spurgeon's suggestion of a doctrinal basis along

9. I discussed this recently available material in Hopkins, "The Down Grade Controversy," 262–78. It has been lodged in the Angus Library of Regent's Park College, Oxford.

the lines of that of the Evangelical Alliance and the Council's probing of Spurgeon's past actions and evidence. Spurgeon refused to give way to the pressure to "name names." He certainly had evidence, most of it in the public domain and known to his opponents—the liberal leader J. G. Greenhough could say he thought he knew most of those targeted, and the often retold story that Booth had given Spurgeon evidence he refused to allow him to use has no factual basis at all. Spurgeon did not present his evidence because he knew this would only create martyrs and make things worse. His sense of betrayal only came out in comments in *The Sword and the Trowel*, in which he talked amongst other things of hidden claws and secret aims.[10] By the time that appeared, Council had already made its own comment on the meeting, not unfairly known among Spurgeon's supporters as the "vote of censure." Since he had failed to substantiate his charges, Council concluded that he should not have made them.

At this stage Spurgeon's more confrontational opponents were in the lead. But in the following meeting of Council, on 21 February, their bid to censure Spurgeon a second time failed, and the floor was finally clear for Joseph Angus, who represented the more conciliatory approach, to present evangelical doctrinal declarations. Unlike the versions prepared for the previous two Council meetings, this one was drawn up in consultation with James Archer Spurgeon, who had emerged as the leader of his brother's supporters in the Baptist Union. Clifford sensed that the majority would be prepared to go along with a revision that removed liberal objections, and distanced himself from the radical grouping by producing such a revision on the spot; after further haggling he and Angus reached a compromise that was acceptable to a large majority of Council—but not to the Spurgeon brothers.

The Spurgeons drew up competing declarations for the Union's annual assembly by assembling all the most conservative bits of Angus' various versions and then adding a little extra reinforcement. When delegates and spectators crowded the City Temple on Monday, 23 April 1888 it was in expectation of a dramatic showdown leading to the fracturing of the Union. But a compromise suggested or at least brokered by Booth and agreed by both Spurgeon brothers was sealed minutes before the debate was due to begin and J. A. Spurgeon ended up seconding rather than opposing Charles Williams on the declaration motion. Neither had

10. Vol. 24, February 1888, 81–83, 91.

an appropriate speech ready: Williams came out with confrontational language of a kind that left J. A. Spurgeon lamely seconding the motion but not Williams' speech. His stronger but absent brother could only say afterward that he would have turned round to oppose the motion as interpreted by Williams.

Charles Haddon Spurgeon's verdict was that they had been "entrapped by diplomatists."[11] Instead of being joined in withdrawal by his supporters—shown by voting returns for new Council members to hold about a quarter of the votes in the Union—or even winkling out a single liberal unable to live with the declarations, he emerged from the controversy with nothing to alleviate his pain. He had to look elsewhere for comfort: cheered by many messages of support from outside the Baptist Union, in his last years Spurgeon took refuge in a vision of conservative ecumenism.

On their side, the Union leadership had achieved their goal of preventing substantial disruption, but the victory was achieved more by coup than true consensus, the price of which was continuing animosity. But to substantiate this assessment, that the Union had merely survived rather than achieving anything of significance, we need to examine how the issues were handled.

Religious Communion and Its Limits

The evangelical consensus which had been dominant in the early nineteenth century, on which Particular and General Baptists had been able to come together freely in the newly established Baptist Union, had come under increasing strain as liberal theology took hold among a growing part of the Union's constituency in the later nineteenth century. The Downgrade Controversy was the result. It came about like an earthquake, for a point had been reached at which something had to give, just as when the pressure between two tectonic plates moving in different directions becomes too great.

In Congregationalism a similar process had moved faster and brought their Union into crisis a decade before Downgrade. The trigger was the organization of a conference on the fringe of the Union's official autumn meetings in Leicester in 1877, to explore putting religious com-

11. Spurgeon to Wright, 27 April 1888, quoted in Kruppa, *Charles Haddon Spurgeon*, 442–43.

munion on a non-theological basis. That conference's lead speaker, J. A. Picton, unabashedly proclaimed himself a pantheist—"but," as he put it, "mark! of the spiritual, not of the materialistic school"[12]—as he tenderly pleaded with his fellow ministers not to cast him adrift. Denominational leaders responded by putting forward a resolution stating that their basis of communion remained the evangelical doctrines to which they had always adhered. To the objection that this was an instrument of pressure on some members, a conservative replied,

> There seems really no limit to the unwarrantable demands made upon us on behalf of liberty. There are men who seem to think themselves justified in trampling upon the rights and liberties of others, under this ever-ready plea that they must assert their freedom. We should be sorry to say that there is consciously any such purpose here, but this is the practical issue. The liberty of those who cling to the old faith is essentially narrowed if they are told that they cannot lay down the terms of their association, so as to make it a Christian body, without becoming persecutors of those who reject the Christian doctrines, and yet may wish to join them.[13]

The problem was insoluble: once differences have reached a certain level, one group's freedom cannot but impinge on another's. Those looking for a broader fellowship find this hard to see, because the more obvious coercion comes from the other side when it tries to draw a line. Picton thought that religious communion could be organized informally by what he termed the "selective action of spiritual affinities,"[14] but this could not work where spiritual affinities were not reciprocal. We shall see very similar dynamics operating in Downgrade.[15]

But before exploring those it will be good to sketch the process of doctrinal revision. We shall take as an example one of the three main doctrines at stake in Downgrade, that of future punishment. The traditional doctrine of eternal punishment came under increasing pressure in the late nineteenth century. This pressure was generated ethically, as was usual with liberalism. The common name for the new views was

12. *Evangelical Independent*, 22 November 1877, 1282.

13. *Congregationalist*, 6, December 1877, 712–13.

14. *Christian World*, 8 May 1878, special May Meeting number, 13.

15. This paragraph distils a part of my account of this controversy in Hopkins, *Nonconformity's Romantic Generation*, chapter 4 "The Leicester Conference Controversy (1877–79)."

"the larger hope"—a vague hope that in the end all or at least most might somehow be saved. It followed the normal pattern of striking the younger generation while their seniors were largely unaffected, and of reaching higher social classes and urban congregations first. George Knight, a graduate of Pastors' College,[16] testified of his Weymouth church that "The doctrine of everlasting punishment, which I unhesitatingly announce, is like gravel between the teeth of not a few among us."[17] He contrasted that with his village chapel at Putton where "among a simple, true-hearted people, the gospel is precious, prayer abundant, and conversions numerous."[18] At theological colleges the new views were spread effectively through student interaction, not lectures. George Howells went up to Regent's Park College from the sheltered valleys of South Wales in 1888 and soon found his traditional views on future punishment shaken by a senior student: "If he had confessed to a murder the shock would not have been so great,"[19] he recalled in old age. The *coup de grâce* was unwittingly administered by an elderly minister who led the college in prayer some months later: "'And, Oh God,' he tenderly pleaded, 'when we hear the shrieks of the damned ascending from the everlasting flames of the bottomless pit, give us grace to shout, Hallelujah, Hallelujah.' This was too much for me . . ."[20]—and Howells is talking of moral outrage at words he found grossly offensive, not the outcome of study of scripture or systematic reflection.

Once this quiet shift in views had reached a critical point, it could be followed by the second and final stage in the process, which may be called "registering" the new views openly in a representative setting. The opportunity fell to James Thew, a member of the small group of Baptist ministers who were very visibly liberal in the years before Downgrade. He was asked to preach a missionary sermon at the autumn meetings of the Union in 1885 (being a Baptist Missionary Society invitation, this escaped the Spurgeon-oriented self-censorship policy of the Union itself). Thew handled the challenge astutely through taking an indirect approach. Rather than ask the direct question concerning the legitimacy

16. A former name of Spurgeon's College.

17. George J. Knight to Professors Gracey and Fergusson, 11 February 1888, MS letter in Spurgeon's College.

18. Ibid.

19. Howells, "Christian Problems," 107–8.

20. Ibid.

of the "larger hope" in the Baptist Union, he discussed whether or not it would decrease zeal for missions, concluding that it need not do so. Spurgeon had a small window in which to try to dislodge Thew and the larger hope from their new perch in the Union, but his fulminations did not amount to a serious attempt—and that particular battle was won and lost there and then.[21] The place of the "larger hope" was already secure when Charles Williams proclaimed its legitimacy in his speech proposing the doctrinal resolutions in April 1888.

Two big issues must be addressed in any discussion of the limits of religious communion. The first is doctrinal: where should the line be drawn between what is acceptable and what is unacceptable? The second is ecclesiastical: how should that line be drawn and enforced? We will take these questions in turn.

As early as 1883 Spurgeon had distinguished differences on essentials and secondary matters, saying that only "when truths which are viewed as vital by a large portion of any society are trifled with by others" is there "an end of fellowship, or else of conscientiousness."[22] The first problem with this was that what he considered rejection of the gospel others took to be a legitimate difference on a secondary matter. The second problem, compounding the first, was that disagreement over the definition of primary and secondary differences was frequently not identified.

The generally accepted shorthand term for what was considered essential was "evangelical." The first aim of the Baptist Union's 1832 founders was "To extend brotherly love and union among Baptist ministers and churches who agree in the sentiments usually denominated evangelical."[23] This was dropped from the constitution in its 1873 revision, which took the minimalist line of making believers' baptism the only condition churches had to fulfill for membership.[24] Nevertheless, throughout the Downgrade Controversy Baptists—like Congregationalists a decade earlier—continued to insist that they must be evangelical: that was primary. But what did it mean to be evangelical in the 1880s? Spurgeon expressed agreement with the conclusion of the leading liberal Nonconformist newspaper, the *Christian World*, ". . . that Evangelicalism, on its intel-

21. Payne, "The Down Grade," 50–51.

22. *The Sword and the Trowel*, vol. 19, 1883, 607.

23. Quoted in Payne, *The Baptist Union*, 61.

24. Payne, *The Baptist Union*, 109–10.

lectual side, lies neither here nor there, but is consistent with the most widespread differences of belief."[25] Yet it was an unvoiced and therefore unresolved difference over the definition of evangelicalism that alienated from Spurgeon William Robertson Nicoll, the influential editor of a more conservative newspaper, the *British Weekly*. Nicoll disagreed with Spurgeon's assessment "that the Congregationalists were *in the main non-evangelical* and that the Baptists were rapidly following suit."[26] He then did much to focus the debate on the question of the number of people whose views were not evangelical. The real difference was not made clear: Spurgeon and Nicoll did not have widely differing impressions as to how many people believed what, but differed on whether or not particular sets of beliefs were within the bounds of what was acceptable, that is evangelical.

As usually happens in theological controversies, more heat than light was generated in Downgrade. Spurgeon bears considerable responsibility, making brief statements couched in offensive language rather than engaging in clear analysis. Defenders of the unity of the Baptist Union had a vested interest in avoiding clarity. Their approach to the formulation of doctrinal definitions was to look for language flexible enough to satisfy everyone: satisfy conservatives that a line was being drawn, while satisfying liberals by making sure they did not find themselves on the wrong side of it. And if the marking of theological boundaries was sketchy, then the reason *why* they should be set where they were was even less evident. We can take the doctrine of Scripture, another of the three focal doctrines of the controversy, to explore these issues.

The article on Scripture in the Baptist Union declarations was not one of those disputed, and it is easy to understand why that was so. It simply proclaimed "The Divine Inspiration and Authority of Holy Scripture as the supreme and sufficient rule of our faith and practice,"[27] along with individual judgment in its interpretation. There was nothing in that to make a contemporary Baptist liberal uncomfortable. The

25. *The Christian World*, 22 November 1888; *The Sword and the Trowel*, vol. 25, January, 1889, 40.

26. *The Sword and the Trowel*, vol. 23, September, 1887, 464; Nicoll to Spurgeon, 29 August 1887, MS letter in Spurgeon's College.

27. The two sources consulted are "Council Report for 1887, Proof Copy for Council Members," and *The Christian World*, 24 April 1888.

Spurgeon brothers' amendment did not touch this article, so although C. H. Spurgeon had headlined Scripture as one of the major doctrines on which there had been unacceptable movement away from evangelical norms, he did not really follow this up.

In the ensuing "mini-Downgrade" struggle in the London Baptist Association conservatives tightened up. The article passed on Scripture was a beefed up version of the Baptist Union's, saying that its inspiration and authority were "full" "in all its parts." There was also an additional introductory phrase, "We maintain that the inspired Scripture of the Old and New Testament is the only complete, authoritative, and infallible exposition of evangelical doctrine."[28] Some liberal eyebrows were raised that John Clifford had been prepared to go along with this, for "full" was equivalent to "plenary" inspiration, widely seen as a corollary of infallibility, whose meaning was then scarcely distinguishable if at all from that of inerrancy. The word "infallible" itself, as it appeared in the introduction, was made somewhat more palatable by being applied only to doctrine.

As the main controversy reached its climax in April 1888 Spurgeon finally expressed his views on Scripture more clearly. Certainty to him was a psychological necessity; as he put it in *The Sword and the Trowel*, "If we have in the Word of God no infallible standard of truth, we are at sea without a compass . . . Infallibility is necessary somewhere; and it is far more to God's glory, and to our safety, that it be found in the Scripture itself than in human judgement."[29]

It is of interest that Jerry Sutton, a participant-historian of another notable Baptist controversy, the successful conservative struggle for control of the Southern Baptist Convention that centered on the 1980s, had a very similar perspective on Scripture to Spurgeon: "Yet the question remained, What did conservatives fear if inerrancy was rejected? The answer was that we wanted a wholly trustworthy Bible. We feared that without it Southern Baptists were open to a watered-down gospel and a deviant soteriology."[30]

A major weakness of this approach is that it rules out possible alternatives by insisting that inerrancy is the only position capable of securing

28. Quoted in *Freeman*, 28 December 1888. The declaration was accepted by the London Baptist Association on 8 January 1889.

29. "Remarks on Inspiration," May, 1888, 205, 207.

30. Sutton, *The Baptist Reformation*, 473.

adherence to scriptural authority. Yet the leading theologians of the early twentieth century in Sutton's own denomination, E. Y. Mullins and W. T. Conner, had argued cogently for such an alternative.[31] Evangelicals have struggled to produce an agreed narrative of the history of their own doctrine of Scripture. Some have seen the deductive approach characteristic of the Scholastics and Puritans of the seventeenth century as normative, with nineteenth-century inerrancy a new stress on this position to counter the new liberal threat; while for others the inductive approach of the eighteenth-century fathers of evangelicalism is the standard, and inerrancy an inferior interloper. A broader perspective is needed: both rationalist (inerrantist) and empirical (non-inerrantist) approaches can be taken to argue for scriptural authority; which dominates at any given time depends in part on swings in philosophy. By focusing on infallibility and inerrancy Spurgeon and Southern Baptist conservatives alike narrowed the historic diversity of evangelicalism and diverted attention from the true heart of the matter, whether Scripture is an authority over us or not. If evangelicals who took the empirical approach had been as militant they might have lumped together inerrantists and liberals as groups that had the temerity to lay down criteria the Bible must satisfy to qualify—or fail to qualify—as God's Word, and turned on both together.

This case study of the doctrine of Scripture suggests that the Downgrade Controversy hardly began to get to grips with *why* doctrinal lines should be drawn here and not there, and the record of its American successor is no better. It is said that doctrinal controversy stimulates doctrinal development, but neither the heat nor the tactical considerations that characterize controversy favors lucidity. Laying down boundaries is better done outside the challenging environment of controversy. But it is not pleasant to see anyone fall on the wrong side of the line, so human nature tends to recoil from such an exercise until the discomfort of sharing with people one doesn't feel any bond with becomes even greater. So it is that religious communion issues tend to be addressed at times when they can be handled least easily.

I have said nothing on the ethical basis of religious communion because there is very little to say. All Spurgeon brought up in the Downgrade articles was a suggestion that increasing theatre-going was a sign of spiritual decline—ideas as to what leisure pursuits were accept-

31. Their views are briefly sketched by Sutton himself in *The Baptist Reformation*, 409–11.

able were slowly changing. Even the Leicester radicals who thought that theology need no longer be a consideration for religious communion maintained substantially the same traditional Christian ethics as conservatives with no thought that these might be up for negotiation. Doubt might be tolerated, but not immorality.

Preserving Religious Communion

We can move on to the other question identified for exploration. Beyond the doctrinal question of *where* to draw the line lies the ecclesiastical question of *how* to draw it. One of Spurgeon's arguments was that the Baptist Union was powerless to stop the process of doctrinal broadening, as it had made believers' baptism its only requirement for membership. This was countered with the observation that there was a provision for Council to remove churches from membership, and rare instances where this was done to churches that had become Unitarian could be pointed out. But an informal doctrinal basis such as that can hardly be considered ideal. In 1904 the Union implicitly acknowledged the weakness of its position during Downgrade by adding doctrinal articles to its constitution—modified in 1906 to ensure that Unitarianism was excluded. It is notable however that these articles did not touch the three most controversial issues in Downgrade, the Bible, atonement and future punishment.[32]

By February 1888 most were agreed that doctrinal declarations were needed to mark out what was considered normative in the Baptist Union. This consensus included Spurgeon, who had not abandoned his skepticism as to how adequate the process would prove, but who realized he had to be seen to be doing something and could not think of anything more constructive to turn his hand to. It also included people like Clifford who were happy with the broadening of the doctrinal basis of the Union that accompanied the growth of liberal theology: they saw others' concern and did not want to refuse to address it. But that still left a question unanswered: were these doctrinal declarations to be prescriptive or merely descriptive?

This was a prominent feature of the story of the development of the doctrinal declarations passed by the Union assembly in April 1888. In December 1887 the original drafter, Joseph Angus, included a statement

32. Payne, *The Baptist Union*, 162–63.

that made them firmly prescriptive: "If any renounce these truths, or are no longer in sympathy with them, they, in the judgement of the Council, have no legitimate place in the Union."[33] This was however replaced in the version Angus prepared for Council's February meeting by a statement that the intention was not to control belief but to show the level of agreement that existed as a basis for working together.[34] Angus wanted to pre-empt the suggestion that he was trying to impose a creed. Even that did not satisfy Council, and a major part of the revision it underwent there was the addition of a decisively anti-creedal introduction. This contained two points. First, the Union's doctrinal beliefs had to be determined by those of its member churches. So, as Pastors' College tutor F. G. Marchant pointed out, if a member church became Unitarian the Union would be obliged to embrace Unitarianism. Secondly, Council disclaimed authority to formulate a new theological basis of union. But, as James Douglas showed, this was a *non sequitur*, for it had had authority to formulate the original one.[35] The removal of this introduction was J. A. Spurgeon's final condition for the last minute compromise. It left the Union with something intermediate, neither obviously prescriptive nor descriptive. As with the Congregationalists a decade earlier, there was no attempt at enforcement. Any action was left entirely to those who might consider themselves outside the line drawn—and no one stepped forward.

What hung in the balance in Downgrade was whether or not there would be a big new division in the Baptist denomination. In the event there was not, so the Baptist Union resumed a calmer existence with substantially the same profile as before. The disturbance had revealed the growing strength of the liberal wing, and the previously covert acceptance of the legitimacy of certain of its tenets was now open: this conservatives had failed to prevent. A few of them thought this development serious enough to require their resignation; many more preferred to ease out their limits of toleration a little further. More than a century later the theological differences are still there. It has been trench warfare: there

33. As reprinted by *The Christian World*, 15 December 1887.

34. *The Baptist* and *The Freeman*, both 24 February 1888; the slight differences between the two versions do not affect the sense in any material way.

35. *The Baptist*, 24 February 1888; F. G. Marchant, letter in *The Baptist*, 23 March 1888; Douglas' comment is reported in "The London Baptist Association and The Baptist Union: Their Relations as to the Down-Grade," in *The Baptist*, 30 March 1888.

are periods when all is quiet, the front line changes shape gradually, and sharp engagements flare up at different points from time to time, but neither side has swept the other away.

Conclusions

My decision to study this period was influenced by a hope that through looking at the issues in the period in which they arose I might find solutions to my own questions. In that I was disappointed. That there was no hidden gold is hardly surprising: if gold had been found, a gold rush would surely have followed. Yet it was while I was engaged in this study that I did start to come across gold elsewhere—and Spurgeon of all people helped set me off on the right path. I will say a few words about that as I close because I believe these discoveries can transform present tensions on the basis of communion—and not only among Baptists.

Spurgeon had a desire I have learnt from, to let each part of Scripture make its own point rather than squeeze it into a predetermined doctrinal mould. It made him an unconventional Calvinist, for he let "Arminian" passages be Arminian as well as "Calvinist" ones be Calvinist. This affected his ability to fit everything together: he pronounced systematic theology something for angels rather than human beings.

This helped me forward on a process of discovery in Scripture that was opened up by two interlinked breakthroughs. Firstly, I chose to believe with Paul in the reality of our sharing in Christ's cross and resurrection: we really, truly die and rise there with him. Secondly, I saw that what God did in Christ brings this world with its time to a close and starts a new one with dimensions of its own. Theology of all descriptions through the ages has gone wrong on both these points: it has woven our time into its basic structure, dividing the story of salvation into past, present and future phases; and then, having ruled out the biblical one, it has looked for alternative ways of linking us to the cross and resurrection. In Paul salvation is one great eschatological event, seen from two perspectives: a hidden one, open only to faith, in which it is accomplished; and that of experience, in which it is in process. These two perspectives show that the death-and-resurrection of Christ both fills and transcends our time.

The results astonished me: the liberal-conservative stand off wasn't the only thing to be transformed. I found new freedom with Paul: I no longer had to put in theological boundaries where he had left them out;

I no longer had to be puzzled by his apparently cavalier use of tenses. And whichever way I looked glorious new perspectives opened up on protracted splits in the Church—between Calvinists and Arminians, Protestants and Catholics, East and West. The analogy I would use is that of a maze I once entered. However hard I tried, working within the universal structures of theology it was only possible to get close to the centre from various angles. I had to go back almost to the entrance to take an unpromising turning which took me to the goal with ease.

Unresolved differences persist in the Church on salvation because no proposal carries complete conviction, none handles all of Scripture well. The doctrine of the Trinity has always been contested, but it has ruled supreme in the Church's various traditions because no competitor has come anywhere near its coherence, its ability to handle Scripture and to nourish spiritually. That no doctrine of salvation has achieved similar dominance is due to the fact that none has reached that target—not even the Reformation doctrine of Luther with its recovery of the vital point that salvation is a gift of God received by faith. But if we can once more find the turning that Paul took all that may change.

Bibliography

Douglas, James. *The Prince of Preachers: A Sketch; a Portraiture; and a Tribute*. London: Morgan & Scott, 1893.

Hopkins, Mark. "The Down Grade Controversy: New Evidence." *Baptist Quarterly* 35 (1994) 262–78.

———. *Nonconformity's Romantic Generation: Evangelical and Liberal Theologies in Victorian England*. Studies in Evangelical History and Thought. Carlisle, UK: Paternoster, 2004.

Howells, George. "Christian Problems: Settled; and Awaiting Further Exploration." *Baptist Quarterly* 7 (1934) 106–22.

Kruppa, Patricia Stallings. *Charles Haddon Spurgeon: A Preacher's Progress*. New York: Garland, 1982.

Murray, Iain. *The Forgotten Spurgeon*. 2nd ed. London: Banner of Truth, 1973.

Payne, Ernest A. *The Baptist Union: A Short History*. London: Carey Kingsgate, 1959.

———. "Down Grade Controversy: Postscript." *Baptist Quarterly* 28 (1979) 146–58.

Spurgeon, Susanna, and Joseph Harrald. *C. H. Spurgeon's Autobiography*. Vol. 2, *1854–1860*. Rev. ed. Edinburgh: Banner of Truth Trust, 1973.

Sutton, Jerry. *The Baptist Reformation: The Conservative Resurgence in the Southern Baptist Convention*. Nashville: Broadman & Holman, 2000.

7

Catholicity and Confessionalism

Responding to George Beasley-Murray on Unity and Distinctiveness[1]

John E. Colwell

I hold it a poignant honor to be invited to participate in this series of lectures in memory of George Beasley-Murray. Firstly, and most obviously, as one of his former pupils I owe a significant debt to his teaching, his influence, and his example.[2] As a member of one of the last groups of students at Spurgeon's College to benefit from his New Testament lectures, I imbibed habits of reading and expounding Scripture which I hope I have never betrayed. Perhaps most profoundly, with all who in those years observed his example, I was challenged (if not intimidated) by his seemingly unfailing capacity for diligent effort and scholarly thoroughness: in periods of *ennui* I have been shamed by the memory of his extraordinary effort and, even in periods of sustained academic labor, I confess that I have not come close to his exacting standards. But beyond the clarity of his teaching and his tireless effort, those who were his stu-

1. This lecture was delivered at the Baptist Assembly in Blackpool on 4 May 2008. It was later published under the same title in *Baptist Quarterly* 43/1 (January, 2009). The cooperation of the editors is here acknowledged. The present chapter has undergone slight editorial changes.

2. I was a student at Spurgeon's College from 1970 until 1974, the final three years of Dr. Beasley-Murray's tenure as principal followed by a year under the leadership of Dr. Raymond Brown.

dents could not have failed to be influenced by his infectious passion for the gospel and for those distinctives that identified him as thoroughly Baptist.

Aspects of this final feature of his legacy will form the focus of this present paper—but this brings me to the second source of my sense of honor in being invited to deliver this lecture. This habit of assembly is one of the aspects of our ecclesial life that marks us as distinctively Baptist; to be invited to address even a fringe meeting of the Assembly betokens a weighty responsibility; and a memorial to the passionate commitments of George Beasley-Murray in such a context affords opportunity to focus on Baptist distinctives at a time when, for a range of reasons, those distinctives may be in jeopardy of being muted. Previous lectures in this series, fittingly and unsurprisingly, have drawn attention to George Beasley-Murray's definitive contribution to a properly theological understanding of baptism and to his evangelistic commitment. As its title suggests, it is my intention in this paper to focus, at least initially, on his seemingly lifelong commitment to ecumenism, a commitment which, to the frequent embarrassment of his friends and to the delight of some who in other respects were his detractors, was as profound and as passionate as those other commitments for which George Beasley-Murray is justly honored.

George Beasley-Murray and Ecumenism

Now having already identified a motivation for this paper as an opportunity, in the context of Assembly, to reaffirm those aspects of Christian witness and discipleship that are distinctively Baptist, this headlined focus upon ecumenicity may appear surprising or even incongruous—this, of course, ought not to be the case since it is precisely in consideration of our catholic oneness as Christ's united body that our distinctive Baptist witness, within that catholic oneness, should attain its sharpest relief rather than its more blurred and embarrassed expression.[3]

The title of Paul Beasley-Murray's fine and appropriately personal biography of his father is *Fearless for Truth* and it would be difficult to think of a more fitting headline for this life and personality.[4] Rather than

3. Here, as elsewhere, I employ the term "catholic" to refer to the Church in its connectedness and continuity, reserving the term "Catholic" as an abbreviated reference to the Roman Catholic communion.

4. Beasley-Murray, *Fearless for Truth*.

militating against ecumenical conversations, this characteristic fearlessness and passion marked George Beasley-Murray as a most appropriate advocate of Baptist distinctives within ecumenical dialogue—indeed, we should recognize that the essential unity of the Church and the commitment to bring that unity to visible expression are themselves gospel truths for which he was a fearless advocate. As witness to this, Paul Beasley-Murray records his father's advocacy of the World Council of Churches during George's first year as a tutor at Spurgeon's College.[5] He was a member of the "Commission of Christ and the Church," a group established by the Faith and Order Committee of the World Council of Churches, serving as Secretary to the Commission from 1957;[6] he was appointed as chairman of the Baptist Union's "Advisory Committee on Church Relations";[7] but it is perhaps in a booklet published in 1965 that his personal ecumenical commitments come to their most clear and full expression.[8]

In introduction to this short essay George Beasley-Murray speaks with marked personal hope, reflecting that "[i]n our days a movement has sprung up for the healing of the divisions of God's people" and observing that "by some it is hailed as the work of the Holy Spirit, by others as the instrument of the Devil."[9] Unequivocally he identifies himself as "one of those who believe they can discern the finger of God in the ecumenical movement,"[10] and to the objection that a true spiritual unity already exists amongst the true people of God he rejoins that "spiritual realities must be given embodiment in this world if they are to count for anything."[11] With characteristic zeal for the Church's mission and echoing the statement made by Visser't Hooft at the Nottingham Faith and Order conference of 1964 he affirms that "the evangelistic task in our day is too vast and too urgent to be undertaken by the Churches in isolation,"[12] and, while admitting that "[t]he obstacles to be overcome in the reunion of the Churches of Christ are immense" (expressing impatience with

5. Ibid., 132–33.

6. Ibid., 133.

7. Ibid., 140.

8. Beasley-Murray, *Reflections on the Ecumenical Movement.*

9. Ibid., 3.

10. Ibid.

11. Ibid., 4.

12. Ibid., 8.

unrealistic goals such as the hope adopted by that Conference to work for unity by 1980),[13] he warmly (and perhaps bravely) acknowledges that "there is no doubt that unprecedented things are happening in the Roman Catholic Church, the outcome of which is unpredictable."[14] The paper ends with the plea that we should not "allow prejudice to hinder the fresh examination of our divisions, their causes and their possible cures."[15]

The depth of that residual prejudice was notoriously exposed in the very public condemnation of George Beasley-Murray by the Protestant Truth Society in response to his sharing of a platform with Father Agnellus Andrew, a Roman Catholic priest, at a Christian Unity Meeting in Ipswich held on 24 January 1967 (Beasley-Murray's address on that occasion was subsequently published in *The Christian* and *Christianity Today*, 10 February 1967).[16] The context for this angry reaction is traced in Ian Randall's refreshingly balanced account of English Baptists in the twentieth Century: while discussions following Vatican II had issued generally in more positive and hopeful views of the Roman Catholic Church, for the Baptist Revival Fellowship and other similar groups this hopefulness engendered an even "stronger anti-ecumenical rhetoric";[17] the Baptist Union and its leadership were increasingly dismissed as "pro-ecumenical."[18]

It was in this highly confrontational context in March 1967—just two months following the Ipswich meeting—that George Beasley-Murray presented the report *Baptists and Unity* to the Union's Council.[19] The report was a considered response to the Nottingham Conference on Faith and Order that acknowledged the particular difficulties of Baptists in such negotiations and aspirations; but that nonetheless acknowledged "that God will break forth more light and truth from His word";[20] and that (among other things) concluded that

13. Ibid., 12.

14. Ibid., 11.

15. Ibid., 13.

16. Beasley-Murray, *Fearless for Truth*, 135ff.; cf. Randall, *The English Baptists of the Twentieth Century*, 341.

17. Randall, *English Baptists of the Twentieth Century*, 338.

18. Ibid., 336.

19. Baptist Union Advisory Committee for Church Relations, *Baptists and Unity*.

20. Ibid., 6.

> . . . for Baptists to weaken their links with either the British Council of Churches or the World Council of Churches would be a serious loss to themselves and would make it more difficult for Baptists to present their distinctive witness and heritage to others; to receive in return from them other insights and corrective truths.[21]

It is this concern to preserve and to present a "distinctive witness and heritage" within the context of a committed quest for unity that was personally characteristic of George Beasley-Murray and that motivates this present paper.

Two years later, during the third session of the 1969 Baptist Union Assembly, on 29 April, George Beasley-Murray presented a paper incorporating responses to *Baptists and Unity* entitled *Baptists and Unity Reviewed* (though only 635 churches had responded to the original report). To the surprise of some (and certainly to the consternation of others) the resolution to accept the report was carried (1125 voted for the motion, 356 voted against)[22] and, perhaps fittingly, the session ended with the singing of Bishop George Bell's hymn "Christ is the King! O friends rejoice," which closes with this verse:

> Let love's unconquerable might
> Your scattered companies unite
> In service to the Lord of light:
> So shall God's will on earth be done,
> New lamps be lit, new tasks begun,
> And the whole Church at last be one.

Ian Randall records that this affirmation of the Union's continued membership of the British Council of Churches and the World Council of Churches issued in ever louder voices within the Baptist Revival Fellowship calling for withdrawal from the Union—a direction which itself led to Geoffrey King and Stanley Voke resigning from the Committee of the Fellowship.[23]

Twenty years later (bar ten days), on 19th April 1989 at the Union's Assembly held in Leicester, the issue was revisited with respect to the involvement of Baptist churches in "Churches Together." For many individual Baptists and Baptist churches the issue was seriously com-

21. Ibid., 49.

22. Randall, *English Baptists of the Twentieth Century*, 342.

23. Ibid., 344.

pounded by the involvement of Roman Catholics in the Churches Together process. The Assembly voted by approximately 74 percent to approve the Union's membership of these new ecumenical bodies (Churches Together in England and the Council of Churches for Britain and Ireland). By this time, of course, George Beasley-Murray was no longer a prominent prime-mover in these proposals—he had resigned the principalship of Spurgeon's College in 1973, spent seven years teaching at the Southern Baptist Theological seminary in the United States, had retired and returned to Britain in 1980, and (since 1986) had been living in Hove and attending the Holland Road Baptist church—yet he acknowledged the irony of his position as a constant advocate of unity but now a deacon in one of the sixty-five churches dissociating from the Union's decision.[24]

Continuing dissent from this ecumenical involvement led eventually to further votes concerning the Union's participation in ecumenical bodies at the Assembly held in Plymouth in 1995. On this occasion the motion for continuing participation in Churches Together in England was approved by over 90 percent and continuing membership of the Council of Churches for Britain and Ireland was approved by over 81 percent.[25] George Beasley-Murray died on 23 February 2000. I would like to believe the he died enormously encouraged by this now overwhelming support within the Baptist Union for ecumenical processes and inter-church engagement, yet I want to sound a note of caution qualifying any too hasty euphoria: such overwhelming approval for ecumenical involvement most certainly can be interpreted as issuing from that gospel commitment to visible unity that George Beasley-Murray so vigorously championed, but it might also be indicative of a blurring of Baptist distinctives, a blurring he would repudiate with equal vigor.

Ecumenism and Baptist Distinctives

I must confess that I retain a marked skepticism concerning the scientific merits of supposed scientific method with respect to church statistics, church surveys, and congregational questionnaires. Taking refuge, therefore, unapologetically in the merely anecdotal, few (I suspect) would dispute the rise of post-denominationalism. The prefix "post-"

24. Ibid., 344; cf. Beasley-Murray *Fearless for Truth*, 195.

25. Randall, *English Baptists of the Twentieth Century*, 495.

seems ubiquitous these days, is frequently misappropriated or misapplied, and is often employed imprecisely and with insufficient definition: by referring to post-denominationalism I am not intending to imply either the culmination or terminal demise of denominational divisions and affiliations; I am not suggesting that denominational distinctives have been abandoned entirely or superseded; but I am suggesting that those distinctives—and thereby those affiliations and distinctions—are becoming muted and relegated in significance. The consumerism and radical voluntarism of contemporary society—a radical voluntarism for which one interpretation of Free Church tradition is at least partly responsible—have infected Free Church life and, perhaps to a lesser degree, Anglicanism, more thoroughly than we might care to admit. On the one hand this consumerism and voluntarism has issued in the multiplication of independent churches (an oxymoron if ever there was such), but more pressingly these contemporary societal traits have affected the regularity of church attendance and the criteria for church affiliation: one is at least as likely to affiliate with a local church for the quality of its crèche, for the attractiveness of its youth work, or for its musical style, as for its denominational connectedness and doctrinal distinctives. Consequently, Baptist churches seem to be increasingly comprised of those who would not readily or without qualification identify themselves as Baptist; their commitment to the local church is genuine enough, but their awareness of its denominational distinctives and affiliations—and thereby their commitment to those distinctives and affiliations—is severely limited. The report *Baptists and Unity* identifies six Baptist distinctives of doctrine and practice, "points about which Baptists have naturally shown special concern":

1. Baptism
2. The authority or autonomy of the local company of believers
3. The Lord's Supper
4. The relationship of any form of episcopacy to the ministry as a whole
5. The use of Creeds and Confessions, whether in worship or as tests for membership
6. The relationship of Church and State[26]

26. Baptist Union Advisory Committee, *Baptists and Unity*, 20–22.

The inclusion of both the Lord's Supper and the use of Creeds and Confessions as peculiarly Baptist concerns may surprise some contemporary readers (and may indicate the inevitable time-embeddedness of all such documents). I will return specifically to the Report's discussion of these later in this paper, not least in order to illustrate the difficulty of identifying distinctively Baptist doctrines and practices with any definitive finality. Notwithstanding the Report's particular discussion of the remaining distinctives—discussions to which also we shall return, most (I hope) would agree that the nature and form of baptism, the integrity of the local church (and the consequences of such for any understanding of translocal ministry and connectedness), and a tradition of dissent with respect to the relationship between Church and State, historically and definitively are distinctive of a Baptist ecclesiology. Yet it is precisely these historically defining distinctives that, anecdotally, appear increasingly muted in this post-denominational context. The last half-century has seen a welcome awakening of interest in the continental Anabaptists of the sixteenth and early seventeenth centuries. No doubt the frequently trumpeted demise of Christendom forms the context of this renewed interest—though one suspects a more general voluntarism and romanticism fuels this fascination—yet, as a consequence of this renaissance together with the presence in many Baptist churches of former members of the Brethren, a tradition of separation has become confused with a tradition of dissent to the detriment and demise of the latter.[27] Perhaps symptomatic of this demise, the report *Pushing at the Boundaries of Unity*[28] presented to the Council of the Baptist Union in March 2006 makes no explicit mention of a tradition of dissent as defining of Baptist life in its discussion of possible obstacles to unity[29]—yet it is possible to argue that this tradition of dissent is even more basic in English Baptist history, rooted in radical British Puritanism rather than continental Anabaptism, than is baptism itself.[30]

27. For a discussion of the distinction between these traditions see my article, Colwell, "In Defence of Christendom," 21–29.

28. Faith and Unity Executive of the Baptist Union of Great Britain, The Council for Christian Unity of the Church of England, *Pushing at the Boundaries of Unity*.

29. Reference to late sixteenth-century Separatists is made on page 8 of *Pushing at the Boundaries of Unity* and the term is used again on page 81.

30. For the finest discussion of British Baptist beginnings, see White, *The English Baptists of the Seventeenth Century*.

The aforementioned presence in many Baptist churches of former members of the Brethren, together with the siren voices of Restorationism (itself more influenced by Brethrenism than is often acknowledged[31]) may explain the now not uncommon flirting with more Presbyterian forms of church government and the similarly not uncommonly expressed embarrassment with traditional forms of the church meeting. That considerations of the appropriateness of the church meeting can ever focus on the merits and demerits of democracy, a vulnerability to loud voices and dominant interests, the boring nature of agendas and minutes, or even the practicalities of convenience, betokens a loss of a distinctive confidence in the promise of Christ to be present to the Church in its gathering. And if this loss of confidence manifests itself with respect to the formal meetings of the local church, might it also apply to meetings of Council and Assembly: to what degree do we recognize such as ecclesial gatherings under the promise of Christ's presence and leading; to what degree have theological notions of prayerful assembly given way to set-piece presentations?

And what of baptism itself? In this respect, at least, one would expect Baptists to remain distinctive, yet the welcome increase in the proportion of open-membership churches—a trend that surely should be welcome in ecumenical context—seems rooted all too often in a relegation of the rite of baptism as secondary to personal confession and a felt experience of regeneration rather than in a gracious (if reluctant) acceptance of the validity of infant baptism within the context of a personal journey of discipleship. As I have noted elsewhere and at far greater length, we find ourselves today enmeshed in the extraordinary contradiction of churches known distinctively for their theology and practice of baptism being among the congregations where baptism is granted the least significance, where it is possible to be a fully communicant member without having been baptized in any form or manner whatsoever.[32] If baptism really is of such marginal significance what conceivable justification can there be for our continued existence as a distinct denomination? Why do we continue to make such a fuss about its supposedly appropriate mode and practice? With baptism seeming to count for so little and with apparent embarrassment concerning

31. For a discussion of Restorationism that draws attention to this dominant Brethren influence see Kay, *Apostolic Networks in Britain*.

32. Colwell, *Promise and Presence*.

the integrity of the gathered church, in an increasingly secular society where the so-called "Established Church" finds itself inevitably in a place of dissent, and while so many amongst us would gladly be part of an Anglican church, a Presbyterian church, a Pentecostal church, or a Methodist church if their youth work was deemed superior or their musical style was more congenial, what is the point of our continued separation? Let's quit these ancient and now redundant habits and unite as a single Church of England?

All this may have the sound of the rant of a grumpy old man—I must plead guilty on all counts—and I have already admitted the anecdotal nature of these observations (though such could easily be demonstrated by supposedly scientific surveys). Without hesitation I rejoice in the friendships, co-operation, and joint projects that have issued through the Churches Together process, in the fruitfulness of so many Local Ecumenical Projects, and in the mutual trust that so remarkably has replaced the suspicion and prejudice (if not bigotry) that marked my youth. But a unity furthered by a blurring of distinctives will be a unity of impoverishment rather than a unity of enrichment; will be precisely not that unity sought through the *Baptists and Unity* report; will be precisely not that unity for which George Beasley-Murray so courageously hoped and labored. With that report and with George Beasley-Murray, I am committed to seek a visible unity enriched by the sharing of distinct traditions and perceptions rather than impoverished by their suppression or demise. The need, then, is not for a blurring but for a renewed appreciation of that which renders us distinctively Baptist. The pressing question for the remainder of this paper is that of how such distinctives might come to sharper expression; how such renewal might be brought about.

Renewing a Distinctive Contribution

In September 1987 George Beasley-Murray participated in a consultation, sponsored by "Mainstream," exploring the question of Baptist identity. The date and sponsorship locate the conversations in specific context and the consultation led to the publication of a booklet, *A Perspective on Baptist Identity*, bringing together seven contributions to the discussion.[33] George Beasley-Murray is the author of the final article in this collec-

33. Slater, *A Perspective on Baptist Identity*.

tion, "Confessing Baptist Identity,"[34] but the editor notes with gratitude his suggestions and revisions of other papers within the booklet.[35] The consultation was, at least in part, a response to Brian Haymes' reflections on Baptist identity,[36] and, accordingly, George Beasley-Murray's article concludes the complementary contributions with a call, echoing "the plea made by Brian Haymes," for "a contemporary Baptist Confession of Faith."[37]

In the light of George Beasley-Murray's participation in the report *Baptists and Unity* this call is a little surprising (perhaps the intervening twenty years had issued in a change of mind; perhaps this later article indicates a limit on Beasley-Murray's influence on the earlier report). As previously noted, the report *Baptists and Unity* lists "the use of Creeds and Confessions, whether in worship or as tests for membership" as "among the points about which Baptists have naturally shown special concern."[38] The report acknowledges that "there is no evidence that Baptists ever used a creed or confession in worship, except on some rare and special occasion," but that the seventeenth-century Baptist Confessions "followed a pattern common to most of the Protestant Churches of the period." A previous statement of the Union in response to the "Lambeth Appeal" of 1920 is cited denying that ancient Creeds, though of historic value, can be accorded "a place of authority comparable with that of the Scriptures."[39] The report goes on to acknowledge that some Baptists view "references to the Apostles' and Nicene Creeds in a number of schemes of union" as "dangerous," that "even the ancient Creeds are not in themselves fully adequate statements of the Christian faith," and that it would be "in the view of many, an unfortunate and reactionary development were they again to become tests of orthodoxy."[40] Moreover, accepting that some would seek for the Declaration of Principle to be "elaborated and made into a more comprehensive doctrinal statement," the report opines that "almost inevitably . . . what are then advanced as possible statements

34. Beasley-Murray, "Confessing Baptist Identity," 75–85.

35. Slater, *A Perspective on Baptist Identity*, 5.

36. Haymes, *A Question of Identity.*

37. Beasley-Murray, "Confessing Baptist Identity," 78.

38. Baptist Union Advisory Committee, *Baptists and Unity*, 20–21.

39. Ibid., 30; cf. Randall, *English Baptists of the Twentieth Century*, 118: this *Reply* was adopted unanimously by the Baptist Assembly meeting at Leeds in May 1926.

40. Baptist Union Advisory Committee, *Baptists and Unity*, 30–31.

are 'party' concerns, representing a particular theological system, or the formulation of certain doctrines in avowedly controversial or partisan scenes."[41] The report concludes that "probably the one matter on which all would say they are united is the danger of apparent agreement on statements which can be variously understood and interpreted."[42]

In sharp contrast to this rather pessimistic (if realistic) earlier conclusion, George Beasley-Murray, in this later consultation, urges the production of a contemporary Baptist Confession of Faith "for God's sake, for our sakes, for the sake of other Churches and for the sake of the world."[43] His paper "Confessing Baptist Identity" begins with the observation that is similarly central to this present essay, that

> . . . when Christians of different traditions come together for discussion or joint action of any kind, they are inevitably led to examine their own beliefs. They have to ask why they are what they are, what it is that is distinctive about themselves and whether their distinctiveness is really very important.[44]

He acknowledges that the first "complication" in such discussions is "the diversity among us,"[45] and this observation provides the impetus, following the example of the American Baptist Convention, to seek to identify those "genes" that, in combination, make "the Baptist body what it is."[46] In calling for a contemporary Baptist confession of faith "for God's sake," Beasley-Murray moves against the historical contention of the report *Baptists and Unity*[47] by proposing that such a contemporary confession could be used within worship.[48] Such a confession is needful "for our sake" in order to "transform the understanding of . . . faith which many . . . hold to be dead" and as "an excellent basis for instructing new converts."[49] For the "sake of other Christians" Baptists "have a responsibility . . . to enumerate our convictions in a clear and

41. Ibid., 31.

42. Ibid.

43. Beasley-Murray, "Confessing Baptist Identity," 78.

44. Ibid., 75.

45. Ibid.

46. Ibid., 76.

47. See earlier reference to Baptist Union Advisory Committee, *Baptists and Unity*, 30.

48. Beasley-Murray, "Confessing Baptist Identity," 78–79.

49. Ibid., 79.

understandable manner" since there are "surprisingly few members of other denominations who have a reasonably accurate knowledge of what Baptists believe."[50] Finally, and "for the sake of the world," Baptists need "a statement that will help Christians to bear an effective witness to the gospel among people outside the Churches."[51]

Initially, perhaps, such a call for a contemporary Baptist confession may seem attractive. In the first place we have the historical precedent of the seventeenth-century Baptist Confessions—few surely would dispute that amongst Baptist congregations today they are barely known and that their language at least would benefit from contemporary revision. But in the second place—and for some among us far more pressingly—there is the perceived inadequacy of our present Declaration of Principle. Dissatisfaction with the present basis of our Union is expressed by more than one of the contributors to the Mainstream consultation, but maybe most sharply by Barrie White in response to its first article:

> That our Lord and Saviour Jesus Christ, God manifest in the flesh, is the sole and absolute authority in all matters pertaining to faith and practice, as revealed in the Holy Scriptures, and that each Church has liberty, under the guidance of the Holy Spirit, to interpret and administer His Laws.

Expressing a long standing "unease" with the article White comments, "That statement about liberty sounds to me all too much like an assertion of unbridled independency. It is a virtually absolute independence which has led to many of our troubles over the years."[52]

I would resolutely argue that this first article is woefully inadequate, if not ecclesiologically erroneous, as a matter of principle, but, as Barrie White continues, it is similarly lamentable "as a statement of unfortunate fact":

> Across three and a half centuries, if Baptists have had to choose between the independence of the local church and cooperation in fellowship with an association, they have chosen independence. This does not mean that most Baptists have been opposed to inter-denominational structures, but rather that they have

50. Ibid., 79–80.

51. Ibid., 80–81; for a similar summary of this article see Beasley-Murray, *Fearless for Truth*, 204.

52. White, "The Practice of Association," 19.

> tended to put their independence first and their cooperation, in any practical or theological sense, a long way second.[53]

In its favor, of course, it must be noted that, in our present context of radical individualism, the article identifies the interpretation of Scripture as the prerogative of the Church, albeit implicitly the local church, rather than the individual Christian in solipsistic isolation. Similarly it confesses Christ as revealed in Scripture as our sole authority rather than Scripture itself in any indeterminate or unfocused sense. Certainly, as Barrie White proceeds to admit, much depends here on how we understand the phrase "under the guidance of the Holy Spirit,"[54] but the phrase is vulnerable to notions of unmediated immediacy and, without some explicit qualification, would seem to be a blatant denial of catholicity (of the Church's essential oneness, connectedness, and continuity) for the sake of a radical autonomy that is itself a denial of a church's essential identity. To affirm the integrity of the local church is not necessarily to deny its connectedness and catholicity: any authentic integrity of a local church is rather an outcome and consequence of its connectedness and catholicity and is nullified without such. Independency ought properly to be understood as a rejection of external domination by State or by supposed ecclesiastical authority rather than as an independency of ecclesiastical disconnectedness; a local church simply does not have the liberty—without denying its true integrity as a local church—to interpret Scripture without respect to this catholic connectedness; the continuity and connectedness of the Church across the ages and across the continents is precisely a means through which the Holy Spirit guides the local church in its interpretation of Scripture. As Barrie White seems to urge, at very least there should be some explicit reference to associating here (and, while we're on the subject, can we please drop this reference to the administering of 'His Laws' which only reinforces naïve notions of Scripture as a book of rules rather than as a transformative narrative). Nor are the difficulties of the Declaration of Principle limited to its first article: the statement on baptism appears to determine the form of baptism (immersion) to be as definitive as the faith and repentance of its proper participants, and surely we can find more appropriate language than that of duty to express the missional

53. Ibid., 20.

54. Ibid., 25ff.

identity and calling of the Church, and thereby of every Christian disciple—we are constrained by love before we are constrained by obligation. A relatively recent trend in ordinations and inductions has been to invite the candidate to express assent to our Declaration of Principle—I suspect that I am not alone amongst my peers in being grateful that this never used to be the case.

Yet, since this Declaration of Principle is quite properly the basis of our Union, the basis of a covenantal relationship between churches, associations, and colleges, the basis of a covenantal commitment of accredited ministers, ought we not belatedly to heed the call of George Beasley-Murray and others at least to the point of revising the wording of this most basic statement? If our covenanting together is to be meaningful, then the basis of that covenanting should be more persuasive and precise. Moreover, if the distinctiveness of our being as Baptists is not to become blurred in a context of post-denominationalism, and if we are to enrich rather than to impoverish ecumenical dialogue, surely this brief and simple statement of distinctives merits revision.

The call of George Beasley-Murray and others was, of course, for something far more comprehensive and robust, something resembling the Confessions of our Baptist forebears—but here, I think, we encounter a series of significant difficulties (not least, the sheer length of those confessions would militate against their use in worship or in the instruction of new Christians). Returning for a moment to the report *Baptists and Unity*, we should firstly heed the warning concerning "partisan" tendencies. That report notes the adherence of some to the Evangelical Alliance statement of faith of 1846 but this particular example is instructively problematic.[55] Firstly, the Evangelical Alliance statement of faith has itself undergone a series of not insignificant revisions over the years, demonstrating again the inevitable time-bounded nature of all such statements and confessions.[56] Secondly, recent and very public debates concerning whether or not a penal and substitutionary notion of the atonement was "implicit" in the version of the statement immediately preceding the current version demonstrates the similarly inevitable vulnerability of all such statements to a range of interpretations and the all too common and presumptuous confusion of an im-

55. Baptist Union Advisory Committee, *Baptists and Unity*, 31.

56. For an account of these revisions and their possible significance see Randall and Hilborn, *One Body in Christ*.

plication and an inference. But finally and most disturbingly, this most recent controversy concerning the significance of the statement in this specific respect demonstrates the tendency (if not the intention) for such statements to become tests of supposed orthodoxy,[57] thereby promoting such statements to an authoritative status without respect to their lack of catholicity, their confessedly partisan nature and purpose, and their blatant inadequacies. Local churches (and colleges) may wish to adopt such statements as a means of affirming their evangelical identity, but the temptation to partisan witch-hunts is ever lurking and with respect to peculiarly Baptist distinctives—which is our present concern—such statements help us not at all.

Note was taken previously of the surprising inclusion of the Lord's Supper within the *Baptists and Unity* report as one of the issues of "special concern" and here we encounter further illustrations of the difficulty in identifying definitive Baptist distinctives beyond our present Declaration of Principle.[58] Questions raised by that report include that of the freedom for "lay presidency" at the Supper, the freedom for a memorialist understanding of the Supper, and the assumption that it would "be generally agreed that it is not satisfactory for there to be participation by any who are not ready to make a Christian profession and publicly to assume the responsibilities of church membership."[59]

Again merely anecdotally, "lay presidency" seems commonplace amongst contemporary Baptist churches but I doubt that this was as universally the case when that report was written and there is evidence that it was not a common practice for our seventeenth and eighteenth-century forebears;[60] there may be few Baptists who have maintained a notion of any transformation of the identity of the elements or held a sacrificial understanding of the Eucharistic rite, but earlier generations of both General and Particular Baptists were seldom merely memorialist in their interpretations of the Supper; and contemporary debates concerning children and communion rightly or misguidedly challenge the

57. Note, for instance, the tone and explicit assumptions of Jeffery, Ovey, and Sach in *Pierced for Our Transgressions*.

58. Baptist Union Advisory Committee, *Baptists and Unity*, 20.

59. Ibid., 26–27.

60. See, for instance, White, *The English Baptists of the Seventeenth Century*, 29, 62, 117ff.; Walker, *Baptists at the Table*, 121ff.; and Winter, "Who May Administer the Lord's Supper?," 129–30.

general assumption of this older report—all which serve to show that, if we move beyond those distinctives identified in our Declaration of Principle, we quickly encounter significant difference and dispute, both historically and contemporarily.

The focus for the Mainstream consultation in which George Beasley-Murray participated was in the call for a contemporary Baptist confession of faith, the plea to "pluck up courage and do for our day what our Baptist forefathers did for theirs."[61] This appeal to historical precedence may be instructive in several respects. In the first place (and to state the blindingly obvious), there was not one but there were several Baptist confessions of the seventeenth century sometimes emanating from local associations or connexions, sometimes reflecting the distinctions between General Baptists and Particular Baptists—but beyond the distinctives of baptism, dissent, and the integrity of the local church (and perhaps even with respect to these distinctives, at least in terms of emphasis and specific understanding) Baptists then would have found it as hard to agree a single confession as would now most certainly be the case.[62] In the second place and as noted both in the *Baptists and Unity* report and in Barrie White's history of *The English Baptists of the Seventeenth Century*,[63] the Baptist confessions were not themselves independent, they incorporated or elaborated upon other Protestant confessions, the Westminster Confession and the Savoy Declaration in particular, and sometimes explicitly acknowledged and affirmed the older catholic creeds—that is to say, in seeking to affirm something distinctive they were also and perhaps primarily concerned to say something catholic, something connected and continuous. Thirdly, as also noted in the *Baptists and Unity* report and as perhaps deriving from the previous point,[64] these Confessions were rarely used in worship. It is with respect to this final point, and inferentially with respect to the second point that I find myself in profound disagreement with George Beasley-Murray concerning the possibility of any such confession ever finding its proper place in corporate worship.

61. Beasley-Murray, "Confessing Baptist Identity," 78.

62. Lumpkin, *Baptist Confessions of Faith*.

63. Baptist Union Advisory Committee, *Baptists and Unity*, 29; cf. White, *The English Baptists of the Seventeenth Century*, 61, 117ff.

64. Baptist Union Advisory Committee, *Baptists and Unity*, 29.

I recognize that I am unrepresentative in this respect, both historically and contemporarily, but I welcome the use of the catholic creeds in our worship: the Nicene-Constantinopolitan creed may have been formulated in the context of controversy but several of its individual affirmations arose in the context of worship and the Church's worship remains its proper context. The roots of the Apostles' Creed are lost to us but the assumption that it emerged as a baptismal confession is not without merit and again locates the creed in the context of worship. Certainly the Nicene-Constantinopolitan creed, together with its accompanying list of anathemas, was formulated specifically to exclude, but its common place in catholic worship (albeit in slightly different forms in the East and the West) tends to a more inclusive outcome—here we can affirm again that which we are called to hold in common through all our distinctions. We do not confess ourselves but Jesus Christ as Lord: confession is appropriate to that which unites rather than that which divides; confession is an expression of confidence in the gospel, not an expression of distinctives, no matter how rooted in the gospel those distinctives may be. If it is the case that we learn by indwelling then it is appropriate that these catholic affirmations should regularly find their place in our worship, as recognition of our unity rather than our distinctiveness. But if it is the case that we learn by indwelling then maybe our Baptist distinctiveness should be demonstrated not in different or non-catholic confession but in confessing differently; a liturgical distinction of manner rather than content.

Most obviously, it should be our practice of baptism, rather than our confession of baptism, that identifies our distinctiveness to all those participating in our life and worship, whatever their ecclesial roots. Similarly, it should be our practice of being Church, our manner of expressing the Church's holiness and catholic unity, that identifies our distinct manner of being Church, whether demonstrated in our manner of celebrating the Lord's Supper or in the manner of decision making, of our corporate discerning of the mind of Christ. And in the manner of our praying for our society, for government, for the world, we should demonstrate neither our subservience nor our separation but our radical and prophetic dissent. If these distinctives are in our Baptist genes they will be demonstrated in our life and worship. Conversely, if these distinctives are demonstrated in our life and worship they will inevitably become part of our genetic identity and of the genetic identity of those who gather with us, whatever their denominational origins. We do not need a distinctive confession to mark our points of difference—confession is an opportunity to celebrate our catholic unity. We rather need the renewal of a distinctive manner of confessing, of worshiping, of being the people of God that demonstrates our distinctiveness within that unity, an enriching rather than a qualifying of catholicity.

Conclusions

It would be naïve to expect a revision of our Declaration of Principle alone to issue in such a renewal of distinctive practice—and the use of any Declaration of Principle in worship or as a test of membership should be resisted—but the mere process (and pain) of conducting such a revision might awaken us to that which renders us distinctive. Were this revision to be undertaken through our representative gatherings in Council and Assembly this in itself would necessitate a refreshing theological rigor that has not always characterized these bodies, and the mere process of pursuing this end in this manner would not only bring these distinctives to the foreground of our collective consciousness; it would itself be a demonstration of a distinct means of ecclesial discernment. In a context when, for whatever reasons, our Baptist distinctives may be threatened, the troublesome process of reviewing our Declaration of Principle may compel us again to reflect on our distinctive understanding of baptism and of the Church, this might prompt a more general awakening of historical and theological consciousness and this, in turn, might issue in a deep and tangible renewal of practice that enriches rather than undermines a true catholic unity. It is fitting to conclude this paper on this positive note and by allowing its subject, George Beasley-Murray, the last word. Commenting on the prayer of Jesus in John 17 he writes,

> In the light of the divisions that have arisen between Christian churches through the centuries, it was inevitable that a movement should arise to call the churches to reverse the trends of the centuries and to seek to experience and express anew their unity in Christ. It was equally natural that this movement should begin within the missionary agencies of the churches (as at Edinburgh, 1910), since the divisions were hindering the carrying out of the missionary task; the nations frequently saw the reconciling power of the Gospel less clearly than its divisive power. . . . reflection on the prayer of necessity leads to urgent consideration how the unity which embraces all Christians within one Body can be expressed within their mutual relations, and how it should be-

come a principle of action in the churches' mission to the world. Perhaps then reflection on the fact that the unity of the Church was the subject of Jesus' prayer to God rather than exhortation to disciples may drive us to our knees in prayer for grace that his prayer may be answered in us, and in our own churches, that the world may be able to perceive in us the reconciling power of God in Christ.[65]

Bibliography

Baptist Union Advisory Committee for Church Relations. *Baptists and Unity*. London: Baptist Union, 1967.

Beasley-Murray, George. "Confessing Baptist Identity." In *A Perspective on Baptist Identity*, edited by David Slater. Knightsbridge: Mainstream, 1987.

———. *John*. Word Biblical Commentary 36. 2nd ed. Nashville: Thomas Nelson, 1999.

———. *Reflections on the Ecumenical Movement*. London: Baptist Union of Great Britain and Ireland, 1965.

Beasley-Murray, Paul. *Fearless for Truth: A Personal Portrait of George Raymond Beasley-Murray*. Carlisle, UK: Paternoster, 2002.

Colwell, John E. "In Defence of Christendom: The Claim of Christ and the Confidence of the Church." *Baptist Ministers' Journal* 298 (2007) 21–29.

———. *Promise and Presence: An Exploration of Sacramental Theology*. Milton Keynes, UK: Paternoster, 2005.

Faith and Unity Executive of the Baptist Union of Great Britain, The Council for Christian Unity of the Church of England. *Pushing at the Boundaries of Unity: Anglicans and Baptists in Conversation*. London: Church House Publishing, 2005.

Haymes, Brian. *A Question of Identity: Reflections on Baptist Principles and Practice*. Leeds: Yorkshire Baptist Association, 1986.

Jeffery, Steve, Mike Ovey, and Andrew Sach. *Pierced for Our Transgressions: Rediscovering the Glory of Penal Substitution*. Leicester, UK: InterVarsity, 2007.

Kay, William K. *Apostolic Networks in Britain: New Ways of Being Church*. Studies in Evangelical History and Thought. Milton Keynes, UK: Paternoster, 2007.

Lumpkin, William L. *Baptist Confessions of Faith*. Valley Forge, PA: Judson, 1959.

Randall, Ian M. *The English Baptists of the Twentieth Century*. Didcot: Baptist Historical Society, 2005.

Randall, Ian M., and David Hilborn. *One Body in Christ: The History and Significance of the Evangelical Alliance*. Carlisle, UK: Paternoster, 2001.

Slater, David, ed. *A Perspective on Baptist Identity*. Knightsbridge: Mainstream 1987.

Walker, Michael J. *Baptists at the Table: The Theology of the Lord's Supper amongst English Baptists in the Nineteenth Century*. Didcot: Baptist Historical Society, 1992.

White, Barrie R. *The English Baptists of the Seventeenth Century*. London: Baptist Historical Society, 1983.

65. Beasley-Murray, *John*, 307.

———. "The Practice of Association." In *A Perspective on Baptist Identity*, edited by David Slater. Knightsbridge: Mainstream 1987.

Winter, E. P. "Who May Administer the Lord's Supper?" *Baptist Quarterly* 16 (1955) 128–33.

8

"Living like Maggots"

Is Preaching Still Relevant in the Twenty-First Century?[1]

Stephen R. Holmes

Preamble

I only once had the privilege of meeting Dr. George Beasley-Murray, listening to him give a paper on the nature of apocalyptic whilst a Research Fellow at Spurgeon's College. What I know of his interests and concerns, and so what I can divine as a fitting way to honor his memory, is limited to what I have read in his own works and in the reminiscences of others—notably, of course, in his son Paul's excellent biography. No current evangelical scholar, however, can fail to be aware of the debt we owe to George Beasley-Murray in teaching the academy that evangelicals could actually think—well, at least one of them could—and in teaching evangelicalism that academic theology could serve the cause of the gospel not just oppose it. When I was asked to consider giving this lecture, then, I seized the chance to acknowledge, if not to begin to discharge, the debt my own calling owes to Dr. Beasley-Murray, despite my acute consciousness that there are so many others who could honor his memory so much better. I am grateful to Spurgeon's College for the

1. This lecture was delivered at the Baptist Assembly in Bournemouth on 3 May 2009.

invitation, and I hope that what I have to offer will be judged appropriate by those better qualified than I.

George Beasley-Murray's academic life was almost framed by a single book: his *Preaching the Gospel from the Gospels* was first published in 1956, the first book to appear after the publication of his doctoral thesis, and appeared in a second edition in 1996, the last monograph to appear under his name during his life with the exception of a second edition of his John commentary.[2] The book was radical when first published: Evangelicals preached the gospel from the epistles, which helpfully told us of human sinfulness, justification through the atoning death of Christ, and so on. The Gospels taught us Christian living. The book challenged such an unhelpful bifurcation and insisted that the whole of Scripture was, in the truest sense of the word, evangelical.[3]

It claimed more than just that, though. Drawing on the methods of form criticism, although wryly observing that Martin Dibelius would probably not have been pleased to see this particular result of his techniques, Dr. Beasley-Murray argued, startlingly, that "*it pleased God by the foolishness of preaching to give men the Gospels*."[4] Scripture is gospel-shaped, and in the case of Matthew, Mark, Luke and John, it is gospel-shaped because it is the result of gospel preaching. The book oozes the urgency of evangelistic preaching in every paragraph, seeing the beginnings of the church, its foundation-document in the New Testament, and the whole of its ongoing life, as built by and on the proclamation of what God has done in Jesus Christ. The book ended, "God has spoken. The Son has risen. The doors of the Kingdom stand open. The hour of opportunity is present. By parable, by entreaty, by every means of driving home the message, let us persuade men that they enter whist they may."[5]

It is not difficult to find many similar claims to the importance of gospel preaching in Dr. Beasley-Murray's writings. Take again the closing peroration of a sermon preached at the Baptist Assembly, in Leeds in 1965: "In such a spirit let us go to our mission. Chicken-heartedness and pessimism have no place in Christianity, nor feeble knees, helpless hands and hang-dog looks. We are the people of the resurrection with

2. Details from Beasley-Murray, *Fearless for Truth*, 221–22.

3. See ibid., 66, for some similar reflections.

4. Beasley-Murray, *Preaching*, 13, italics original.

5. Ibid., 127.

the message of life for the world. Share the faith of Jesus. Do not fail or be discouraged. Set the gospel in the earth. For the earth shall be full of the knowledge of the glory of the Lord as the waters cover the sea."[6] George Beasley-Murray believed in the importance and urgency of preaching, and strove to send able preachers into the world, and to convince others that it mattered.

With preaching in view, however, we cannot just examine what George Beasley-Murray had to say on the subject. Preaching, at least potentially, needs to be alive to contemporary culture to be effective; at the very least the challenges to the ministry of preaching are different in each new cultural context. So it seemed to me, when Nigel and I agreed on a theme of preaching for this lecture, that it would be more faithful to Dr. Beasley-Murray's memory to think about how we can make preaching more honoring to God and effective in human lives in the first decades of the twenty-first century, than to think about how he himself worked to do the same thing in the middle decades of the twentieth. In *Preaching the Gospel from the Gospels,* he tackled head-on one of the limitations imposed on preaching by the assumptions shared widely within the evangelical churches of his day; I take it a better task to try to do the same for our day, than to rehearse arguments that are long-won, not least because of Dr. Beasley-Murray's powerful intervention. After all, we live in a time when preaching is under more sustained attack within evangelicalism than any other point in history of which I am aware. St. Paul compared the minister of the gospel to an ox treading out grain—one of his more flattering images for us preachers, I always thought; it would take a modern writer to compare us to maggots, however. Let me introduce you to the words of Scotland's greatest twentieth-century poet, and a near contemporary of George Beasley-Murray, Hugh MacDiarmid.

"Living like maggots"? The Failure of Preaching

> . . . as I spoke with these five thousand people
>
> Each of us was more or less lost
>
> In the midst of events so powerfully presented.
>
> All who should help to open the way for true expression

6. From a sermon on Isa 42:4, given at the 1965 Baptist Assembly in Leeds, quoted in Brown, "George Raymond Beasley-Murray," 17.

> —The teachers, the ministers, the writers—are living like maggots
>
> On dead words in an advanced state of decomposition,
>
> Big words that died over twenty years ago
>
> —For most of the important words were killed in the First World War—
>
> And Edinburgh has not given birth to any new words yet
>
> In which it can say anything worth saying, make anything but animal noises . . .[7]

So wrote MacDiarmid in his 1945 poem "Talking with Five Thousand People in Edinburgh." In his account ministers sit alongside teachers and writers as those "who should help open the way for true expression," who should give the culture a language in which it can articulate its deepest and nameless desires and aversions. (The earlier part of the poem has been about the lack of such a language in Edinburgh.) The failure, in MacDiarmid's terms, of the ministers, writers, and others, is their—our—lack of realization that the world has changed, that a world, a culture, a language, has died, gunned down and gassed on the plains of Flanders, so that now we live like maggots, gorging ourselves on its rotting carcass, giving no language and no life to Edinburgh, or anywhere else.

Over the last generation or so in the United States, a similar complaint has been heard, specifically about preaching, and a significant scholarly industry has grown up attempting to give an answer, which goes by the name of the "new homiletic." The generally-accepted starting point is Fred Craddock's devastating first chapter to his book, *As One Without Authority*.[8] Craddock wrote:

> As a rule, younger ministers are keenly aware of the factors discussed above, and their preaching reflects it. Their predecessors ascended the pulpit to speak of the eternal certainties, truths etched forever in the granite of absolute reality, matters framed for proclamation, not for discussion. But where have all the abso-

7. MacDiarmid, "Talking with Five Thousand People in Edinburgh," 248. This extract is used with the kind cooperation of Routledge & Kegan Paul.

8. The term "new homiletic" was first used in print a couple of years before Craddock's book. It was coined by David James Randolph, in his *The Renewal of Preaching*.

> lutes gone? The old thunderbolts rust in the attic while the minister tries to lead the people through the morass of relativities and proximate possibilities. And the difficulties involved in finding and articulating a faith are not the congregation's alone: they are the minister's as well . . . No longer can the preacher presuppose the general recognition of her authority as clergy, or the authority of her institution, or the authority of Scripture.[9]

Craddock's solution, hinted at in this quotation and widely followed, has been to suggest that the failure was not a failure of preaching *per se*, but of an older tradition of preaching, which assumed certain structures of authority, and so found its characteristic mode of discourse in proclamation, the ringing declaration of non-negotiable truths. This is what has failed. In Craddock's new "inductive" model of preaching, the preacher guides her people through a reflection on the collision between text and life, not telling them what to think, but coming as a questioner amongst questioners, and seeking to help them to discover their own truth, rather than demanding that they hear and believe hers.

Now, we need to be careful here. Thus far, it is possible to hear Craddock as recommending a change in style, not in theology. It is quite possible to believe that the Word of God comes to us refusing to be questioned and demanding to be believed, but also that in our present culture, the best way to present that uncompromising demand is to let people discover it for themselves—popular evangelical catechetical material such as the *Alpha* Course offers obvious examples of such a stance, as does much criticism of preaching that appeals to cultural modes of discourse and educational theory. In these discussions we are routinely told that evidence demonstrates that an uninterrupted monologue is an extremely poor way of communicating information, particularly in the context of a culture that has had its attention spans reduced by television entertainment. Craddock points to the collapse of authority structures: the preacher occupied a cultural location as a professional or an expert who could expect to command attention by virtue of his office. Deferential respect for authority figures is long-gone from our culture, however, pummeled by the newly-invented teenagers of the 1950s, and killed by a thousand sharp stabs of satire in the 1960s. If we are inspired by teachers today, it is inspirational personalities, not accredited expertise, that will be the key quality they possess. They will encourage us to

9. Craddock, *As One without Authority*, 13–14

be ourselves, to take responsibility for our own learning and flourishing. These are tasks not easily essayed in a deferentially-received monologue.

MacDiarmid accuses us of using dead language; modern critics challenge our styles of delivery; but Craddock's complaint is much deeper than either of these. His call was for a new theology of preaching, which eschewed proclamation simply because it no longer found the doctrine of revelation that undergirded proclamation credible. He says:

> Rarely, if ever, in the history of the church have so many firm periods slumped into commas and so many triumphant exclamation points curled into question marks. Those who speak with strong conviction on a topic are suspected of the heresy of premature finality. Permanent temples are to be abandoned as houses of idolatry; the true people of God are in tents again. It is the age of journalistic theology; even the Bible is out in paperback. The transient and the contingent have moved to the center of consciousness.[10]

At the heart of Craddock's book was a demand that preaching should start where the people are. Preachers should name the questions, hopes, and fears, of their congregations, and work from there; Scripture and theology have relevance only insofar as they adequately interpret these starting points. Preaching, perhaps, has finally caught up with Frei's observed shift in hermeneutics: it has ceased attempting to read the world into the text and started, if it deals with the text at all, to read the text into the world. And the world it finds is confused, fragmented, shattered and multiply partial. MacDiarmid's complaint was, appropriately for 1945, characteristically modern: the concern that there are at present no convincing ways of narrating the world; Craddock's is classically postmodern: he has given up believing that the world, as a whole, can be convincingly narrated.

In the discussions started by Craddock all that was wrong with the old modes of preaching is summed up under the word "proclamation": it refers to an assumption of certainty and authority that is incredible in modern culture and illegitimate in modern theology; to a practice of homiletics that ignores the needs and locations of the hearers and assumes, utterly wrongly of course, that a congregation might actually be attentive to the preacher's analysis of the text of Scripture; to bombastic

10. Ibid., 11.

monological discourse that regards its own ideologies as more central than the lived reality of human lives.

MacDiarmid's poem points to the core problem identified by Craddock: the loss of any shared language that can narrate the world in a publicly convincing manner. (We could, I suppose, speak of an "incredulity towards metanarratives," but I suspect that such discourse fails to capture just how complete the collapse of shared meaning has become.) MacDiarmid in 1945 pictured preachers, along with writers and teachers, proceeding in complete ignorance of this loss, assuming that the world may be narrated the way it always was, living like maggots on the rotting remains of long-dead metanarratives. Craddock, a generation later, also notes the attempt to live as if old narrations remained convincing, but also imagines a new homiletic which does not pretend to easy explanations, but which instead attempts to reflect authentically the problematic process of living in an unnarrated world, of acting out a play not just without knowing the script, but knowing that whatever script there is lacks any perceivable narrative structure, any coherence or inner logic. And so we use the pulpit, sometimes to amuse, sometimes to fend off despair, whilst waiting, perhaps, for Godot to come and make whatever sense may be made of it all. The preacher in this pulpit is not to pretend confidently to describe the world, but to come timidly, like a frightened boy, called by Mr Godot to mind the goats—or perhaps to feed the sheep—but not understanding the task, or the message he is given to deliver.

The one who comes today proclaiming a deposit of truth, pretending to some uncomplicated access to a privileged narration of the world, to a script that makes sense, and expecting it to command assent, is necessarily deluded. Craddock's evidence for this claim can be as simple as an appeal to MacDiarmid's poem: culturally, such a claim is merely risible. It seems risible to our hearers and, perhaps more importantly, it seems risible to us. No averagely intelligent and culturally aware preacher would dare to preach like this anymore. As Craddock says, "the difficulties involved in finding and articulating a faith are not the congregation's alone: they are the minister's as well." We don't believe in metanarratives that describe the world adequately; how can we preach as if we did?

The preacher who engages in proclamation is living like a maggot whilst imagining he is roaring like a lion; he is a dangerous and pathetic creature who should be first banned from doing any more psychological damage to congregations, and then pitied for his delusional state. In his place? Discussion, of course—much discussion; encounter groups; experiential learning; the sharing of practical insights that derive authority from being lived, not from being learned. George Beasley-Murray taught two generations of Baptist pastors how to preach; is it a lesson now best consigned to the pages of the journal of the Historical Society?

Words That Inspire

Before we despair of the task, let's pause for a moment. "I see a cloud, the size of a man's hand," and I see it, bizarrely, in the murky business of political electioneering. There has been a surprising renewal of the power of speech-making in our time. On 2 October, 2002, a virtually unknown politician spoke at an anti-war rally in Chicago. His speech was about five minutes, 926 words. It transfixed, astonished, and inspired the crowd. Jennifer Spitz, one of the organizers of the rally, recalls, "I stood there and listened to him give that speech and said, 'who is this guy? . . . He needs to be president.'"[11]

He now is. Eighteen months later, Senator Obama spoke at the 2004 Democratic National Convention, and in the course of less than an hour moved from being just a junior senator to being one of the front runners for the party's next presidential nomination. It is not unreasonable to claim that Barak Hussain Obama started rewriting the pages of history with a single speech—a monologue, delivered to a silent crowd, from a podium higher and more remote than any Baptist pulpit I have ever seen. What, then, of the educational theory that says monologues are bad ways of communicating information? Well, it happens that the evidence is rather less compelling than sometimes claimed; but much more importantly, Obama almost never uses speeches to communicate information: the content of his election campaign was not a set of detailed policy proposals, but a mood, a confidence, a belief that change could happen—if you had to sum it up in his own slogan, rather less impressive for those of us who grew up on British children's TV, he spent nine months traveling America saying, of Iraq, of the economy, of inequality, of healthcare, of the Middle East, of trade negotiations, of racism, of every social and political problem "Can we fix it? Yes we can!" Obama's speeches didn't inform—but they did inspire.

11. Quotation and statistics taken from Weissman, *The Power Presenter*, 163–64.

In the run-up to the 1997 British General Election the same thing happened. Tony Blair is not in Obama's class as an orator, but he had around him one of the most successful and sophisticated communication machines ever assembled. And after all the planning and informing and policy decisions and everything else, as the 1996 Labour conference closed, the last session rolled away the screens and the technology, and Blair stood up and spoke directly to the audience, and the aim was simply inspiration. He wanted them to go out one more wet April evening knocking on doors. To stuff a hundred more envelopes. He was not telling them how to campaign—they knew that—but inspiring them to act on what they knew.

Is politics a special case? Let me tell you about Nancy Duarte. Nancy Duarte runs a design company in California that specializes in designing presentations. She prepared the script and Power-point for Al Gore, for his "Inconvenient Truth" tour. Anyone who can produce a Power-point presentation that can both become a blockbusting film and win a Nobel peace prize has got something to teach us about communication! Talking to businessmen, she recommends that information be communicated through a memo; but if you want to "get others to adopt your point of view," she says, use a presentation.[12] And it's not about the visuals or anything else, it's about personal, face to face, human contact. Duarte is not alone in recommending this. There is an extensive and big-selling genre of business books on giving presentations that convince, inspire, change hearts and minds and actions. People claim results worth hundreds of millions of dollars from well-planned speeches. And some of that planning is scarily basic—one of the biggest books in the genre, much referenced by other writers, including Nancy Duarte, recommends, as an important, ground-breaking insight, dividing every speech up into three clear points![13]

And so the sermon: it may be that a sermon is a bad way of transferring information to people; but if current political and business thinking is right—and I acknowledge that that is a big "if"—then preaching might be a very good way of inspiring people. George Beasley-Murray again: "by every means of driving home the message, let us persuade men that they enter whilst they may." To persuade might just be the proper work of preaching.

12. Duarte, *Slide:ology*, 6–7.

13. Atkinson, *Beyond Bullet Points*, 148.

Words That Enliven

This is not enough, however. A gifted orator might persuade us to vote this way rather than that; she might inspire us to take out a stock option. But the man who has lain paralyzed for thirty-seven years will not be inspired to leap into the pool when the waters are stirred; those who are dead in their trespasses and sins will not be persuaded into new life. Unless we are simply Pelagian, preaching that inspires is not enough: we need preaching that transforms, enlivens, converts.

Now, of course, it is a basic truth that human acts, of themselves, do not and cannot transform, enliven, or convert. This is the work of God's Spirit alone. We should not make the mistake, however, of separating the work of God's Spirit from creaturely events—to take precisely our point, "it pleased God, through the foolishness of our preaching, to save those who believe," or so claims Paul in 1 Cor 1:21.[14] We are here into the mystery of the concurrence of divine sovereignty and human freedom, and we must be careful to steer the right course: human acts do not cause divine action—of course not!—but nor are they irrelevant to it. God has chosen to use our words in his sovereign work of salvation.

Strikingly, one way or another, every side of the various Reformation debates over the nature of salvation knew this. When the Council of Trent located the office of the keys in the sacrament of penance rather than in the pulpit,[15] the debate concerned the location of the words that have the power to redefine and re-narrate the life of the sinner, not the existence of such words. The Lutheran symbols, collected in the *Book of Concord*, are eager to stress the difference between the preaching of the law and the preaching of the gospel, and to determine where the call to repentance properly belongs; this is important because it safeguards the Lutheran conviction that the preaching of the gospel is not a giving of information about how forgiveness may be obtained, but an effectual proclamation that the hearers are, in Christ, forgiven.[16]

14. My translation.

15. The point is repeated, but see, e.g., Canon III on the Sacrament of Penance: *Si quis dixerit, verba illa Domini Salvatoris: Accipite Spiritum Sanctum; arequorum remiseritis peccata, remittuntur eis; et quorum retinueritis, retenta sunt: non esse intelligenda de potestate remittendi et retinendi peccata in sacramento pœnitentiæ, sicut Ecclesia Catholica ab initio semper intellexit; detorserit autem, contra institutionem hujus sacramenti, ad auctoritatem prædicandi evangelium: anathema sit.*

16. See especially Article V, in either the *Epitome* or the fuller text.

In Reformed symbolics, finally, the pure preaching of the Word of God is mostly mentioned, without definition, as one of the two/three marks of the church, alongside the right celebration of the dominical sacraments and (sometimes) the exercise of biblical church discipline. When the question of definition is raised, however, the answer given is striking, and it is given in a central and influential document, the *Second Helvetic Confession*, which asserts that *praedicatio verbi Dei est verbum Dei*. The preaching of the Word of God is the word of God.[17] As simple as that. The article under this head spells out that the one who hears gospel preaching hears the true and actual word of God.

Now, as far as I can see, the Word of God does not propose itself for discussion, speak hesitantly, or convene a study group. Nor does the Word of God operate in inductive mode. In the beginning, God speaks, and in obedience to the Word of God, worlds spring into being. But—crucially—nor does the Word of God as it is described in Scripture simply announce propositional truth. For the prophets, the Word of God comes with all the power of transforming event. When the Word of God names a thing or a person, the existence of that person or thing is transformed. As Klappert says, the Word of God even in OT usage refers to '[t]he prophetic word of promise which shapes history, the directive word of the covenant which takes possession of men [*sic*] and the creative word of God which determines nature and its order."[18] If the preaching of the Word of God is indeed simply the Word of God, the proper mode of preaching is proclamation, the uncompromising announcing of new truth that will be transformative of the being and life of the hearer, whether that hearer is an idolatrous monarch or a not-yet existent galaxy.

Let me suggest that, if we actually take this seriously, and try to understand the claim of the Confession in these terms, the problem with the forms of proclamation decried by MacDiarmid and Craddock is that they failed to be proclamatory enough. Craddock again, words I have already quoted: preachers once "ascended the pulpit to speak of the

17. The slogan is, of course, a title added later to the text of the confession. The actual text reads: *Proinde cum hodie hoc Dei verbum per prædicatores legitime vocatos annunciatur in Ecclesia, credimus ipsum Dei verbum annunciari et a fidelibus recipi . . . atque in præsenti spectandum esse ipsum verbum, quod annunciatur, non annunciantem ministrum, qui, etsi sit malus et peccator, verum tamen et bonum manet nihilominus verbum Dei*. The title is clearly an adequate summary of the content.

18. Klappert, "Logos," 3:1087–1117.

eternal certainties, truths etched forever in the granite of absolute reality, matters framed for proclamation, not for discussion." Well, perhaps they did, but if so, their preaching was inadequate, if measured strictly by the canons of the *Confessio Helvetica Posterior*. The preacher who merely declaims "truths etched forever in the granite of absolute reality" has far too small a conception of the preaching task, far too weak an account of the authority of preaching, far too little trust that the *praedicatio verbi Dei est verbum Dei*.

"The Word of God is living and active" affirms the writer to the Hebrews.[19] As I have said already, worlds spring into being in obedience to God's Word. When God speaks, the Word spoken does not do anything so trivial and impotent as revealing the fundamental truth about things; necessarily not—there just are no things to reveal the truth about apart from the Word of God. The preaching identified in the Second Helvetic Confession does not merely announce eternal truths etched forever on granite; rather it etches new, hitherto unimagined, truths, on—not granite, but on something far harder, stony human hearts, and on the powers and principalities of this evil age. Preaching understood properly as proclamation claims the ability to narrate human lives—and the grand sweep of history—not because the preacher pretends to have read the script, but because preaching, as the Word of God, is called to write the script.

Ingolf Dalferth has somewhere described the proper mood of theological discourse as the "eschatological indicative": where much human discourse describes what is, and some describes what should be, theology announces the reality of things as they will be, in the good purposes of God.[20] I do not want to consider here the adequacy of this account of the nature of theology, but it seems to me that this describes the proper mood of preaching very well: preaching is not called to accommodate itself to the broken and confused realities of this age, or meekly and impotently to implore people to be different, but confidently to announce the coming truth of God—and, in the sovereign will of God, to take its part in bringing this truth to pass. Preaching is, precisely, proclamation. It is speech that merely by being spoken creates a new order. As a proclamation may make a woman a queen, or free a prisoner, so the word preached changes reality. On every side of the Reformation debate this

19. Heb 4:12.

20. Dalferth, "Creation," 127.

was understood. "It pleased God, through the foolishness of our preaching, to save those who believe"—and it pleases God still to do that thing.

Dr. Beasley-Murray was right, then, to see gospel preaching as central and urgent: it pleases God to use it to re-write human stories, using words like "life" and "hope" and "forgiveness"—and "justice" and "peace" and "holiness" and many others—where once was written "death" and "guilt" and "sin." Too many of the forms of preaching proposed by the new homileticians assume that the self-understanding and self-narration of sinful human people is something to which preaching should conform itself and even celebrate. But the Fathers, the schoolmen, the mystics, and the Reformers would unanimously and clearly teach us to deconstruct the world's self-narration as idolatrous lies. The failure here is sheer faithlessness: understanding the world as a blunt given, preaching is asked to accommodate itself to that cold, hard *factum*. But preaching, the sort of preaching imagined in the Helvetic Confession, does not approach the world as a blunt given; it approaches the world as something that finds its only legitimate existence in being shaped anew by the Word of God. Preaching that understands itself rightly knew, antecedently of any postmodern condition, that the world as we encounter it is broken, fragmented, unnarratable—we use the word "fallen." And preaching that understands itself rightly does not attempt to explain this world, but rather recreates it. Preaching, rather precisely, is called to make sense of the world—with the emphasis, of course, on the making. The preacher who understands her calling knows that in preaching, Word and world collide, and that when they do the world will inevitably be broken and healed and changed.

Finding Words

So much for the theology; if all this happens to be true, how do we preach? The message will be defined theologically: Christian preaching is the announcement that God's decisive action in Jesus Christ has changed everything; it is the enumeration and explication, through disciplined exposition of Scripture, of the particularities of that change, in each human context and for every human life. It is, finally, the proclamation that this change is now, even in part as a result of the preaching, the decisive reality for the life of each person hearing. Of course, some who hear may faithlessly reject the message, may attempt to live as if the divine Word does not have any claim on their lives. In the mystery of God's providence, such rejection of God's work may even appear to be successful; that is not our business, except in so far as, by preaching well, we can, under God's providence, encourage joyful reception of the message. This means that we also need to discuss the mode of preaching: remembering the issues I raised earlier about God's sovereign choice to work through human agency in certain areas, we are called to make the truth we preach luminously clear, winsomely attractive, and utterly convincing. Let me say some more, as I come towards the close, about both the message and the mode.

Everything I have said in this lecture has assumed that the message of preaching is the truth God has revealed about the reality of human life in this fallen world, and the reality of redemption in Jesus Christ. I take it, without further defense here, that these realities are revealed in the text of Scripture. The content of preaching, then, ought to be determined only and decisively through exegesis. In the words of the Confession that has guided this lecture, it is the preaching of the Word of God, Holy Scripture, that is the Word of God, and so can hope to proclaim the truth. Preaching is not made preaching by virtue of ordination, or licensing, or liturgical context, or education, or doctrinal orthodoxy, or anything else except its basis in and utter dependence upon the written Word.

The message of preaching must be exegesis applied to the hearers, however. Exegetical conclusions will typically be phrased in the third person—"Jesus Christ died to save sinners"; in preaching this must move into the second person—"Jesus Christ died to save you," and it must be applied with all the eloquence and rhetorical skill we can muster. The basis of any preaching that is preaching, and not merely the delivery of a religiously-themed lecture, will be exegesis; this does not mean, however, that the form of real preaching must be exposition. It might be; but equally, exegetical lessons might better be driven home in other ways.

This is where we can learn from Barak Obama, Nancy Duarte, and the other professional communicators I have cited. The task of a preacher, as I have said, is to make the new truth we proclaim about the lives of our hearers luminously clear, winsomely attractive, and utterly convincing; it is not to show our working so that we get full marks from the exegesis class. Let me cite you just one more: in his classic e-book *Really Bad Power-point*, Seth Godwin talks about being at a meeting discussing urban pollution. The speaker showed slide after slide of PM-10 statistics (items of "particulate matter" polluting the air) and the like, showing all her working; Godwin asked if he could have a go—he began the next meeting by saying, "I want to talk to you about the problem of air pollution," and filled the screen behind him with a photograph of a dead bird. Clear. Powerful. Emotive. Convincing.

Whether we use Power-point or not when we preach is a matter of homiletic and theological indifference, but if we do we should use it in ways that convince our people. The use of words in preaching is essentially not an option, famous stories about Watchman Nee or St. Francis notwithstanding, but the same criterion applies: we must use words in ways that convince our people and drive home the truths of the gospel we are called to proclaim. And, if the best practice politics, PR and business is any guide at all, that means we preach in extended monologues, naming issues that connect with people and telling stories they can follow.

For these reasons, whilst wanting, as I have indicated, to disagree profoundly with much of Fred Craddock's diagnosis of the problems of preaching, I want to commend the cure that he and others—Eugene Lowry, Barbara Brown Taylor, you know the list, the cure that he and others have proposed. The plotted moves, Lowry loops, and inductive methods of the new homiletic get something profoundly right—they connect, engage, draw in the listener, that the truth of the gospel may be heard and believed.

In preparing for this lecture I tried to reread everything Dr. Beasley-Murray published concerning the ministry of preaching, or at least everything of which I was aware; I also found myself reading as many of his sermons as I could lay my hands on. It goes without saying that in our four hundred years of history we Baptists have not produced a better exegete of Holy Scripture than George Beasley-Murray; and his sermons are without question rigorously exegetically founded. They are not, however, dry expositions of the meaning of texts, but passionate, pressing, urgent appeals for decision and action. I dare to hope that he would have recognized something of the defense and definition of preaching that I have attempted this afternoon, and so that this has been an appropriate way of seeking to honor his memory.

Bibliography

Atkinson, Cliff. *Beyond Bullet Points*. Redmond, WA: Microsoft, 2008.

Beasley-Murray, George. *Preaching the Gospel from the Gospels*. London: Lutterworth, 1956.

Beasley-Murray, Paul. *Fearless for Truth: A Personal Portrait of George Raymond Beasley-Murray*. Carlisle, UK: Paternoster, 2002.

Brown, J. J. "George Raymond Beasley-Murray: A Personal Appreciation." In *Mission to the World*, edited by Paul Beasley-Murray. Didcot: Baptist Historical Society, 1991.

Craddock, Fred B. *As One without Authority*. 4th ed. St. Louis: Chalice, 2001.

Dalferth, Ingolf. "Creation—Style of the World." *International Journal of Systematic Theology* 1 (1999) 119–37.

Duarte, Nancy. *Slide:ology: The Art and Science of Creating Great Presentations*. Sebastapol, CA: O'Reilly Media, 2008.

Klappert, Bernhard. "Logos." In *New International Dictionary of New Testament Theology*, edited by Colin Brown, 3:1087–1117. Grand Rapids: Zondervan, 1968.

MacDiarmid, Hugh. "Talking with Five Thousand People in Edinburgh." In *The Hugh MacDiarmid Anthology: Poems in Scots and English*, edited by Michael Grieve and Alexander Scott. London: Routledge & Kegan Paul, 1972.

Randolph, David James. *The Renewal of Preaching*. Philadelphia: Fortress, 1969.

Weissman, Jerry. *The Power Presenter*. Hoboken, NJ: Wiley, 2009.

9

In Praise of Incompetence

Ministerial Formation and the Development of a Rooted Person[1]

Ruth M. B. Gouldbourne

It is a great honor to be invited to present this year's Dr. G. R. Beasley-Murray Memorial Lecture. I have not managed to attend them all, but those I have heard have impressed and delighted me by being erudite, interesting and provocative of further thought. Further, they all appear to have started with at least a memory of or reference to George Beasley-Murray himself—and usually with much more, a gracious tribute and an expression of gratitude for what he meant, both as a friend and as a scholar in the life of the lecturer.

That I am here today to offer this lecture is in itself a tribute to George Beasley-Murray as a significant scholarly presence in our community—not because I ever knew him directly, or because I have made a particular study of the issues with which he engaged so creatively, but because not the least part of his impact upon Baptists in this country was to be part of the creation and sustaining of a context where ideas matter, questions are important and reflection and discussion together is taken seriously—the context in which, to my deep gratitude, I have been nur-

1. This lecture was delivered at the Baptist Assembly in Plymouth on 2 May 2010. It was subsequently published under the same title in *Baptist Quarterly* 44/2 (April 2011) and is reproduced here with minor editorial changes and with the cooperation of the editors.

tured. I did not know him. I can certainly make no claim to be a serious student of his writings. But I am one of those whose life and ministry has been profoundly shaped by this context. And so I have been delighted to accept this invitation this year and to stand in the line of those predecessors I have mentioned; erudite, thought-provoking, stimulating and serious scholars whose work I have benefited from.

The experience of doing it in such a context provokes me to an important question—why me, and what I am supposed to do? Lest you think that this is a falsely modest attempt to win your sympathy, let me disclaim any such intention and reflect instead that this question comes so easily to my mind on this occasion because it is the question that is almost always in my mind, particularly when considering questions of calling, formation and the practice of ministry. And since it is that context which is, for the purposes of this lecture, my link to George Beasley-Murray, it is the question that is going to be unavoidable. I do not intend to interact directly with Beasley-Murray's thinking on these topics, but at least to indicate a possible beginning for doing in my context what he did so importantly for Baptists in his—to ask, as a minister, and as one who has been, and to some extent still is, involved in the initial and continuing formation of ministers, and as a member of a church, and so one who looks for ministry, why am I here, and what am I supposed to do?

Questions of Ministry

The question of what a minister is, is a perennial among Baptists. That we need, or better, are given[2] ministers was accepted among Baptists from very early on. The actual title, to say nothing of the role, has been and remains a matter of constant negotiation and renegotiation. We have argued about whether ministers are linked to only one congregation, or whether there is an appropriate form of wider ministry—perhaps even with some kind of oversight authority. We have argued—sometimes bitterly—about whether our ministers should be trained. And even when we have agreed that they should be trained, we have argued about in what—languages and sciences, or only Scripture and preaching?: sometimes even getting ourselves into the position where these come to be seen as mutually exclusive. We have argued over ordination, should it happen or not? And if it does happen, what does it mean?

2. Eph 4:11–16.

It is this argument that is probably the most common area of discussion among us at the moment, though it is by no means new. But in its current form, it presents itself as a choice between ministry as functional or ministry as sacramental—simplistically, is a minister somebody who is called to do certain things, and is therefore set apart by a community in order that these functions should be carried out? Or is a minister somebody whose ordination is an "action of the Spirit, mediated through human instrumentality?"[3] and so to be so ordained means, "It is not merely that I have been called to do or to perform; I have been separated to this ministry; this is now the manner and focus of my life."[4]

It is important to notice that the difference between these two is not necessarily visible in what any individual minister actually *does* day-to-day. The difference in this discussion, is in whether, in the act of ordination and the context which it therefore creates for the continuing practice of ministry, God is at work in a particular way. It is not even a question of whether God is at work or not—an ordination or commissioning service includes prayers, therefore there is at least an implicit assumption that God is working. The difference might be best expressed as "am I a minister because I do certain things, dependent on the grace of God, and in order to serve God and the people of God, or do I do certain things because, through the grace and action of God, I am a minister, called to serve?"

It is a difference that exists among us, and people write eloquently on both sides and will no doubt continue to do so. One of our charisms is being able to live in the light of such questions, to continue the discussion and, on good days, not to fall out but to hear each other, and seek to discern the voice of Christ within the discussion of the community. I refer to it as one of our charisms, our gifts in and to the wider church, but there are times when I wonder if, despite the fact it is a gift, a grace of God to us, we use it as an excuse, the perception that we will argue becoming the reason to avoid serious theological reflection and discussion, yes, and argument. There is a great deal of theological reflection going on in the studies of individuals, and in small groups of discussers. But there is a difficulty in finding a place where we can have the wider discussion, meeting those we disagree with, engaging in sustained, and

3. Colwell, "The Sacramental Nature," 238.

4. Ibid., 244.

long-term consideration of the issues that matter, or should matter to us about who we are as part of the people of God.

As we will go on to reflect, if you stay with me, we live in a social and professional context which is deeply functional and pragmatic, and which is shaped by patterns of measurement, meeting targets, and being efficient. And it has to be said that arguing, slowly, carefully, with respect and with enough time and hope of finding a way forward together is not culturally the norm. Nor is it efficient. Nor does it give quick results. It can look very inward focused—and in a setting where we are all too aware of our shrinking capacity, and the loss of numbers, it is natural that looking inwards, towards questions that seem to be navel-gazing and irrelevant to those who have not been introduced to lively faith seems unimportant. That is to say nothing of the fact that all too often we are not able to argue well, to sustain relationships through disagreements (or at least we fear that this may be the case). So we have both set up and allowed ourselves to be drawn into a situation in which we know there are disagreements among us, and even more, that we actually have little in the way of a common mind regarding the questions, about which we might then disagree. There are various issues about which we have allowed this pattern to develop. We have shied away from sustained theological—and I mean theological not pragmatic—discussion on various issues, and one of them is ministry.

There are two positions, or better, a spectrum, which I have characterized as more and less sacramental. Both are among us, and we go on discussing—or, not discussing—without finding a way to explain ourselves to each other. But by allowing ourselves to be in a position where these two answers have shaped the discussion about ministry, there has arisen a particular area of confusion. Paul Goodliff's research work indicates that for a majority of those in ministry a more rather than less sacramental view of being a minister prevails; that is, an emphasis on being a minister preceding doing whatever it is a minister does.[5] The phrase "ministry as a way of being," which came into being with the report *Forms of Ministry*,[6] is, for many, central to their self-perception. We can see it having an impact, as Chris Ellis points out in the language we use in one of our colleges for example.[7] We talk about "ministe-

5. Goodliff, *Ministry, Sacrament and Representation.*

6. Faith and Unity Executive Committee, *Forms of Ministry among Baptists.*

7. Ellis, "Being a Minister," 57.

rial formation" rather than "ministerial training," a shift which he says moves "away from seeing ministerial training as primarily the acquisition of knowledge and skills to a more holistic view in which character and calling are important perspectives." However, as he goes on to point out, with the "emergence of leadership studies and a tendency to professionalize ministerial identity, then the wind is set fair for a task-focused approach to ministerial training."[8] And since most of those in our churches are not those whose primary previous formational context has been self-consciously theological, but who have been trained and effective in professional and work-based skills, for them, quite sensibly, a more task-focused and functional view of ministry prevails.

This is certainly visible among those who come to talk to ministers and colleges about the future possibility of training. It is not uncommon, though it is not of course universal, but it is not uncommon, for people to look for training in order to do the things that a minister needs to be able to do. It is the way people expect to approach a job and it is the way those of us in congregations who are helping people discern a call to ministry are accustomed to think, because it is how we think about helping others find their way professionally and developmentally. And denominationally, such an approach is further reinforced by the need to satisfy a set of competences in order to complete initial training.

It is of course from that aspect of this whole discussion that I have taken the title of this lecture. Much of what I have just said I am about to explain in more detail, but let me make some things clear first. It is not that I suggest that those who are ministers should be incompetent. It is, I believe, right and proper that our churches should be able to depend on and assume that those whom we accredit and recognize are "competent" in appropriate things. I believe that the work done by the Ministry Office, between the Ministry Office and the colleges, and within the colleges has been creative and effective. And of course the competences that are required and worked at, for which people are held accountable, are by no means a minimalistic list of tasks that the bare title "competences" might suggest. This is not simply about being able to conduct a wedding, lead a baptismal class, write the letter for the church magazine or organize a holiday club. Issues of ethics, of personal growth, of prayer, all the things that make people into people rather than automata doing

8. Ibid., 58.

things, are either included or at least hinted at in the way this work is developing. And yet . . .

And yet it seems to me there are two areas open for further consideration: Firstly. if most ministers gravitate towards the more rather than the less sacramental end of the spectrum, why is there this confusion that those who come forward exploring a call to ministry, presumably shaped within our churches, seem much more concerned with developing skills in appropriate tasks? Secondly, what happens if we are not competent?

Trajectories of Understanding

So, where do we, and why do we, get the idea that ministry is primarily functional and ministerial training is to do with developing particular skills and gaining appropriate knowledge? It is, in my experience, one of the most frequent points of challenge with incoming students, to help them grasp that their time at college is not only, perhaps not primarily, to educate them in ideas or equip them with skills, but rather to engage with them as people and explore that growth and depth. And it is similarly a challenge with churches who are exploring working with ministers who are students on placement, that at the heart of the process is more than simply gaining practice in the various functions.

Indeed, this tendency can be so hard to resist, that it is important to ask if in trying to challenge it we are going in the wrong direction. If it is our conviction that the local church is the primary, not the only by any means, but the primary place where we discern the mind of Christ for who we are called to be, then we need to ask the question seriously: If the discernment of the churches is that ministry among us is ultimately functional, focused on *doing* rather than *being*, then perhaps those of us who regard being as primary are guilty of over-complicating matters, or even worse, of a creeping, or perhaps galloping clericalism. It may be so. The distinction between doing and being is of course a false one; understanding ministry as primarily doing is itself a way of being, a way shaped by action and defined by function. Understanding life as a way of being of course involves doing; it is not about sitting around passively. Nonetheless, it is a distinction that is significant, and one that divides us. But I want to suggest another possibility, well-rehearsed in the discussion, but nonetheless important in my overall theme.

In viewing our ministry as primarily doing rather than being, I suggest it is less the mind of Christ we are discerning, than the spirit of the age, and that in two ways. Firstly, in an unhealthy emphasis on productivity, on people as units of production, judged on the basis of what they achieve and, this is the important bit, in the light of the overall aims of the organization. And this arises, secondly, from a loss of, or an ineffective theology of the nature and purpose of the church, and therefore derivatively of ministry. It is a commonplace to polarize discussion around whether the current mode of making explicit use of good business and managements practice in church life and structure is healthy or unhealthy. For many, the skills and practices of understanding how organizations work and how to help them work well and purposefully is a significant gift of our age, to be used judiciously certainly, but gladly and gratefully. For others, this constitutes an invasion which distorts and damages the life of the community of the people of God, and it is to be resisted. At the heart of both positions however, is the conviction that unless good theology is being done about church, its purpose and its being we are in trouble. I want to suggest that this is in fact the issue. We are in danger of not doing good theology about the church. And without such good theology, then we are all too open to an uncritical use of models and practices from various structures without their contextual constraints. Thus, unless we have thought through theologically what the church is for, the practices we adopt to make it work well and therefore the understanding and expectations we bring to those who operate within it, and in particular ministers, will be driven by models that do not fit.

I suggest, for example, that evidence for this is visible in our language about how we pay our ministers. Always an issue of contention and debate from the beginning, for a long time the language of "stipend" was used, and indeed, still is in our formal language. A stipend is a sum of money, a grant, as it were, paid over to an individual to free them from the necessity of earning their living, so that without that constraint they are available for the service of the community. A salary, the language that is now much more commonly used, is proper reward for fulfilling a task. It is paid to an employee by an employer, and it carries with it certain expectation of what those tasks will be.

Again, I am not arguing against proper living conditions. Our ministers need to live free from financial worries. But the change of language both indicates and shapes the way, as congregations, we think about what the minister is for the church, all the more so because, as far as I can tell, it is not much talked about within churches. A similar shift is visible in discussion of working hours, of time off, of availability, and so on. Now, I am deeply grateful for some guidelines on such things. I am profoundly grateful to serve in a church, as many of us do, which is careful of its minister, taking seriously, even when she does not, her need for rest, refreshment and self-care. I do not want to suggest that such care and attention is anything other than good and godly, but nevertheless it is a shift, and it is a shift into the viewing of ministry as a profession and functioning as such *vis-à-vis* the congregation. I am left with the question of whether this is a theological shift, or rather, recognizing that it is a theological shift, that is, a shift with theological implications. Is it a theology that is coherent with the rest of our theology? I suggest it is not. At least, I suggest that, if Paul Goodliff's research is accurate, and the majority of ministers do have a more rather than a less sacramental view of ministry, and do view their calling as primarily a way of being that then results in various kinds of doing, then we are seeing a lack of congruence between how our ministers see themselves and how our churches see both our ministers, and themselves. My suggestion is that this is significantly because we have forgotten how to think about what it means to be the church.

All sorts of tributaries feed this. The functional ecumenism with which we live, good in so many ways, does mean that our reason for being involved with a particular congregation is likely to have less to do with ecclesiological convictions and more to do with overall feel and style, activity and even ease of access. None of these are wrong reasons for being in a particular church, but in terms of being part of that particular church's thinking-through of issues around ecclesiology and ministry, it does lead away from the commitment to the convictions that have shaped us in the past. The emphasis on a mission identity, again absolutely right, is another tributary. Of course mission is our agenda. We are the people of a God whose intention is the reconciliation of all creation; but living as we do in a wider context of value through productivity, and identity through function, our mission identity can be subverted in ways that reinforce rather than challenge such notions, leading to the conviction that "successful church is productive church" and its entailed statement "successful ministry is productive ministry" with productivity defined in a very particular way. A third tributary is another of our strengths, our capacity and depth of lay-leadership and our failure too often to offer them the theological resources that we might.

Last year, I went to Nigel Wright's seminar on what it is to be a Baptist church, and it was packed to overflowing. Now, of course, this is all credit to Nigel and his skills as a thinker and a communicator. But I think people's interest also reflects a recognition among those in our churches that it helps to have these theological tools, because without them, the only available instruments for thinking about the church, how to be the church and all the rest of it come from other places, perhaps from other theological traditions, perhaps from other organizational contexts all together.

There are other tributaries. Time precludes. My basic point here is that the mismatch between how the majority of our ministers think about ministry and how our churches are thinking is significant and it has an impact. The idea that ministers should be trained in certain competences makes perfect sense to most people in the churches—as does the idea of review, of continual personal development and of all the other skill based paraphernalia. And, as I hope I have made clear, I certainly do not want to dismiss these, or suggest that somehow ministry is in some kind of rarefied sphere that is beyond such things or even that all ministers inevitably imbibe such things, and no competence and no accountability is necessary. But, I do want to go further, to suggest that this professionalization of ministry, while it brings all sorts of goods with it, is not something we should walk into theologically blindfolded. If we come, together, theologically, to the conclusion that ministry is defined by and contained within doing, then this model of competence, of appropriate skill and knowledge, of a salary and line management may well be perfectly justified and healthy. But at the moment, the sense among many ministers is the conviction that they are called to be and therefore to do, rather than the fact that they do certain things making them a minister. And if this is so, then a formation that focuses on competences, a community that judges them on the basis of their doing and productivity, and a set of skills that structure what we do rather than who we are is not going to be enough.

This is where my original question comes from. Why am I here, and what am I supposed to do? And if the way I answer that question is different from my congregation's, and my Union's, then where does that leave me? And what resources do I have and what resources does my congregation have to make sense of it all? This leads me into the second part of my discussion, what happens if I am incompetent, unproductive, ineffective?

Understanding Incompetence

Clearly, at one level, the answer is completely straightforward. If I make a mess of my job, then either I have to increase my skills and/or knowledge, or I have to get out. While accepting that the training in and testing of competences and skills is part, and even an important part, of the training of a minister, I am convinced that it cannot be the whole. And I recognize that those who have taken responsibility for working out what these competences should be, and those who have worked to include them in the curriculum are by no means saying that that this is all there is to being a minister. However, in a world where worth is all too easily defined by productivity, and activity is primarily measured by effectiveness, and where the role of a minister in wider society is not at all clear, and can feel very insecure, we cannot afford to give hostages to fortune. Many of those who offer themselves as ministers come from a work context in which these models predominate. Many of those in our churches experience this as their context, and without anything to resist it have no reason to think of their ministers otherwise. So, *faute de mieux*, our day-to-day understandings of ministry become functionalist and competence based only.

I want to suggest however that ministry often happens at the very edge of (or even beyond) competence. In those moments when the preacher comes face to face with the mysteriousness of Scripture, when having used all the tools of analysis, criticism, rhetoric and all the other skills we develop, there is finally the confrontation with the Living Word that invites us to dare to speak what cannot be spoken and to trust that the Living Word will communicate, there is a moment of ministry. In those moments when the pastor is confronted by the mystery of another person in the reality of question, grief or joy, and when despite all the skills of counseling and care, there is in the end simply the meeting of one human being with another in the presence of the Presence that is greater than them both, there is a moment of ministry. In those moments when the overseer or leader is silenced by the complexity and intractability of the community, and despite all the administrative and managerial skills available, there is no obvious way to make something happen, but simply the invitation to watch, wait and forego control, there is a moment of ministry. In those moments when the evangelist loses the words, runs out of arguments, cannot engage a response through all the gifts and talents expertly deployed, but gladly and breathlessly observes as the Spirit transforms a life, there is a moment of ministry. In those moments when a person of prayer falls into silence, loses touch with the images, has no conviction of the presence, but can only offer themselves to allow the prayer to happen, there is a moment of ministry.

Being skilled and competent matters. Skills and competences will sustain us through significant parts of our daily activities. They will allow our congregations the relaxation of knowing they can trust us and not to worry about us or for us. But if skills and competences define our ministry, we run the risk of fearing to go beyond what we know we can do, what we are confident we can accomplish, and our activity and service become what we can do rather than our openness to what the Spirit is doing through us. It is in our incompetence, our "unskilledness," beyond who we think we are and what we think we can safely do, it is there I suggest that we discover the country of the Spirit's ministry and the transformational activity of the everlasting Love.

Here is where the conviction about ministry as sacramental begins to take particular shape. For those of us with a more sacramental view of ministry, our starting point tends to be that the act of ordination is a sacramental act, a means of grace; that in the prayers and the laying on of hands, God is active, and grace is mediated. Paul Fiddes in *Participating in God* takes this further.[9] Citing Austin Farrar he reflects on the idea of the minister as "a walking sacrament," what Fiddes further defines as a living symbol of the sacrificial and persuasive love of Christ. He continues this discussion thus, "The whole point of a sacrament is that it is a piece of weak, created and fallible stuff in itself, but it is a doorway into the life of the Triune God. Precisely in its frailty the sacrament symbolizes an ultimate value."[10] Those moments I referred to earlier, when ministry happens beyond our competences and outside our control are these moments of sacramental ministry; when the weak, created and fallible stuff becomes the means of grace and the locus of God's action. The conviction that ministry is sacramental is the conviction not that

9. Fiddes, *Participating in God*, 294.

10. Ibid., 295.

somehow the minister is more special, more graced, or more set apart than not-ministers. It is the conviction that ministry is God's activity, and that just as water becomes more than it is in the act of baptism, and bread and wine become more than they are in the act of communion, without ceasing to be water, bread and wine, created stuff, so the minister becomes more than she is not by doing, or even in order to do, but because God moves through her in grace. And just as moments of covenant promise renewal, forgiveness and nourishment are not limited to the acts of baptism and communion, but can happen wherever the freedom of God chooses, so the ministering grace of God is not limited to the minister. But a conviction about this kind of sacramental ministry entails the conviction that this is one of the places where God promises to be graciously present to the people of God.

Water, bread and wine require certain characteristics to be water, bread and wine. Without appropriate physical attributes, they would be something else. There is no reason why something else should not, in the freedom of God, be a means of grace. But the physical attributes of water, bread and wine, are not enough, in themselves to make them the means of grace that they are in baptism and communion. Our competences are necessary, but they are not sufficient. In free grace, God ministers among us. In the economy of God, there are appointed those who carry particular promise of the gracious presence and action. The competences may be understood to provide some of the basic stuff, but the promised gracious ministry of God that is mediated through these sacramental presences is not competence, but something of a different order altogether!

Thus far we might compare the sacramental nature of ministry with that of water, bread and wine, in the acts of communion and baptism. But, unlike water, bread and wine, we are not inert and unreflective. We are conscious and self-conscious beings with wills and intentions. We have things we are able to do, and things we cannot do. We have activities we undertake and points where we fail. A concern with developing competences quite rightly looks to minimize the points of failure, but on the basis of this understanding of sacrament and of the activity of God in ministry, I also want to argue that when a minister goes beyond the limits of competence and fails, there is also a Kingdom moment, or at least the possibility of it if we dare to trust that a "piece of weak, created and fallible stuff . . . is a doorway into the life of the Triune God."

There are two consequences of this that make it daunting. The first is the possibility that, by going beyond what we know we can do, we will fail. Indeed, it is more than a possibility, it is a certainty. At least sometimes, and possibly more frequently than that, when those who are ministers dare to move beyond what they know they can do, at the very least it will not work or it will not work in the way that we plan. The sermon will not be powerful, the pastoral care will not bring healing, the oversight will not energize the congregation, the evangelism will not create revival. The Kingdom is not yet.

Sometimes it happens, sometimes what we long for and trust in happens around, through and even despite us. But sometimes it does not, and we are simply incompetent. And my question is, does this matter? We talk, sometimes too glibly, about the important thing not being success but faithfulness. And it is true. Ours is to serve faithfully and leave the harvest to God. But how radically dare we embrace this? Can we trust ourselves to a gracious love that loves us in our incompetence? Can we, as ministers, model to and for our congregations the reality that the grace we give ourselves to is not affected by success, failure, competence or incompetence? Can we, as congregations trust in this kind of grace enough to forgive an incompetent minister who has dared to go beyond and failed? I realize that this is very risky stuff. We know, too many of us have experienced, the pain that incompetent ministers can inflict on individuals and on congregations. Such hurt is not to be ignored or dismissed. The disrepute into which the Church and the gospel are brought when people get it badly wrong is not something that we dare take lightly. So I do not want to be heard to say that our competences and skills are unimportant. But if we create a context where the fear of failure prevents the openness to possibility, the willingness to move beyond what we know we can do, the daring to take a risk, and fail, then I suggest we are undermining one of the truths of the gospel: that before God we are all failures.

And that is not the point. It is not the point because our standing before, our life within God arises not from our achievements or our successes, but from grace, forgiveness and redeeming love. To take this seriously is for sure not to condone willful carelessness or unthinking risk-taking, which will cause intentional or even unnoticed damage to others or to ourselves. But it is to insist that the preaching of the grace of God calls us as ministers and congregations also to explore living in that grace and extending it to each other. A model of ministry that is task or function focused can allow the growth of a judgmental approach—if these tasks are not fulfilled, then not only is there failure, there is blame, or disappointment, or dismissal and a break down in trust.

To admit that we are wrong, to be able to accept this, to apologize and to keep going is surprisingly difficult, not only to do it, though that can be hard enough, but for it to be heard. To admit that we have been wrong as ministers, to accept our failure and its consequences without defending ourselves, trying to deny the mistake or the failure is, as all such recognitions and apologies, hard. Saying sorry is not easy. But hearing a sorry is also not easy. Not only because those who are hurt have to then discover the capacity to forgive, and that in itself is a grace, but also because it is so counter cultural. To hear an apology and not try to comfort the apologizer, or add to the blame, or, at its simplest, treat this as something major, unusual and strange, is surprisingly difficult. And yet, for most of us, most times we meet for worship, we include in our being together prayers in which we confess our sin and failure, and ask for (and expect) forgiveness from God. Why then should it be hard to do it with and before each other? One of the gifts of failure, if, as ministers we can dare to live with it, and as congregations we can trust the faith we live by, is the discovery of the meaning of confession and forgiveness not simply as a liturgical act, all too easily glossed over as words we say with no meaning other than ritual, but as who we are and how we live.

Ministry That Is Graced

If we are truly willing to embrace a foundational theology of grace and forgiveness and resurrection, then we will discover the capacity to allow for and recover from failure. By recovery, I do not simply mean knowing better how to do it next time, though that will be involved. I am more concerned with recovery in the sense of maintaining relationships, exploring forgiveness and trusting in the renewing, indeed, resurrecting grace of God; the transforming of deadly failure into life. So, I also wish to argue that when the minister goes beyond the limits of competence and fails, there is also, or at least can be, a Kingdom moment. If we dare to trust what Fiddes says of the way a piece of weak stuff is a doorway into the life of the Triune God, then we glimpse, and are brought into the life of God, into greater Christ-likeness, as we dare to live trustingly in and offering each other not judgment and blame, but forgiveness, renewal and nourishment for the journey to continue. Within this model, then it is not just the act of ordination that is sacramental, but the life of ministry itself; the life given to ministry becomes, in grace, not through special skill or other capacity, a sign of grace and an encounter, for others, with grace.

If one fearful aspect of taking our incompetence seriously is discovering the grace to fail, another is that what matters is not what we do but who we are. What makes the ministry is not activity but the person. Ministry as a way of being has become an important phrase in this discussion, and it is not the easy option. Developing Fiddes' notion of the fallible "stuff-ness" of sacrament, ministry as a way of being is to do with the minister learning in the very depths of her being that she is not God, that in all the ways that finally matter, she is incompetent, that it is in and through her radical incompleteness that God uses her, and in her "unskilled-ness" that grace is mediated. To understand ourselves as competent is to know ourselves as self-contained, autonomous, as, in some way self-sufficient. And the story in Genesis tells us that in this is our alienation from God. Central to the definition of competence is the capacity to manipulate the world and achieve a desired outcome. There are two aspects of this that cut across the sense of radical incompleteness that I have just mentioned. The sense that in any final or complete sense we can manipulate the world is a dangerous delusion.[11] It is, ultimately, the attempt to be like, or even to be God, to take final control into our own hands, to embrace the conviction that we know what the desired outcome in any situation may be. We may know what we desire, but can we claim authoritatively to know in detail what God desires? Such a self-understanding and such a way of acting is, in the end, to make ourselves as gods, to desire to be those who are in control and are complete.

But the truth of being human is that we are not God. And to live as a minister in the truth of the radical incompleteness and radical uncertainty of this existential reality is both fearful and to discover the gift that is incompetence. It is to live the truth of being human joyfully, trustingly and without denial. Such a position is a profound shift in anybody's sense of self, and, more to the point, it is a profoundly counter-cultural sense of self. In a context in which self-determination, self-definition or

11. Part of the writing of this lecture happened while I was in Prague, stuck there (and extremely well looked after) because of the suspension of all flights due to the Icelandic volcanic ash cloud. An interesting experience of being out of control!

invention, and autonomy are held as fundamental goods; and in a world in which achievement is measured by targets met, and systems adhered to, the conviction of and willingness to live in the reality of incompleteness and incompetence puts us at odds with those around us. But it is a gospel truth—that we are humans, and that we are sinners. Both truths about us are not any more easily spoken in our time than at any other time. Fundamental to speaking such truths is the willingness, the daring to live them. The conviction that the Church is a gathered and gathering people of God contains within it a conviction that such a community is a place for experimenting in how to live the life of the Kingdom and a place of apprenticeship for the discovery of how to live this life; the life of a human person in relationships with God, with other people and with the creation. It is the exploration of what it is to be human, freed from the burden of trying to be God, and daring to trust in forgiving, redeeming grace as our identity, and as the gift we offer one another. To explore this identity entails being willing to embrace the existential reality of ultimate and radical incompetence. And for the minister to do this in full view of and without defense against the congregation and the wider world, is profoundly a matter of being.

Conclusion

The English term "parson" as a denominator for the clergyman is the same word and derives from the same root as person (diagrams of the Great English Vowel shift can be supplied on request!); and here is one of the vital aspects of being a minister: it is to be a person, not a set of functions, not a "meeter of needs" or a provider of services, but a person in relation to God and to other people. And so who we are as ministers matters, knowing ourselves and living as those who are as fully human as they can be, living out this human life in God before and for our congregations so that it can be seen as possible.

This in itself challenges our culture of achievement, productivity and consumption. In a context where human reality and worth are defined by these things, where identity and security are bound up with them, the minister is called to a way of life that is not so shaped. "Wasting" time in prayer, offering space and time to intractable problems without needing to solve them, and without giving up when they cannot be solved, refusing to allow our worth to be expressed, limited, by what is achieved on a to-do list; all of this requires a basic commitment to being incompetent, unskilled, in the sense of not forcing the world to be what we choose, and not abrogating to ourselves the self-sufficiency that asserts our autonomy. Such incompetence is not easily achieved, not straightforwardly maintained. The pull of doing what we can do, and the draw of being seen to be able to cope is huge. But this kind of incompetence, the acceptance of what it is to be human; to be weak, created and fallible, is I believe, in the end, the heart of ministry, for it is the heart of discipleship. Why do I believe it? Because it is, in the end, the way of God with us, if the incarnation is true. In the incarnation, we see the second person of the Trinity embrace and live in the reality of incompetence, incompetence in both its senses; a ministry and a movement for transformation that ends with a criminal's execution is not a success. A life lived as fully human, with its refusal of self-determination and self-definition, even for protection's sake, is a life that lives fully the incompetence of incompleteness. And if this is the way God chooses to minister to us, why should we choose to minister to each other any differently?

Bibliography

Colwell, John E. "The Sacramental Nature of Ordination: An Attempt to Re-engage a Catholic Understanding." In *Baptist Sacramentalism*, edited by Anthony R. Cross and Philip E. Thompson, 228–46. Studies in Baptist History and Thought 5. Milton Keynes, UK: Paternoster, 2003.

Ellis, Christopher J. "Being a Minister: Spirituality and the Pastor." In *Challenging to Change: Dialogues with a Radical Baptist Theologian: Essays Presented to Dr. Nigel G. Wright on His Sixtieth Birthday*, edited by Pieter J. Lalleman, 55–70. London: Spurgeon's College, 2009.

Faith and Unity Executive Committee and the Doctrine and Worship Committee. *Forms of Ministry among Baptists: Towards an Understanding of Spiritual Leadership*. Didcot: Baptist Union of Great Britain, 1994.

Fiddes, Paul S. *Participating in God: A Pastoral Doctrine of the Trinity*. London: Darton, Longman & Todd, 2000.

Goodliff, Paul. *Ministry, Sacrament and Representation: Ministry and Ordination in Contemporary Baptist Theology and the Rise of Sacramentalism*. Centre for Baptist History and Heritage Studies 2. Oxford: Regent's Park College, 2010.

10

Renewing a Vision for Mission among British Baptists

Historical Perspectives and Theological Reflections[1]

Brian Stanley

Introduction

When I chose this title for the G. R. Beasley-Murray lecture, I was not aware that George Beasley-Murray's theme for his presidential address for the Baptist Union in 1968 was "Renewed for Mission."[2] It was an address which Patrick Baker, then in his final year of ministerial training at Spurgeon's College, considered in retrospect to have been a turning point in the life of the Baptist denomination in Britain.[3] In so far as the Baptist denomination is the only one of the historic Free Churches in Britain to be more or less holding its own against the corrosive impact on membership rolls of the surging tides of de-Christianization, the vision held out by George Beasley-Murray in 1968, and indeed throughout his ministry, must be reckoned to be one of the sources of that spiritual vitality. In terms of new and creative initiatives for presenting the gospel to Britain's multi-ethnic and thoroughly materialistic society, Baptists

1. This lecture was delivered at the Baptist Assembly in Blackpool on 1 May 2011.

2. George Beasley-Murray, *Renewed for Mission*, cited in Paul Beasley-Murray, *Fearless for Truth*, 117–18.

3. Beasley-Murray, *Fearless for Truth*, 68–69.

have renewed, and are continuing, to renew their vision for mission, and for that we should be thankful to God. Nevertheless, there is no room for complacency as Baptists contemplate the missionary challenges of contemporary Britain. We are nowhere near the trajectory achieved by Baptist membership in the wake of the Evangelical Revival, which saw Particular Baptists more than double their proportion of the rising population of England between 1800 and 1851.[4]

Moreover, by "renewing a vision for mission" I mean, not simply expanding and deepening our commitment to evangelism within Britain, but, more fundamentally, bringing into the very centre of our church life a passionate absorption with the theme of God's missionary purposes for the world. It is no accident that the era in which Baptist membership grew most rapidly in Britain was also the era in which Baptists led the way in new initiatives in world mission through the formation of the Baptist Missionary Society (BMS). The traditional bifurcation between world *mission* and domestic *evangelism* is theologically indefensible, and is not to be found at the roots of the British Baptist missionary tradition. William Carey's famous *Enquiry into the Obligations of Christians to Use Means for the Conversion of the Heathens* (1792) was at root a protest against the supposition that the boundaries of European Christendom had any theological validity in determining Baptist thinking about the nature of the Church's calling in the world. Hence, until as late as 1815–16, the BMS sponsored itinerant preaching tours in various parts of England.[5] Of course, there was little more than a shadow of a Baptist Union in those days, but the point I am making is about the need for an integrated missionary vision, not primarily about institutional relationships. How prominent in the worship, preaching, and prayer life of our Baptist churches is a lively sense of what God is doing, and calling us to do with him, in the *world*? How aware are our church members of the fact that about two-thirds of the world's Christians now live in what used to be (and still, sadly, sometimes are) called the "mission fields" of Africa, Asia, Latin America, and Oceania?

4. Gilbert, *Religion and Society in Industrial England*, 37. Particular Baptist membership was 0.45 percent of population in 1800, and 1.12 percent in 1851. General Baptist New Connexion membership was 0.17 percent of population in 1851, and obviously considerably less in 1800.

5. Stanley, *History of the Baptist Missionary Society*, 18–19.

In this lecture I shall be drawing on historical resources from time to time, but we should not idealize our denominational history. In the year 1850–51, which was close to the peak of Baptist numerical growth in real terms, fewer than 44 percent of Particular Baptist churches in England supported the BMS, and many that did so did not do so consistently from year to year.[6] Baptist missionary enthusiasm over the last two centuries has been sporadic and far from a model of theological purity. There can be, and should be, no going back to the days when British commitment to overseas missions was tinged with imperial overtones of the supposedly distinctive role of the British Empire in the purposes of God for the world. I should be very surprised to hear that BMS missionaries overseas celebrated last Friday's major event in the life of the British monarchy by processing through the streets proudly wearing rosettes of red, white, and blue, behind a trio of elephants, as they did in Udayagiri in Orissa on the coronation of George VI in 1937.[7] But the loss of Britain's empire has, undoubtedly, made it more difficult for the Society, and all other mission agencies, to present the claims of world mission upon the attention of church members. The late South African missiologist, David Bosch, urged that the appropriate mindset for Christian mission was "mission in bold humility."[8] European-led mission in the imperial context of the late nineteenth and early twentieth centuries had plenty of boldness, but precious little humility. Since the postcolonial crisis of the 1960s, mission in most of the churches of the northern hemisphere has had plenty of humility, but very little boldness. How might we recapture some of that boldness without losing our postcolonial humility in the process? I should like to suggest three answers.

Rediscovering the Missionary Purpose of God

Missiologists nowadays talk a great deal about the mission of God, or *missio Dei* (it sounds more impressive in Latin). They wish to remind us that mission originates with God, belongs to God, and is broader in scope than the mere multiplication of church members. This emphasis would not have been news to William Carey. The Introduction to the

6. Stanley, "Home Support," 194–95.

7. Stanley, *History of the Baptist Missionary Society*, 301. The royal wedding of Prince William and Kate Middleton took place two days before this lecture was delivered.

8. Bosch, *Transforming Mission*, 489; see Saayman and Kritzinger, *Mission in Bold Humility*.

Enquiry grounds the call to action in mission, not in the command of Christ, but in the universal salvific purpose and loving character of God.[9] Section I of the *Enquiry* goes on to argue that the commission given by Christ to the apostles remains binding on all Christians to the end of the age. But Carey's appeal is not to the commission alone, but to an implicitly Trinitarian understanding of the *missio Dei*. Behind the command of Christ lay the purpose of God, and that purpose was confirmed by evidence from many quarters of the globe (and here Carey drew on Jonathan Edwards) that "the universal down-pouring of the Spirit," proclaimed in the book of Joel as a sign of the last days, had already begun.[10] The protests of hyper-Calvinists that no initiative to bring the gospel to those beyond the frontiers of Christendom could be contemplated until God signaled a resumption of the apostolic age by the renewal of the miraculous gifts were thus silenced. Carey's appeal was for obedient action to the command of Christ, but also for earnest prayer that the purposes of God for the world would be fulfilled: "The most glorious works of grace that have ever took place, have been in answer to prayer; and it is in this way, we have the greatest reason to suppose, that the glorious outpouring of the Spirit, which we expect at last, will be bestowed.[11]

The origins of the BMS lie in the institution within the Northamptonshire Baptist Association in 1784 of monthly prayer meetings for the world-wide spread of the gospel. The united prayer movement was itself a response to Jonathan Edwards's pamphlet, *An Humble Attempt to Promote Explicit Agreement and Visible Union of God's People in Extraordinary Prayer*, published in 1747.[12] In the *Enquiry* Carey follows Edwards in using Zechariah chapters 12 and 13 to teach that "a universal conjunction in fervent prayer" would be the prelude to "copious influences of the Spirit" being shed upon the churches, and hence to the fulfillment of God's saving purposes by the establishment of his kingdom among all nations. Carey is insistent that the deployment of all human means in mission without the accompanying blessing of the Spirit will be ineffectual.[13]

9. Carey, *Enquiry*, 3–6.

10. Ibid., 12.

11. Ibid., 78–79.

12. Stanley, *History of the Baptist Missionary Society*, 4–5.

13. Carey, *Enquiry*, 77–78.

We may have questions about the postmillennial eschatology that underlay these arguments. But the point to notice is Carey's belief in the sovereign and gracious redemptive purpose of God for humanity, perfectly revealed in Jesus, and effected in history by the Spirit of God bestowed on the people of God down the ages. That belief was the basis of Carey's confident, but not self-confident, missionary action, and it can be so of ours as well.

Behind Carey's pamphlet lies the evangelical Calvinism of Andrew Fuller, with its finely struck balance between divine sovereignty and the responsibility of Christians freely to offer, and of non-Christians freely to respond to the offer, of the gospel.[14] Nearer the surface of the *Enquiry* lies also, of course, the Gospel texts, not simply of Matthew 28, but also of the long ending of Mark 16, both of which Carey cites as the source of "the Commission of Christ."[15] We should note in passing that neither the phrase "The Great Commission," nor any exclusive linkage between the Commission and Matthew's version, may be found in Carey: both the stock phrase "The Great Commission" and its exclusive attachment to Matthew 28:18–20 are later developments in Protestant tradition.[16] Nevertheless, it is Matthew's version that is to the forefront of Carey's mind, and it seems to me that his exegesis of the words of Christ is exactly right: "All authority is given to *me*—therefore *you* go." If we forget the first part of that statement, mission becomes just another process of human persuasion or propaganda, an attempt to capture or colonize the minds of men and women so that they should all think just like us. That is not authentic Christian mission. But equally, if we forget the second part of Christ's statement, we end up with a view of the *missio Dei* which leaves the Church comfortably marginal to the salvific activity of God. That is a view which is now most assiduously promulgated, not so much in our day by hyper-Calvinists, but by advocates of a radically secular view of mission that places little emphasis on the necessity for the actual proclamation by Christians of the good news of the reign of Jesus.

What might this reminder of the theology that undergirded the genesis of our missionary tradition as British Baptists have to say to our contemporary church scene? Allow me to suggest three interrelated reflections.

14. Haykin, "Andrew Fuller on Mission," 25–41.

15. Carey, *Enquiry*, 7–9.

16. Wright, "The Great Commission," 149, 153–57.

(1) A trinitarian understanding of God nurtured by consistently trinitarian worship is the only secure basis for churches to undertake mission to the world.

This may sound like a truism, but I notice that a major policy document produced by BMS World Mission in January 2007, "Towards 2010: Where BMS is Heading," made only one explicit reference to the mission of God in an eight-page document, and no mention at all of either the Father or the Holy Spirit, whereas "Jesus" or "Christ" appeared eight times.[17] An emphasis on mission as obedience to the command of Christ without an accompanying emphasis on mission as the gracious sovereign intention of a loving God will induce a frenetic and guilt-laden approach to evangelism that can only lead to frustration. Without an adequate trinitarian framework, we will be unable to grasp ourselves and present evangelistically to others a doctrine of the atonement that avoids grotesque caricature.[18] Without a continual recognition of the gracious power of the Spirit, as we have already observed, evangelistic mission becomes propaganda, mere human persuasion. If all authority belongs to Jesus, the mission of the church is not to convert people—only the Spirit who mediates that authority in the world can do that. It is only through the presence of the Spirit that the authority given by the Father to the Son is made available to us. Without the presence of the Spirit it simply makes no sense for us to go when the authority belongs to Jesus, and not to us. But with the indwelling presence of the one through whose power the Father raised the Son from the dead, and through whose power men and women can be raised to new life in Christ, obedience to the "Great Commission" becomes possible.

(2) The mission of God is an overflowing of the incessant dance of self-giving in relationship (what Moltmann and other theologians call perichoresis), which characterizes the inner life of the triune God, into the community of the people of God, and from them into the world.

Worship that is consistently focused on God who is Three in One will build churches that are able to combine cultural diversity with unity and have a vision of a plural world made one in Christ. Conversely, worship

17. BMS World Mission, "Towards 2010."

18. I am, of course, alluding here to Steve Chalke's controversial statement in 2004 that the doctrine of penal substitution was liable to be regarded as "cosmic child abuse."

which is preoccupied with "Jesus and Me" will surely encourage atomistic and self-absorbed rather than mission-minded Christians. Those of us who lead worship, and those of us who preach, need to be asking ourselves continually whether our choice of songs and the content of our sermons are equally honoring to Father, Son, and Holy Spirit, and are regularly encouraging our people to focus on the missionary purposes of our triune God for the world.

(3) A third reflection relates to the centrality of organized corporate prayer for the world in the movement that transformed Baptist life in much of England in the 1780s and 1790s.

Without the monthly prayer meetings that began in 1784, there would have been no BMS, and no London Missionary Society either, for the movement spread to Congregationalists.[19] Without prayer, insists Carey, there will be no outpouring of the Spirit, and no building of the kingdom. This is no new message for a gathering of Baptists, but I wonder whether the place of prayer, and especially of intercessory prayer for the world, has become marginal to the life and worship of too many of our churches. Congregations which regularly and imaginatively engage in bringing the world to God in prayer will also be congregations which are committed to bringing the gospel of Christ to the world. Conversely, congregations whose prayer life is introspective will not be missionary congregations. If we do not Sunday by Sunday implore God for the outpouring of his Spirit on the world church in its witness to the world, can we be surprised if our members seem uninterested in the life of churches overseas, or even in the next association? If we do not regularly bring before God in our Sunday services the needs of a world riven by conflict, hunger, poverty, environmental catastrophe, and epidemic disease, can we be surprised if our church members appear to see little connection between these subjects that dominate their television screens and what they imagine Christian mission to be all about? As N. T. Wright in particular has reminded us, God's redemptive and restorative purpose extends ultimately to the renewal of the entire created order, leading to the new heaven *and* the new earth of which the Book of Revelation speaks.[20]

19. Payne, *The Prayer Call of 1784*, 11–12; Lovett, *History of the London Missionary Society*, 1:12–13.

20. See Wright, "New Heavens, New Earth," 31–51; also idem, *Surprised by Hope*.

The scope of our prayers should be no narrower if we are to be true to the mission of God.

Restoring the Centrality of Missionary Discipleship

A second ingredient in my recipe for the renewal of our vision for mission is the priority of restoring the centrality of missionary discipleship. This is a priority which is already reflected in the strategy document adopted by the Baptist Union Trustees in 2008, which lists "making disciples" as the first component of "the heart of the strategy," and makes the encouragement of missionary disciples in "radical, life-long missionary discipleship" its primary strategic objective. Nevertheless, I find it interesting that the document lists "mission" as a separate component of the heart of the strategy from making disciples.[21]

The conservative evangelical tradition that has so fundamentally and fruitfully shaped British Baptist life, especially in the four decades since George Beasley-Murray's presidential address of 1968, seems strangely reluctant to appropriate Matthew's emphasis that Christian mission is essentially to do with making disciples. Evangelicalism, ever since its eighteenth-century origins, has instead placed the call to conversion at the centre of its understanding of mission.[22] The call to turn to God in repentance and faith was certainly at the heart of the message that Jesus proclaimed, and should equally be so in ours. But the Gospels know nothing of mere converts: the call of Jesus was to take up one's cross and follow him (Matt 16:24). In our exegesis of Matthew 28 we sometimes seem to miss the obvious: we are sent to make not converts, but disciples, of all nations. The commission is not discharged once commitments to follow Christ have been made. The sixteenth-century Anabaptist tradition, with its emphasis on the call to costly discipleship, has something to teach us here. Hans Kasdorf has aptly said that while the mainline Reformers rediscovered the great Pauline term *Glaube* (faith), it was the Radical Reformers who "rediscovered the evangelists' word *Nachfolge* (discipleship). People cannot, they maintained, call Jesus Lord unless they are his disciples indeed, prepared to follow him in every way."[23] Something of the same emphasis can be found in the early years of the

21. Baptist Union Trustees, "Strategy."

22. See Bebbington, *Evangelicalism in Modern Britain*, 5–10.

23. Kasdorf, "The Anabaptist Approach to Mission," 53.

English Particular Baptist tradition. Benjamin Coxe, Hanserd Knollys, and William Kiffin went so far in 1645 in their *A Declaration Concerning the Publike Dispute . . . Concerning Infants-Baptisme* to put discipleship logically prior to baptism, thus virtually collapsing the identity of the missionized into that of the disciple. They did so on the basis of a literal reading of the Greek text:

> The onely written Commission to Baptize (which is in Matth. 28:19.) directeth us to baptize Disciples only, *Go ye and Disciple all Nations, baptizing them*; that is, the disciples: for this is the onely construction and interpretation that the Greek word can there beare; and Infants cannot be made Disciples, because they cannot learne.[24]

The missionary responsibility of the church is to make not converts, but disciples whose communal life together will be a visible embodiment of "all that I have commanded you"—in other words, the mind of Christ and the values of his kingdom. Hence the Church as a missionary community is called to be what Lesslie Newbigin loved to refer to as "the hermeneutic of the gospel," an icon or exemplification of what the gospel of the kingdom is all about.[25] "Making converts" implies replication, domination, and the colonization of the mind—and the world imagines that this is what we are aiming to achieve in Christian mission. "Making disciples," on the other hand, can only mean calling others to follow the One whom we have found to be supremely worth following: the disciple is one who *chooses* to follow. We who are ourselves continual learners in the school of Christ invite and appeal to others to join us in traveling along the road of discipleship. This was an emphasis dear to the heart of George Beasley-Murray. His sermon on Matthew 10:24 preached on 10 October 1970 on the occasion of the ordination to Baptist ministry of his son, Paul, noted that "The disciple is sent out to be a teacher. But he always remains a disciple—a learner."[26] That is an indispensable emphasis in mission, where too often the missionary teacher has forgotten that he or she remains a disciple, and has became a dominator as a result. Christian nurture is not to be seen as a separate business from

24. Coxe, Knollys, and Kiffin, *A Declaration*, 19, cited in Haykin, "Andrew Fuller on Mission," 27.

25. For Newbigin's fullest exposition of this theme see his *The Gospel in a Pluralist Society*, 222–33.

26. Cited in Beasley-Murray, *Fearless for Truth*, 107.

evangelism, as too often it is in the Protestant evangelical tradition. The evangel we are called to proclaim is itself a call to follow Christ, and to *go on following* him.

German mission theorists in the early twentieth century, who were the first to grapple seriously with the problems of Christianity and culture, developed the idea, which can claim some basis in the New Testament, that the call to discipleship has a corporate as well as an individual reference. Influenced by German Romantic notions of the national *Geist* or spirit, they noticed that Matthew's record strictly does not say "go and make disciples *from* all nations," but "go and make disciples *of* all nations" (*panta ta ethnē*). The idea that the gospel might be addressed, not to individuals alone, but to nations as collective entities, was taken up by the pro-Nazi "German Christian" movement in the 1930s to suggest that there was a peculiarly German way of being Christian, a distinctively Germanic pattern of Christian faith, rooted in the *Blut* and *Boden* (blood and soil) of German national life.[27] Karl Barth, that stalwart opponent of the German Christian heresy and of all nationalistic distortions of the Christian faith, regarded such teaching as "painful fantasies," and so in a celebrated exegetical study of Matthew 28 expressed his contempt for the idea that the nations as such are called into their own unique patterns of discipleship, a view he dismissed as "worthless."[28]

However, the German missiologists' interpretation was not entirely killed off by Barth. A similar position was taken up by Donald McGavran, founder of the church growth school. As a Disciples of Christ missionary in India from 1923 to 1954, McGavran observed the remarkable people movements of his day, which saw people of the same caste unit or village moving towards Christian faith through corporate decisions, led by the natural leaders of the community.[29] McGavran drew the conclusion that India would never be won for Christ by piecemeal individual conversions, but only by a mission strategy that enabled people groups (his interpretation of the *ethnē*)[30] to move towards Christ

27. Pierard, "Volkish Thought and Christian Missions, 138–49; Ustorf, *Sailing on the Next Tide*.

28. Karl Barth, "An Exegetical Study of Matthew 28:16–20," in Gallagher and Hertig, *Landmark Essays*, 24–25.

29. Tippett, *God, Man, and Church Growth*, 10, 21–25.

30. McGavran, *Understanding Church Growth*, 40.

without having to cross the barriers of caste or culture. That was the origin of what we know as church growth theory. It was not borrowed from the German missiology of nations, although McGavran later became familiar with one of its leading exponents, Christian Keysser, and endorsed his approach.[31] McGavran's methodology was the seed-bed of all those subsequent seeker-friendly strategies in church life, with which we are now so familiar, that endeavor to make it easier for people to follow Christ by customizing the presentation of the gospel, or the experience of Christian worship, to their existing cultural frame of reference. The famous, or (depending on your point of view) infamous, "homogenous unit principle" affirms that people prefer to become Christians without having to cross a cultural barrier, and thus leads to the logical conclusion of Christian congregations that are culturally or ethnically homogeneous.

There is a lot to be said for McGavran's view, but his theory made a fatal and exegetically dubious distinction between discipling, understood as the initial process of evangelization, and the supposedly separate second stage of "perfecting" ("teaching them to observe all that I have commanded you").[32] Church growth theory deduces a whole series of apparently logical steps from the apparently attractive initial premise that the most important thing in mission is to maximize the rate of conversions. But Jesus does not command us to maximize conversions, but to enable people of all ethnic and cultural backgrounds to become true and lasting disciples. Integral to that process of discipleship is learning to walk the road alongside other disciples of different ethnic or cultural allegiance. That difficult lesson is not some advanced-level Christian education module to be bolted on to profession of faith at some later stage, but is rather an integral part of becoming part of the disciple community.

What does this mean for our approaches to mission, whether at home or overseas? It certainly does not mean that we should throw out our handbooks on inculturation, or contextualization. If our mission is to be profoundly incarnational, following the pattern set by Jesus himself, then we must take with utmost seriousness the patterns of life

31. McGavran's foreword to the English translation of Keysser's classic study, *Eine Papuagemeinde*, reveals that he was unaware of Keysser's work until about 1958; see Pierard, "Volkish Thought and Christian Missions," 145.

32. Tippett, *God, Man, and Church Growth*, 27–31.

and thought of those to whom we are sent. An incarnational emphasis in mission is conventionally associated with Catholic theology, but it is also one that has recently been advocated by the Australian Baptist missiologist, Ross Langmead.[33] However, it does mean that, for every new mission strategy proposed as the answer to our current ineffectiveness, the question we should be asking from the beginning is not, "Will this strategy maximize our rate of initial professions of faith?" but rather, "Will this strategy lead under the blessing of God's Spirit to lasting growth in not merely the size, but also the spiritual depth and cultural breadth of the community of Christian disciples? Will this strategy enable our church to reflect more fully the biblical vision of the body of Christ which knows no division between Jew and Gentile, slave and free, rich and poor, male and female?"[34] What we have come to label "culture" is always an approximation to reality, an attempt to freeze within one photographic frame an elusive entity which is always fluid and always a composite of the differing perspectives of old and young, male and female, native and newcomer. This is all the more the case in our globalized and electronically inter-connected world. The history of the twentieth century, in which both German Nazis and Afrikaner Christians erected abhorrent ideologies of racial supremacy on the basis of philosophies that absolutized cultural differentiation, should warn us against any approach to mission that on the basis of an unmediated appeal to culture elevates converts above disciples.

We come to the third and final ingredient in my recipe for the renewal of missionary vision:

Re-envisioning the Shape of Missionary Fellowship

In the *Enquiry*, Carey advocated that "in the present divided state of Christendom," a national voluntary society of Baptists dedicated to the global spread of the gospel, though not necessarily the ideal way of doing mission, was the most feasible step of missionary obedience at that time.[35] This recognition was duplicated in the founding minute of the BMS, which stated that "in the present divided state of Christendom

33. Langmead, *The Word Made Flesh.*

34. See Padilla's fine article, "The Unity of the Church and the Homogenous Unit Principle," 23–31; republished in Gallagher and Hertig, *Landmark Essays in Mission and World Christianity*, 73–92.

35. Carey, *Enquiry*, 84.

it seems that each denomination by exerting itself seperately [*sic*] is most likely to accomplish the great ends of a mission."[36] Baptists, unlike Christians of Catholic persuasion, do not believe that there is only one revealed and authoritative way of being church and doing mission. Rather, in conformity with the diversity within the New Testament record, they believe that structures should be continually reshaped by the dialogue between the enduring values of the kingdom and the plurality of contexts within which the church is called to embody the gospel of the kingdom. Baptists in every age and every national setting therefore face the challenge of seeking God's guidance about what the most appropriate structures are for fulfilling our part of God's mandate for mission here and now. There are several dimensions to this challenge.

The First of These Is an International Dimension

Baptists, no less than other Christians, now live in an age of multi-directional missionary traffic between the continents. Mission no longer flows solely, or even primarily, from North to South or from West to East. This is, however, not quite as new as we sometimes imagine. At the great World Missionary Conference held at Edinburgh in 1910, one of the delegates of the American Baptist Foreign Mission Society was a Telegu Baptist from South India, John Rangiah. Rangiah was in fact a missionary sent by the Telegu Baptist Home Missionary Society to work among the Telegu indentured laborers in the sugar plantations of Natal. An early example of what we now call "south-to-south" mission, he is remembered today as the primary architect of the Indian Baptist community in Natal.[37] But what was occasional and of exotic interest a century ago is now of regular and central importance in the ongoing story of world mission. Brazilian Baptist missionaries serve in Lusophone Africa and in Portugal. Kingsley Appiagyei from Ghana has served as the president of our Baptist Union from 2009–10 and has founded two of the largest Baptist congregations in the United Kingdom. Other gifted Baptists from the global south such as Joe Kapolyo at Edmonton are enriching our denominational life. Multi-directional missionary traffic is here to stay. It makes for much more interesting journeys, but also occasional collisions! British Baptists are gradually learning what it means

36. BMS Committee Minutes, 2 Oct. 1792, 1–2, Angus Library, Regent's Park College, Oxford.

37. Stanley, *The World Missionary Conference*, 100.

to be humble receivers in mission, as well as continuing to be givers. Learning to receive in humility does not come easily when we have been long accustomed to be donors. Experience within the United Reformed Church of receiving missionaries sent from the majority world to work in Britain under the auspices of the Council for World Mission (heir to the old London Missionary Society) suggests that church members naturally expect such missionaries to talk about the life of their churches overseas, but find it much more difficult to invite them to comment on what they may have noticed about our own church life.[38] Of course, non-Western missionaries working in Britain will make cultural mistakes, and may even attempt to impose their cultural readings of the faith on us. But British Christians did precisely the same in the reverse direction in the past.

Like other denominations in Britain, Baptists have some way still to travel in this respect. Although Fred George (a Sri Lankan), Kate Coleman and Kingsley Appiagyei (both Ghanaians) have served as presidents of the Union in 1997–98, 2006–7, and 2009–10 respectively, we have not yet seen any Christian from the global south appointed to a senior staff position in either the Union or in BMS World Mission. Although a contrast might be drawn with the Church of England, which not simply has an archbishop of York born in Uganda, but as long ago as 1989 had a Pakistani, Michael Nazir-Ali, as general secretary of the Church Mission Society,[39] Baptists now compare very favorably with other British denominations in terms of the ethnic range reflected in their ordained ministry, including at regional team leadership level. In BMS World Mission in 2011 the election of Nabil Costa, a Lebanese Baptist leader, as a trustee and the appointment of an Indian evangelist, Benjamin Francis, as associate regional team leader for India, are strategic and welcome steps.[40]

38. Maxey, "Learning to Receive Missionaries," 16.

39. The Church Mission Society was known as the Church Missionary Society until 1995.

40. http://www.bmsworldmission.org/news-blogs/archive/bms-trustees-given-global-dimension.

The Second Dimension to the Challenge Is an Ecumenical or Ecclesial One

British Baptists developed their denominational tradition in the context of European, and specifically Anglican, Christendom, marked by a union of church and state which even the Anglican Church has, happily, found to be not permanently exportable. Christendom has now largely dissolved, and the Baptist tradition is now found in a great variety of cultural contexts, and its ecclesial character has transmuted, sometimes quite radically, as a result. We have Baptist bishops in countries such as Georgia. Once again, however, this is not quite so novel as might at first sight appear. It would be plausible to claim that there were Baptist bishops in India as long ago as the early nineteenth century. They were not called bishops; they were called BMS missionaries, yet they exercised most of the functions of episcopacy. The "Form of Agreement," a statement adopted by the Serampore missionaries in 1805, stated that Indians ordained to the ministry of the word and sacraments must be allowed to fulfill that ministry

> as much as possible without the interference of the missionary of the district who will constantly superintend their affairs, give them advice in cases of order and discipline, and correct any errors into which they fall; and, who joying and beholding their order, and the stedfastness of their faith in Christ, may direct his efforts continually to the planting of new churches in other places, and to the spread of the gospel in his district, to the utmost of his power.[41]

If that is not a statement of episcopal functions, I do not know what is. It is not surprising that some of the families of churches planted by BMS missionaries have rather more of the episcopal or presbyterian style of polity about them than the congregational independency which we in Britain sometimes identify as a defining mark of Baptist identity. The globalization of the Baptist tradition, as of other Christian traditions, has placed high on the agenda the question of exactly which elements in Baptist identity are of universal, non-negotiable, significance and what of merely local or temporal, significance.

41. *Periodical Accounts Relative to the Baptist Missionary Society* 3 (1804–9) cited in Brian Stanley, "Planting Self-Governing Churches," 381.

Lastly, There Is a Specifically Relational Challenge which Faces Us as British Baptists

The challenge is to be willing to re-conceive the mutual relations, and perhaps even the structures, of our national Baptist missionary fellowships (Baptist Union of Great Britain, Baptist Union of Scotland, Baptist Union of Wales, and BMS World Mission) in the same spirit of godly and prayerful pragmatism which Carey demonstrated in the *Enquiry*. We have come a long way since the Baptist Union was a tenant of the BMS, occupying a few rooms in the Society's headquarters in Furnival Street in London, as it was until the opening of Baptist Church House in Southampton Row in 1903.[42] There is a protracted and not particularly edifying history of relationships between the Union and the Missionary Society, but if there is one lesson to be gleaned from that history, it is that much depends on the personal relationship between the heads of the two bodies. In Jonathan Edwards and David Kerrigan[43] we are currently blessed with a pair of denominational leaders who are not only gifted, but also united by a common vision for mission. They deserve our prayers and encouragement as they work together at developing the relationship in directions appropriate to the state of church and society in Britain today. None of us knows what the shape of British Baptist structures for mission will be in one hundred years' time, though, if granted a vantage point from glory, I would be surprised, and depressed, if they turned out to be precisely the same as we have now. The architecture and geography of denominational identity are changing profoundly, both within Britain, and globally. The challenge for British Baptists will be to renew their vision for mission in this fluid context in ways that hold fast to those values that are integral to the gospel, while sitting lightly to everything else.

Bibliography

Baptist Union Trustees. "Strategy." Didcot: Baptist Union of Great Britain, 2008.
Beasley-Murray, George R. *Renewed for Mission*. London: Baptist Union, 1968.

42. Stanley, *History of the Baptist Missionary Society*, 386.

43. At the time of this lecture respectively General Secretary of the Baptist Union and General Director of BMS World Mission.

Beasley-Murray, Paul. *Fearless for Truth: A Personal Portrait of George Raymond Beasley-Murray*. Carlisle, UK: Paternoster, 2002.

Bebbington, David W. *Evangelicalism in Modern Britain: A History from the 1730s to the 1980s*. London: Allen & Unwin, 1989.

BMS World Mission. "Towards 2010: Where BMS Is Heading." Didcot: BMS World Mission, 2007.

Bosch, David. *Transforming Mission: Paradigm Shifts in Theology of Mission*. Maryknoll, NY: Orbis, 1991.

Carey, William. *An Enquiry into the Obligations of Christians to Use Means for the Conversion of the Heathens*. [1792.] Edited by E. A. Payne. London: Carey Kingsgate, 1961.

Coxe, B., H. Knollys, and W. Kiffin. *A Declaration Concerning the Publike Dispute . . . Concerning Infants-Baptisme*. London: 1645.

Gallagher, Robert L., and Paul Hertig, eds. *Landmark Essays in Mission and World Christianity*. Maryknoll, NY: Orbis, 2009.

Gilbert, A. D. *Religion and Society in Industrial England: Church, Chapel and Social Change, 1740–1914*. London: Longman, 1976.

Haykin, Michel A. "Andrew Fuller on Mission: Text and Passion." In *Baptists and Mission: Papers from the Fourth International Conference on Baptist Studies*, edited by Ian M. Randall and Anthony R. Cross, 25–41. Milton Keynes, UK: Paternoster, 2007.

Kasdorf, Hans. "The Anabaptist Approach to Mission." In *Anabaptism and Mission*, edited by Wilbert R. Shenk, 51–69. Scottdale, PA: Herald, 1984.

Keysser, Christian. *Eine Papuagemeinde*. Published as *A People Reborn*. Pasadena, CA: William Carey Library, 1980.

Langmead, Ross. *The Word Made Flesh: Towards an Incarnational Missiology*. Lanham, MD: University Press of America, 2004.

Lovett, Richard. *History of the London Missionary Society*. 2 vols. London: Henry Frowde, 1899.

Maxey, Sheila. "Learning to Receive Missionaries." *Articles of Reformed Faith and Religion* 8 (1999–2000).

McGavran, Donald A. *Understanding Church Growth*. 3rd ed. Grand Rapids: Eerdmans, 1990.

Newbigin, Lesslie. *The Gospel in a Pluralist Society*. London: SPCK, 1989.

Padilla, René. "The Unity of the Church and the Homogenous Unit Principle." *International Bulletin of Missionary Research* 6 (1982) 23–30.

Payne, Ernest A., ed. *The Prayer Call of 1784*. London: Baptist Laymen's Missionary Movement, 1941.

Pierard, Richard V. "Volkish Thought and Christian Missions in Early Twentieth-Century Germany." In *Essays in Religious Studies for Andrew Walls*, edited by James R. Thrower, 136–54. Aberdeen: University of Aberdeen Department of Religious Studies, 1986.

Saayman, Willem, and Klippies Kritzinger, eds. *Mission in Bold Humility: David Bosch's Work Considered*. Maryknoll, NY: Orbis, 1996.

Stanley, Brian. *The History of the Baptist Missionary Society, 1792–1992*. Edinburgh: T. & T. Clark, 1992.

———."Home Support for Overseas Missions in Early Victorian England, c. 1838–c. 1873." PhD diss., University of Cambridge, 1979.

———. "Planting Self-Governing Churches: British Baptist Ecclesiology in the Missionary Context." *Baptist Quarterly* 34 (1991–92) 378–89.

———. *The World Missionary Conference, Edinburgh 1910*. Grand Rapids: Eerdmans, 2009.

Tippett, Alan, R., ed. *God, Man, and Church Growth: A Festschrift in Honor of Donald Anderson McGavran*. Grand Rapids: Eerdmans, 1973.

Ustorf, Werner. *Sailing on the Next Tide: Missions, Missiology, and the Third Reich*. Frankfurt: Peter Lang, 2000.

Wright, David F. "The Great Commission and the Ministry of the Word: Reflections Historical and Contemporary on Relations and Priorities." *Scottish Bulletin of Evangelical Theology* 25 (2007) 132–57.

Wright, N. T. "New Heavens, New Earth." In *Called to One Hope: Perspectives on the Life to Come*, edited by John E. Colwell, 31–51. Carlisle, UK: Paternoster, 2001.

———. *Surprised by Hope*. London: SPCK, 2007.

11

Sustaining Evangelical Identity

Faithfulness and Freedom in Denominational Life[1]

Nigel G. Wright

The Dr. G. R. Beasley-Murray Memorial Lecture was established in 2002 with the intention of extending the scholarly legacy of George Beasley-Murray (1916–2000), the leading British Baptist New Testament scholar of the twentieth century, into the twenty-first century. The series was intended to last for a decade (2002–12) and so today's is its eleventh and final lecture. The lectures have not set out simply to explicate and expound the thinking of an influential figure. Rather, by taking clues from the theological concerns of that person they have sought to extend his legacy into the twenty-first century in creative ways, in ways that give pointers to what Baptist thought and practice might look like in the future.

In pursuit of this goal the lectures have picked up the themes of baptism, the Church, the priority of mission, preaching, ministry and ecumenism. They have often referred to George Beasley-Murray's life story and to relevant aspects of denominational history. All in all, then, the lecture series has succeeded in addressing, as intended, many of the subjects that belonged to Dr. Beasley-Murray's theological contribution.

1. This lecture was delivered on Friday 4 May 2012 at the beginning of the Baptist Assembly held in Westminster Central Hall, Westminster, London. Time and place are of particular significance in this lecture.

I am conscious in this final lecture of the point in time and the location in space at which it is delivered. Four hundred years ago this year, in 1612, the first Baptist congregation on English soil was founded in this very city, in Spitalfields at no great distance from this building, under the guidance of Thomas Helwys on his return from Amsterdam. We therefore celebrate in this year's Baptist Assembly the 400th anniversary of Baptists in England and with that the spread of Baptist life across the globe as an evangelical and evangelizing movement. But one tenth of that time ago, in 1972, another significant event took place, also in London and in a location even nearer to this place, in Westminster Chapel, an event which forms the starting point for this lecture and in which George Beasley-Murray played a significant part. This was a motion in Assembly, strongly supported by those present and voting, and firmly re-asserting the Union's theological position as both orthodox and evangelical as a means of averting a potential schism.

A previous lecture in this series, given by Dr. Mark Hopkins, was titled "The Downgrade Controversy: Reflections on a Baptist Earthquake." The reference was to a nineteenth-century controversy in which C. H. Spurgeon played a leading role, convinced as he was that the Baptist Union was on the theological slide and in danger of losing its evangelical identity. Somehow the specter of theological "downgrade" has lingered with the denomination throughout the twentieth century, kept alive by those within and without the Union who doubted its full commitment to evangelical faith. These suspicions were strongly confirmed for some when in 1971 Rev Michael Taylor, then Principal of the Northern Baptist College in Manchester, and afterwards a distinguished Director of Christian Aid, delivered an address entitled "The Incarnate Presence: how much of a man was Jesus Christ?" The address was given in plenary session at the invitation of the Union President for that year Dr. G. Henton Davies, Principal of Regent's Park College. If the Downgrade Controversy was a Baptist earthquake, Michael Taylor's address came somewhere near it on the Richter scale and for a time threatened to break the Union asunder.

The primary issue concerned the person of Christ. Taylor imagined himself being asked to draft a paragraph on Christ for a new denominational confession. He saw his suggestion as a "modern replacement" for the article on Christ in the Nicene creed and put it in these terms.

> The story of Jesus makes such an overwhelming impression that I am not content to say he was an extraordinary man. I believe that in the man Jesus we encounter God. I believe that God was active in Jesus, but it will not quite do to say categorically: Jesus is God. Jesus is unique but his uniqueness does not make him different in kind from us. . . . The difference is in what God did in and through this man and the degree to which this man responded and co-operated with God.[2]

Now, it is worth noting that in his address Taylor did not see himself rejecting the words of the Nicene Creed (which he in fact describes as "splendid"). His point was that those who penned that creed did so in the language and thought forms of their own day and that their words are not necessarily binding on us. The challenge of these words for those of us who live in different times was that, "We have to re-write them without playing false to the reality which led them to speak as they did." For Taylor, the reality was the sense of an encounter with God through Jesus, an existential reality which in our day is appropriately expressed in different thought forms and language than the fourth century. Taylor's thinking at this point reflects that of others at the time such as John Hick (1912–2012). Hick describes in his autobiography a visit he made with various academics to the church in Nicaea, Turkey where the Council had met in 325 AD. "Someone there," he says, "suggested that we should all, standing on the ruined wall, recite the Nicene Creed. Some did this in Greek, some in Latin, some in English, and some (including me) in inverted commas!"[3] For Hick as for Taylor, "the language of the divine incarnation, in which we speak of Jesus as God incarnate, God the Son, Son of God, Second Person of the Trinity living a human life, is symbolic, mythological, or poetic language."[4] This is a point he drove home at depth and with erudition in his book *The Metaphor of God Incarnate.*

Yet here is the challenge, and here is the justification for the subtitle of this lecture. It concerns the interplay of faithfulness and freedom. Are we confronted here with legitimate diversity or with illegitimate deviation? To what extent and in which regards are we free to change the language and therefore the content of Christian tradition; and at what

2. The address has never been published. It is available however as appendix 8 in Hill, "The Baptist Revival Fellowship" which covers this period. The quotation is from page 238 of this work.

3. Hick, *Autobiography*, 251.

4. Ibid., 231.

point in so doing do we become unfaithful to Christ and the Church's confession of him? How do theological faithfulness and theological freedom interact? And how does a denomination both remain true to its theological core beliefs in a way which sustains its continuing identity whilst also allowing for the creative freedom which will perceive new depths in its beliefs and allow for their faithful re-expression in new generations of its continuing life?

In my own case the issues here identified are professionally and personally important. They have a particular interest because the 1971 Assembly of the Baptist Union was the first I ever attended, being then in my first year of study at Spurgeon's College. My own introduction to organized Baptist life was therefore in the midst of an earth tremor, if not an earthquake. Much that has since happened in Baptist life has been shaped by the aftermath of the Assemblies of 1971 and 1972. Moreover, being at Spurgeon's College meant that I was aware of the part played by Principal George Beasley-Murray in the intervening year. I therefore intend to examine the events of this year briefly before returning to the overall theme of the lecture.

The Assemblies of 1971 and 1972

The impact of Michael Taylor's address was immediate and intense. Responses to it divided into the two tendencies already outlined. Some saw it is as a denial of the divinity of Christ and therefore as unfaithful to fundamental Christian beliefs. They pressed therefore for a repudiation of its content by the Union. Others defended the freedom to explore the content of Christian belief and to advance new constructs; they admired the fact that Taylor understood himself to be on a pilgrimage and himself acknowledged his capacity to be wrong.[5] They appealed to the canon of tolerance and feared a witch hunt. As far as I can see, few if any of this group actually agreed with what Taylor had said, or if they did, did not say so publicly. I am aware of no theological defense of his expressed Christology. Amongst this group of tolerationists was Dr. E. A. Payne (1902–80), a former General Secretary of the Baptist Union, who considered the address "one of the most impressive and moving given from the Baptist Union platform for many years," whilst at the same time believing the Assembly program was "a very unwise one."[6] Amongst the

5. Hill, "The Baptist Revival Fellowship," 242.

6. Randall, *English Baptists of the Twentieth Century*, 367 and references.

former group was George Beasley-Murray who at the meeting of the Union Council (of which he was Chair) on the Thursday of Assembly week suggested a notice be entered into the *Baptist Times* to indicate that views expressed from the platform were not necessarily representative of the Council's position. At Payne's instigation this debate was adjourned. It is not difficult to characterize this controversy as a head to head between Payne and Beasley-Murray, although this would, of course, be an immense simplification.

The tension between the desire to affirm faithfulness to the theological tradition and that of affirming tolerance of differing theological opinions was to emerge several times in the ensuing debate. Both can make their claim out of Baptist history. At a meeting of the General Purposes and Finance Committee of 5 October 1971 Beasley-Murray once more attempted to put a proposal expressing the view that Taylor's position fell short of New Testament teaching. This was defeated but the G. P. and F. did invite the Council to reaffirm unequivocally both the deity and humanity of Christ. The Council of 9 and 10 November 1971 included with this, at Payne's suggestion, an addendum noting that "the Union has always contained within its fellowship those of different theological opinions and emphases, believing that its claim for toleration included tolerance and respect within its own ranks." It was around this statement that further controversy was to rage. A proposed amendment to this section put forward by Sir Cyril Black (1902–91), a leading Baptist layman, Conservative Member of Parliament for Wimbledon and former President of the Union, sought to include the words "consistent with acceptance of, and loyalty to, the doctrinal clauses of the constitution." However, this amendment was heavily defeated.[7] It was at this point that George Beasley-Murray resigned as Council chairman in order to be the more free to argue his case. This action was itself regarded by some as inflammatory and subsequent opinion was divided as to the wisdom of this action. Some saw it as an escalation of the controversy, others as the step which enabled Dr. Beasley-Murray to take the action which would subsequently resolve it.

Ernest Payne's concern was to safeguard the Baptist commitment to liberty and its aversion to prescribed beliefs. On the other hand the addendum for which he had argued offers no indication that there can be beliefs that are intolerable to the Baptist mind. This was the posi-

7. Ibid., 374.

tion emerging from the leadership of the Union and being advocated by Payne and by the serving General Secretary, David Russell. It was now to be vigorously opposed by Sir Cyril Black on the grounds that it set no limits to tolerance. In a letter to the *Baptist Times* he was to accuse the addendum as implying:

> [T]here is no limit to the "tolerance and mutual respect" to be accorded to people within our own ranks. The warning given by Jesus and His apostles regarding "false prophets" and "false teachers" are no longer to be heeded. No heresy can be so great that "tolerance and mutual respect" are to be withdrawn.[8]

In the same letter he expressed the view that this would be the issue over which the parting of the ways would be reached. And this indeed is the nodal issue in the whole debate. If the specter of a witch hunt haunted the dreams of the tolerationists, the fear of a slide into Unitarianism, similar to that which had happened to the General Baptists in the eighteenth century, motivated their opponents.[9] It might be added that there is probably no issue which is potentially more crucial for Christians than how we are to speak of Christ. What was at stake in this controversy, as indeed in the Nicene debates of the early Church, was whether Christ is to be worshiped as God manifest in the flesh or simply to be venerated as a human agent of the divine. This was and is a profoundly existential issue. No denomination can exist without a degree of latitude and tolerance in the views that its members may hold. But a movement that has no limits to what can be deemed acceptable is in danger of losing its identity and bringing about its own dissolution.

In the event, a significant number of churches and ministers did leave the Union at this point, most of them never to return. But a more serious schism was averted. All attempts to resolve the issue through the leadership structures of the Union appeared only to make things worse, unwilling as they were to set a limit to what might be tolerated. But a decisive reversal on the part of David Russell took place in January 1972 when, after a General Purposes and Finance Committee in which Henton Davies himself disagreed with Taylor's views as "insufficient and defective,"[10] Russell promptly changed his view that opposition to the

8. *Baptist Times*, 2 December 1971, 3.

9. Brown, *The English Baptists of the Eighteenth Century*, 57–64.

10. A full account of Davies' criticism is given in Hill, "The Baptist Revival Fellowship," 179–80. Hill indicates that Davies' statement was not publicly revealed at the time.

addendum was only a misunderstanding and gave his support to other initiatives calculated to clarify the position. Resolution of the whole affair was now to come by the bold actions of Sir Cyril Black, supported by George Beasley-Murray, in appealing to the Assembly of 1972.[11] In the Assembly debate of 25 April 1972 (forty years ago) the following paragraphs were included in a resolution proposed by Black and seconded by Beasley-Murray and passed by 1800 delegates voting in favor, with only 46 against and 72 abstentions:

> Following the example of the Council, we gladly and explicitly affirm our wholehearted acceptance of and belief in the Declaration of Principle set out in the constitution. We thereby unreservedly assert our belief in God the Father, Son and Holy Spirit, into whose name are baptized those who have professed repentance toward God and faith in Our Lord Jesus Christ, who "died for our sins according to the Scriptures, was buried and rose again the third day." We acknowledge this Jesus Christ is both "Lord and Saviour" and "God manifest in the flesh" (understanding these words as expressing unqualified faith in His full Deity and real humanity). We recognize Him as the sole and absolute authority in all matters pertaining to faith and practice as revealed in the Holy Scriptures, and acknowledge the liberty of each Church under the guidance of the Holy Spirit to administer and interpret His laws.
>
> We firmly and unhesitatingly place on record our conviction that the Declaration of Principle represents the basic requirement for fellowship in the Baptist denomination and that we attach high importance to the loyal and wholehearted acceptance of it. In particular we assert the unacceptability of any interpretation of the person and work of Jesus Christ our Lord which would obscure or deny the fundamental tenet of the Christian faith that Jesus Christ is Lord and Saviour, truly God and truly Man.
>
> We recall that a rule of Ministerial Recognition stipulates that "all persons who become or remain Ministers or Probationers accredited by the Union are required to accept the Declaration of Principle as contained in the Constitution of the Union."[12]

In so far as the confession of Christ in the Union's Declaration of Principle as "God manifest in the flesh" had been near to the heart of the

11. Randall, *English Baptists of the Twentieth Century*, 379.

12. Baptist Union Minutes for 25 April 1972, Angus Library, Regent's Park College, Oxford as cited by Hill, "Baptist Revival Fellowship," 256–57.

controversy, its more precise interpretation having been in contention, the Assembly resolution is properly read as an authoritative statement as to how that clause is to be interpreted. This re-establishes a strong Trinitarian core to Baptist life and worship. It is therefore perhaps regrettable that in a document jointly published in 1996 about the Declaration of Principle by the then Principals of the Baptist colleges, no reference is made to this Assembly resolution despite an otherwise reasonably comprehensive survey of the history of its interpretation. Given that the Assembly is the gathering which most widely represents the Baptist mind and therefore has considerable moral authority, this guide to its interpretation might well have figured in the historical account.[13] However that booklet does assert in its introduction that the Union unites around, "a strong Christ-centred framework of basic convictions directed towards authentic Christian discipleship and mission."[14]

In short, the outcome of the Christological controversy sparked off by Michael Taylor's address was that a more radical schism within the Union was averted by means of a strong and unequivocal reaffirmation of orthodox and evangelical doctrine. Granted that many may have believed that this was never in doubt, whatever the rights and wrongs of the Assembly address, my evaluation is that this was a positive step in the life of the Union and that it bore fruit in a variety of ways. One of these was in strengthening the Union as a Union of firm theological and Christological conviction and this in its turn has enabled the Union to withstand somewhat better than some other historic denominations the corrosive acids of the second half of the twentieth century. On the other hand it did not lead, as some might have feared, to any form of witch-hunt or theological McCarthyism.

In a later part of this lecture I wish to return to a discussion of faithfulness and freedom and their place in sustaining evangelical denominational identity and to use the painful experience of the Christological controversy as a way of informing this. Before I attempt this, however, it is to my mind significant that the events of forty years ago have not received more attention from historians. No full scale study has been attempted. Ian Randall devotes eighteen concise pages to them in his twentieth century history of Baptists published in 2005.[15] Paul Beasley-

13. Fiddes et al., *Something to Declare.*

14. Ibid., 8.

15. Randall, *English Baptists of the Twentieth Century*, 366–88.

Murray gives them fair and even-handed treatment in his memoir of his father and brings some facts to light which might not otherwise be known, most of all his father's determination to avoid personalizing the controversy.[16] The most extensive enquiry into the events of which I am aware is the 2011 University of Wales MPhil thesis of Phil Hill entitled "The Baptist Revival Fellowship (1938–72): A study in Baptist conservative evangelicalism." Hill brings a number of new facts and documents to light and gives a blow by blow account of the controversy. Almost certainly, the lack of scholarly attention to these events other than these accounts is owing both to an unwillingness to re-open old wounds and to a sensitivity to those who lived through these events and were or are still living.

My claim in this lecture is that the action taken in re-asserting the Union's theological orthodoxy was a necessary and right act and that it was achieved without opening the door to intolerance. In itself this is an indication that it is possible to maintain faithfulness to the doctrinal tradition whilst not stifling the proper freedom that belongs to theological enquiry. It is proper however in denominational life to acknowledge that freedom will always be within certain boundaries.

Faithfulness and Freedom

The resolution passed by the Assembly of the Baptist Union forty years ago was well-judged and timely. The fact that it was passed overwhelmingly was a sign that the Union of that day was both clear about its Christological and Trinitarian doctrine and anxious to put an end to distracting and destructive controversy. What is striking in reading the historical accounts given by Randall and Hill is that although there were those who defended Michael Taylor's right to think and speak as he did, there were none who rushed to defend what he actually said. In fact the weight of theological reflection in the controversy was much against what he said.

In part this was because for many who heard or later read the Assembly address and who had any kind of background in historical theology, its Christology was plainly at variance with Christian orthodoxy. Amongst his many strengths, Michael Taylor has the gift of lucidity. He writes and speaks with exceptional clarity and what he intends

16. Beasley-Murray, *Fearless for Truth*, 145–65.

is rarely in doubt. This gift is supported by his tendency to speak in the first person and therefore existentially, with directness and challenge. In the address he argues for the replacement of an ontological Christology, such as is laid out in the Nicene Creed, with a degree Christology. Christ is not essentially different from other humans but only in the degree to which he offers himself to be used by God and to which God uses him. Such a Christology has much in common with the Ebionite and adoptionist christologies rejected by the Early Church as inadequate expressions of the truth as it is in Jesus. In short despite the promise of the title of the address, "The Incarnate Presence," Christ is not the incarnation of God but merely the supreme example of a person open to God and used by God. Such a Christ is worthy of emulation but not of divine worship.

Taylor can justify this claim as being consistent with the Nicene Creed only by defining the language of that creed as a contextual attempt to express the significance of Jesus for us, or a way of capturing the impression Jesus makes upon us. But it is not necessarily ontologically true. As we have seen, this is not far from the Christology put forward by John Hick in the book *The Metaphor of God Incarnate.17*

I referred above to a personal statement by Gwynne Henton Davies to the G. P. and F. meeting of 11 January 1972 and not at the time made public. This is described by Hill as "a scholarly Baptist assessment of Taylor's Christology,"[18] one of the few attempts to subject the address to theological critique. Davies finds that Taylor had abandoned the theology of the divine presence in Jesus which was the starting point for Davies' own theology; that he had "democratized" the presence of God in Jesus by making God to be present in him only in the way that he is present in us all; and that he had deemed God not to be present in Jesus in any essentially different way from the ways he is always present. So Davies concluded, "If the statement denies that an incarnate fullness of God began in Bethlehem and ended on the cross, then I am bound to reject it." In effect Davies came out on the side of those who found Taylor denying the deity of Christ.[19] One wonders what the effect of this critique would have been had it been made public at the time.

Concurrently with this private circulation, an impassioned theological assessment of the implications of the address was offered by

17. Hick, *The Metaphor of God Incarnate.*

18. Hill, "The Baptist Revival Fellowship," 179.

19. Ibid., 180.

George Beasley-Murray to the *Baptist Times* and when rejected was circulated as a booklet in January 1972. Beasley-Murray clearly argues that were Taylor's interpretation of Jesus to be allowed its place, Christianity would be reduced to the status of a Reformed Judaism. The New Testament teaching that God was uniquely present in Jesus as the Son of God was the pivotal belief of the whole of the Christian faith such that were it to fall all other aspects of the faith would fall with it. Much of the New Testament would have then to be recognized as "one long appalling mistake." With the doctrine of the incarnation would go the doctrines of the Trinity, the vicarious and atoning sacrifice of the cross, the experience of life "in Christ," and the idea of prayer through and in the name of Jesus. It would lead to the rejection of most of our hymns, the abandonment of both baptism and Lord's Supper as means of communion with the risen Christ and the loss of the church as the Body and Bride of Christ. Logically the continuance of the Baptist denomination would then itself be called into question. Taylor's interpretation was not therefore one that could be embraced and the only option was to stand against it.[20]

My contention here is that that these judgments are true and that Beasley-Murray and those who thought like him were right to insist that the Union re-affirm its position in strong and unambiguous terms. This judgment has only been strengthened by reading Michael Taylor's latest book, titled *Sorting Out Believing: Not Alpha but Omega, an Alternative Guide*.[21] One wonders if there is any significance in this book's being published in 2011, forty years after the Assembly address, or whether this is merely accidental. At any rate Taylor writes with his usual lucidity, clarity and directly personal style.[22] He demonstrates, unsurprisingly, a close acquaintance with the Church's life and with its doctrinal and intellectual traditions. He is able to give a fair and accurate account of Christian believing, (even if others might express it differently). And he shows that he is generally of the same mind as forty years ago with the

20. Beasley-Murray, *The Christological Controversy*.

21. Taylor, *Sorting*.

22. "Over many years now I have engaged from time to time in refining my faith, casting doubt on some of its more easily targeted tenets, adjusting it to challenges from without and within, criticising its institutional expressions, joining with others in trying to renew the church, secularising the gospel, relativising Christianity alongside other faiths, and generally bringing it, as I thought, 'up to date', until these days there is precious little left of what as a young theological student I firmly believed in" (ibid, 4).

exception that his self-confessed skepticism has taken him even further.[23] His key insistence is that religion is a human affair and his methodology is to divide between that which he finds credible and that which he finds incredible in the narration of the Christian story. Some things are, to him, eminently credible, such as Israel's story and the story of Jesus narrated in the Gospels, pre-eminently the events of the passion narrative from Palm Sunday to Gethsemane.[24] But Taylor wishes to dissent, for instance, from the idea that there is another world beyond this one, from the resurrection, from the divinity of Christ, from the once for all nature of the atonement, the crucial nature of decision for Christ or the universal saving significance of Jesus. To imagine that Christ is actually with us in, say, communion may be helpful for us to imagine, but not to believe as a reality. In all these areas he outlines the ways in which he is at variance with the Church's liturgy, Scriptures and hymnody.[25] Of particular interest for our purposes are his words on the divinity of Christ:

> My unbelief in the divinity of Christ was publicly expressed some 40 years ago in an address to the national assembly of my church (Baptist). It was encapsulated at the time in the observation that I could not confess that Jesus was God but could say that God was in Christ and that I preferred to see God's active presence in all of us as a difference in degree but not in kind. That was certainly regarded by many at the time as a resigning matter![26]

To the best of my knowledge these are the first substantive public words that Taylor has uttered in forty years on the controversy around his address. They are also the only instance of which I am aware of Taylor's acknowledging himself to be an "unbeliever" in the divinity of Christ. Now, because he believes that religion is a humanly constructed affair[27] Taylor is able to treat all beliefs and doctrines as relative with none having more authority than others. He does acknowledge that human religious constructs can come as response to experiences or realities that are given to us seemingly beyond ourselves.[28] Yet his skepticism goes as far as questioning in strong terms whether there *is* anything beyond ourselves.

23. Ibid., 105.
24. Ibid., 22–23.
25. Ibid., 6–24.
26. Ibid., 9–10.
27. Ibid., 45–47.
28. Ibid., 47.

Christ is not risen in the way in which Christians have depicted this idea but only in the sense that there were "stories and rumours flying about which strongly suggested that Jesus and all his works were by no means dead and buried but had generated so much new life that it justifies talk of a new creation."[29]

One wonders therefore whether Taylor still believes, as he did at the time of his address, that God was supremely active in the person and humanity of Jesus the Christ. To claim that religion is human is only to say what must necessarily be the case and is not the end of the discussion of the difference between religion which is true and faithful and that which is not, as Taylor acknowledges. To humanize is not to falsify.[30] But forty years on Taylor is by no means sure that there is a God. For him, "the jury is out" as to whether God exists.[31] "I cannot in all honesty definitely rule God in," he says, even though he also cannot rule God out.[32] So although there are many elements of Christian tradition that Taylor continues to value, that he finds inspiring and that are "nurturing" and "sustaining" for him,[33] he is also astute enough to recognize that if God does not exist there is no guarantee that even the things he values, such as hope and the power of costly love, have any substance to them. "Without a belief in God very little of the rest makes much sense."[34]

My conclusion is that the Assembly of the Union was acting with right judgment when forty years ago it rejected the interpretation of Christ that Taylor was offering as both defective and insufficient. The further exposition of his views in his most recent writing confirms the assumptions with which he was working and the trajectory of his thought when further extended. However interesting and stimulating it may be, and those who enjoy intellectually testing their faith will enjoy reading his book, it falls short of robust and rounded Christian belief and is certainly not where Baptists collectively would wish to stand. Were his views to be categorized historically they would properly be defined as classical Liberal Protestantism. Were they to be defined denomination-

29. Ibid., 102.
30. Ibid., 47–48.
31. Ibid., 82.
32. Ibid., 105–6.
33. Ibid., 91–92.
34. Ibid., 104.

ally they would place him on the most explicitly Christ-focused end of the Unitarian and Free Christian spectrum.

The resolution in the Baptist Union Assembly of 1972 saved the day and prevented an earthquake in denominational life, though not an earth tremor. It says something to us about commitment to doctrinal and spiritual faithfulness. Did it open the door to intolerance and the curtailment of freedom? In the eyes of some it certainly represented a turn to the "right." But it should be noted that in passing the resolution the Assembly explicitly rejected by a vote of four to one an amendment calling for the discipline of those who denied or contradicted the Declaration of Principle.[35] Whereas the small number of those on the radical end of the Union undoubtedly felt marginalized by the Assembly's action, and no doubt have continued to do so, having done its necessary work the Union clearly wanted to move on from controversy to constructive action. The fact that it declined to take disciplinary action should not therefore be seen as a carelessness concerning the issues but as an unwillingness to act in a heavy handed fashion.

One significant sign of this is that despite all that had happened, Michael Taylor himself has remained within the life of the Union and has never ceased to be an accredited Baptist minister even though, almost inevitably and rightly so in the light of his unchanged views, he has not taken a prominent role in its affairs. He continued as the innovative Principal of the Northern Baptist College till 1985 and then served successively as Director of Christian Aid, President of the Selly Oak Colleges and Professor of Social Theology at Birmingham University until 2004. His choice to remain within the Baptist circle says a great deal about the man.[36] It also helps that although he is prepared to share his views as a personal pilgrimage he is not out to persuade others to see things his way. Whatever disagreements there may be, his personal honesty and integrity are widely recognized. Despite the buffetings of controversy his conduct has been honorable. Staying within the Union says a great deal about his approach to Christian unity, also a significant theme throughout his ministry. Whatever the differences between Christians, the confession of Christ as Lord is what unites them. As he

35. Hill, "Baptist Revival Fellowship," 186.

36. "Talking of love, I believe in being with people and staying with them, getting inside their world as far as possible, standing by them for better or worse through thick and thin, without necessarily approving of all that they do" (Taylor, *Sorting*, 97–98).

indicated within the address which is at the heart of the controversy, that commitment is primarily to a Person: "I am not committed to a confession of faith, I am committed to a Person, and the truth about that Person is not carried for me by a number of intellectual propositions. The truth about him is carried by a story."[37] This was his view forty years ago. Taylor retains enormous respect for Jesus.[38] But what it means to call Jesus Lord in the light of the fact that he is not risen in any objective sense we are left to ponder.

The Baptist Union has shown itself to be firmly committed to Christian orthodoxy but not at the cost of an inquisitorial spirit. It has sought to nurture both faithfulness and freedom. What is particularly interesting in the part played by George Beasley-Murray in the account we have given is that, firmly evangelical though he was, he was not a person simply to toe lines. Paul Beasley-Murray's biography of his father, as also the first lecture he gave in this series, sets out to demonstrate not only that George showed impassioned and great courage in the Christological controversy but that this had been characteristic of former positions he assumed. This was true in his adoption of interpretations of the New Testament which risked his reputation for conventional orthodoxy,[39] of his willingness to cross boundaries in the cause of ecumenism attract criticism though this might,[40] and of his willingness to translate Rudolf Bultmann's commentary on the Gospel of John.[41] Freedom to think beyond and in advance of what might be expected was understood to be part of being faithful to Christ and therefore the truth. George Beasley-Murray was in himself an example of both faithfulness and freedom.

The Nature and Scope of Tolerance

As we have seen, a core issue in the controversy alongside its Christological aspects was to do with tolerance. Significant voices in the Union argued not in favor of Taylor's views but of his right to explore them. E. A. Payne was a prime example of this. Hill records that he held a firm view of toleration in the history of the Baptists and that, "Baptists

37. As recorded in Hill, "Baptist Revival Fellowship," 243.

38. Taylor, *Sorting*, 100–101.

39. Beasley-Murray, *Fearless for Truth*, 73–76

40. Ibid., 134–39.

41. Ibid., 143–44.

have shown themselves opposed to subscription to theological statements as a test of discipleship or even orthodoxy."[42] This was a sentiment often expressed at the time of the controversy. A review of Taylor's latest book in the *Baptist Times* and recalling the controversy began in similar fashion: "A denomination that trumpeted its commitment to freedom of belief suddenly discovered the truth of that old saying, 'Be careful what you wish for.'"[43] However, Sir Cyril Black astutely pointed out that in the ordination service for Baptist ministers, candidates are asked to confess their faith in the following words:

> [In] the presence of God and of this congregation, it is necessary that you should answer, in all sincerity of heart, the questions I now ask of you: Do you believe in One God, the Father, Son and the Holy Spirit; and do you confess anew Jesus Christ as your Saviour and Lord? *Answer*: I do.

To rub the point home, Black went on to point out that these words were co-written by Ernest Payne himself in the then much-valued service book, *Orders and Prayers for Church Worship.*[44] What is this if it is not a verbal test and, according to Payne, a "necessary" one? Once more, the place of verbal affirmations of faith subordinate to Scripture was one of the contentious issues in the Salters' Hall controversy of the eighteenth century. The refusal to subscribe to articles of faith was for many a stage on the road to Unitarianism.[45] But whenever a movement distinguishes between beliefs that are compatible or incompatible with what it stands for a creedal test is in play. It is not possible to dispense with verbal tests altogether. The issue concerns "the bounds within which freedom could be enjoyed."[46]

Baptists certainly prize freedom. But the freedom they prize in the wider society differs from the freedom they celebrate in their own churches and communion. Humans do not choose to be born and they have no alternative but to live in society. To be excluded from society therefore is to be deprived of the goods and provisions that make life viable and livable. To apply religious tests to one's right to participate fully

42. Hill, "Baptist Revival Fellowship," 174 citing Payne's letter to *Baptist Times*, December 9, 1971, 2.

43. Docker, "Key Questions," 14.

44. Payne and Winward, *Orders and Prayers for Church Worship*, 218.

45. Brown, *The English Baptists of the Eighteenth Century*, 58.

46. Hopkins, *Nonconformity's Romantic Generation*, 245–46.

in society, or to participate in it at all, is therefore to threaten a person's well-being and possibly their very existence. For this reason Baptists have opposed subscription to religious tests as a necessary condition of citizenship. They have argued that society should be non-sectarian, "secular" in the sense that religious tests are not a condition of participation and acceptance. But they have not adopted this position with regard to their churches. Within society people are free to believe what they choose within the bounds of decent behavior. Within the church they are free to believe but within the bounds of a confessional community. Membership of the church, for Baptists (and others have followed them), is voluntary and depends on the willingness to make confession of faith. If the faith is not confessed then participation is denied, hence the doctrine of believers' baptism and the practice of self-examination prior to communion. Baptists distinguish between what might be expected in society and what should be expected in the church and understand this distinction as important and beneficial. It is important to society because the rejection of compulsory religion means that none are denied the wherewithal for life on religious grounds. It is important for the churches because the existence of secular space means that those who belong to the church do so not because they have no alternative or for fear of discrimination or because they are compelled but because they sincerely choose to do so. Yet to be in the church is to share in a different kind of freedom. We are bonded to Christ "whom to serve is perfect freedom."

Even as Baptists at the communion table are invited to examine themselves and pass judgment on themselves as to whether they can share in the bread and wine, so they prefer to reserve judgment on people's ability to give assent to even such a minimalist document as the Declaration of Principle. Affirming faithfulness to the tradition of Christian believing has not meant adopting an inquisitorial stance and there is a good reason for this. The higher and fuller our doctrine of the Christ the more we have to take seriously his significance for us in action. If indeed he is the "all-gracious personal embodiment of the way the truth and the life,"[47] then how he acted towards others is not only normative but mandatory. Sometimes it is necessary to be dogmatic in order to safeguard that which will keep us generously wholesome.

47. The words of C. H. Spurgeon as cited in Backhouse, *The Autobiography of C. H. Spurgeon*, 186.

Tolerance is not an undifferentiated good, neither is Jesus an example of unqualified toleration. I am impressed by the words of Ronald Goetz:

> Religious tolerance is not always a sign of good will . . . During the Nazi era, for example, arguments for Christian openness to other perspectives were used by German Christians in an attempt to neuter the church's protest against the neo-paganism of Hitler and his minions. The Confessing Church in Germany found in John 10 a theological basis to stand against Hitler. *There are times in which the only way to keep alive the non-vindictive, nonjudgmental, self-sacrificing witness of Jesus Christ is to stand with rude dogmatism on the rock that is Jesus Christ, condemning all compromise as the work of the Antichrist.*[48]

Faithfulness is not only a matter of holding fast to the truth as it is in Jesus but to the moral truth in him that is to be lived out in integrity and grace. Faithfulness and freedom belong together since, properly understood, freedom comes from being in harmony with the truth not in departing from it. Resonating with God in Christ enables us to be at our most free.

In the four hundredth year of their existence it might reasonably be argued that freedom in Christ is of the essence of Baptist identity: freedom from state control, freedom from ecclesiastical domination, freedom of religious expression and of the informed conscience and yet always freedom within constraints, freedom in Christ, by Christ and for Christ, freedom and faithfulness. This is how we sustain our identity and prove, truly, to be gospel people.

If this lecture is entitled "Sustaining Evangelical Identity," what might we say that could help guide us into the next stage of our denominational pilgrimage? I am mindful of a certain tendency denominations have to take for granted the fundamental convictions and doctrines on which they are founded. Their founding documents are overlooked and forgotten and rarely revisited. Because doctrines are regarded as both difficult and potentially divisive, the stuff of argument, there is a tendency to want to bypass them on the way to working the work or fulfilling the mission. Yet the story is told of some Mennonite denominations: The first generation believed and proclaimed the gospel and thought that there were certain social entailments. The second generation assumed the gospel and advocated the entailments. The third generation denied

48. Goetz, "Exclusivistic Universality."

the gospel and all that were left were the entailments.[49] One might imagine that the fourth generation lost the entailments because they had already lost the gospel.

To sustain an identity a denomination needs to be clear about what is important to it and vital for its existence. It would be easy at this point to list the usual Baptist distinctives and encourage each other to celebrate them. But actually even these things are secondary to our cause. Logically prior to our Baptist identity is our evangelical identity rooted in confession of a creative God who is revealed in his Son Jesus Christ, who has purposed the redemption of human beings through the incarnation of Christ and his atoning death on a cross, who has raised Christ to life so that he may be the means of our present and eternal salvation and who is about the work through the Holy Spirit of electing a people for himself and for his purpose. These are the convictions and doctrines that will sustain us and which we simply assume or neglect at our peril. We have freedom to elaborate and interpret these teachings in many and various ways, but the future of this denomination requires us to be faithful to them with all our hearts. The words of the Barmen Declaration, emerging in 1934 out of the same context that gave rise to Ronald Goetz's words already quoted, are worth recalling:

> Jesus Christ, as he is attested to us in Holy Scripture, is the one Word of God which we have to hear, and which we have to trust and obey, in life and in death.[50]

Bibliography

Backhouse, Robert, ed. *The Autobiography of C. H. Spurgeon*. London: Hodder & Stoughton, 1994.

Beasley-Murray, George. *The Christological Controversy in the Baptist Union*. Privately published, January 1972.

Beasley-Murray, Paul. *Fearless for Truth: A Personal Portrait of the Life of George Beasley-Murray*. Carlisle, UK: Paternoster, 2002.

Brown, Raymond. *The English Baptists of the Eighteenth Century*. London: Baptist Historical Society, 1986.

Docker, Michael. "Key Questions: Getting to the Bottom of Christianity." Review of *Sorting Out Believing—Not Alpha but Omega, an Alternative Guide* by Michael Taylor. *Baptist Times* (May 20, 2011).

49. Gibson, "Assumed Evangelicalism," 1.

50. Leith, *Creeds of the Churches*, 520.

Fiddes, Paul, et al. *Something to Declare: A Study of the Declaration of Principle*. Oxford: Whitley, 1996.

Gibson, David. "Assumed Evangelicalism." *From Athens to Jerusalem*, 3/4 (2002).

Goetz, Ronald. "Exclusivistic Universality." *Christian Century*, April 21, 1993.

Hick, John. *An Autobiography*. Oxford: One World, 2002.

———. *The Metaphor of God Incarnate*, London: SCM, 1993.

Hill, Philip D. "The Baptist Revival Fellowship (1938–1972): A Study in Baptist Conservative Evangelicalism." Master of Philosophy diss., University of Wales, 2011.

Hopkins, Mark. *Nonconformity's Romantic Generation: Evangelical and Liberal Theologies in Victorian England*. Studies in Evangelical History and Thought. Carlisle, UK: Paternoster, 2004.

Leith, John H., ed. *Creeds of the Churches: A Reader in Christian Doctrine from the Bible to the Present*. Louisville: Westminster John Knox, 1963.

Payne, Ernest A., and Stephen F. Winward, eds. *Orders and Prayers for Church Worship: A Manual for Ministers*. London: Baptist Union of Great Britain, 1960.

Randall, Ian M. *The English Baptists of the Twentieth Century*. Didcot: Baptist Historical Society, 2005.

Taylor, Michael H. *Sorting Out Believing: Not Alpha but Omega, an Alternative Guide*. Brighton: Open House, 2011.